Multicultural Science Education

Studies in the
Postmodern Theory of Education

Joe L. Kincheloe and Shirley R. Steinberg
General Editors

Vol. 120

PETER LANG
New York • Washington, D.C./Baltimore • Bern
Frankfurt am Main • Berlin • Brussels • Vienna • Oxford

Multicultural Science Education

Theory, Practice, and Promise

EDITED BY
S. Maxwell Hines

PETER LANG
New York • Washington, D.C./Baltimore • Bern
Frankfurt am Main • Berlin • Brussels • Vienna • Oxford

LIBRARY OF CONGRESS CATALOGING-IN-PUBLICATION DATA

Multicultural science education:
theory, practice, and promise / edited by S. Maxwell Hines.
p. cm. — (Counterpoints; vol. 120)
Includes bibliographical references and index.
1. Science—Study and teaching—United States.
2. Multicultural education—United States. I. Hines, S. Maxwell.
Q183.3.A1 .M85   507'.1073 21—dc21   99-043781
ISBN 0-8204-4540-1
ISSN 1058-1634

DIE DEUTSCHE BIBLIOTHEK-CIP-EINHEITSAUFNAHME

Multicultural science education:
theory, practice, and promise / ed. by: S. Maxwell Hines.
–New York; Washington, D.C./Baltimore; Bern;
Frankfurt am Main; Berlin; Brussels; Vienna; Oxford: Lang.
(Counterpoints; Vol. 120)
ISBN 0-8204-4540-1

Cover design by Joni Holst

The paper in this book meets the guidelines for permanence and durability
of the Committee on Production Guidelines for Book Longevity
of the Council of Library Resources.

© 2003, 2005 Peter Lang Publishing, Inc., New York
275 Seventh Avenue, 28th Floor, New York, NY 10001
www.peterlangusa.com

Printed in the United States of America

ACKNOWLEDGMENTS

Although I cannot hope to acknowledge all of the people who were instrumental to the production of this volume, I would certainly like to publicly recognize the assistance of those who had nothing to gain from lending their assistance in various forms. All of my colleagues at Hofstra University demonstrated their support of this project. I would especially like to thank my colleague Dr. Susan Semel, who upon hearing of my desire to produce this volume, offered her expertise and introduced me to editors and publishers who would be receptive to this topic. I am also grateful to my colleague Dr. Alan Singer, who provided a great deal of moral support.

I would also like to thank my graduate assistants, Kristin Mantione and Andrea Vicale, for their assistance with correspondence between my office and the prospective chapter authors. They demonstrated great organization, poise, and patience as the papers and editorial comments flew back and forth. I am certain that they will be excellent multicultural science teachers, and their school districts should feel privileged to have them.

The authors of these chapters have put a great deal of work into this project and are deserving of many thanks. I asked them a lot of critical questions about their work and often played devil's advocate about their positions on issues. They handled this with great grace and willingly worked on this project through completion. I am especially appreciative of their patience throughout the long process of book conception to publication.

The people who work at Peter Lang have been marvelous. Christopher Myers, Bernadette Alfaro, and Cornelia Faifar waited patiently while the chapter authors and I worked through difficult issues in order to improve this volume. I thank them for all their support.

My greatest acknowledgment must be paid to my family, however. As I spent long hours working on this volume, my husband, George Milliken, tended to the needs of our twin sons, Robert and Lawrence, without a single complaint. Although George has an active and important career in his own right, his steadfast support has helped to further my career and continues to enrich my life. Robert and Lawrence can now look forward to having a more participatory mommy who will have the energy to read them more than one story per day. Finally, a special thank you to my mother, Edna Hines, who has always been my most staunch supporter and the greatest educator I have ever known. Thank you for showing me that all things are possible with hard work and Divine intervention. It has been my most important life lesson.

CONTENTS

PREFACE

As we enter a new millennium, we face a world fraught with the ever-increasing complexities associated with the teaching and learning of science. Although we are inundated with statistics that warn us of the disparity in achievement in science for students of color, females, the poor, those with limited English proficiency, and those living with physical and mental challenges to learning (National Center for Educational Statistics, 1995; National Science Foundation, 1996), we must also acknowledge that these populations of students are increasing (Estrada, 1993; National Center for Educational Statistics, 1997; U.S. Bureau of the Census, 1993). Conversely, the number of science teachers from these populations is decreasing. The majority of high school science teachers in the United States are White males in their forties (Atwater, 1993; Weiss & Boyd, 1990). Few of these teachers have engaged in extensive study of how to teach science to this increasingly and demographically culturally diverse student body. Despite many nationally recognized documents to the contrary (Carey, 1993; Gilbert, 1997; National Research Council, 1996), many science teachers still subscribe to the notion that only a talented few can achieve in scientific enterprises. This deficit model belief is reflected in statistics indicating that only 0.2% of typical American high school students continue on to pursue terminal degrees in science (Hassard, 1996). Traditionally, higher income White males have constituted the majority of people engaged in science and science-related professions in the United States. With the increase in underrepresented populations in American classrooms, new considerations must fuel science education reform. Multicultural science education has been touted as a means of providing equity of opportunity for all students.

Multicultural science education as a field of serious scholarly inquiry is in its infancy. As with any other infant, it is difficult to predict its direction as it grows and evolves. Many scholars are grappling with pedagogical issues that underpin the complex and interconnected factors associated with teaching science to students who historically have been underrepresented in science classrooms (Eide & Heikkinen, 1998; Grubbs, Rosenthal & Lee, 1998; Noordhoff & Kleinfeld, 1993; Santos & Larke, 1998). Multicultural science education and the newer cultural inclusion models consider these interconnected factors holistically and seek to address them in a more integrated fashion (Banks & Banks, 1997). Should this infant be investigated using modern or postmodern paradigms? Will it have its own lexicon or should it incorporate and modify the existing science education lexicon? Should its curriculum be traditional or emancipatory? Should the goals for multicultural science education be different from those espoused by more traditional forms of science education? How will science teacher educators assist their students in understanding and practicing science teaching differently from the manner in which they learned science? How are practitioners implementing the principles of multicultural science education to advance student learning? These questions provide the impetus for beginning the discussion and the framing of future research in multicultural science education.

This volume brings together scholars on the leading edge of the developing field of multicultural science education. These scholars were selected because of their divergent research and opinions on multicultural science education. They represent a mix of traditional, modern, and postmodern theorists, practitioners, teachers, and teacher educators. As a result, this volume designed to provide multiple perspectives and stimulate lively debate around these complex issues. It is in no way a comprehensive treatment of this emerging field. Space constraints did not allow for chapters engaged in focused study of the issues associated with gender, limited English proficiency, and socioeconomic status, though many of their essential considerations are embedded within multiple chapters. Perhaps those will be included in a future volume, but their omission should not be construed as an indicator of lesser importance. I even had to omit my own chapter. The following paragraphs describe the chapters that follow.

Chapter 1 by Carter, Larke, Singleton-Taylor, and Santos provides us with a historical overview of many of the key issues in and constituents of multicultural science education. Through the examination of multiple typologies and teaching methods, the authors call on teachers to shed the deficit model beliefs that result in low teacher expectation and embrace culturally relevant science by focusing on the cultural capital that diverse students bring to the classroom.

In Chapter 2, Rodriguez examines the contradiction between the call by the National Research Council's *National Science Education Standards* for "science for all" and its omission of a serious treatment of ethnicity within the document. He explores the impact of this omission on preservice and inservice teachers and offers examples of how the standards could have taken a stronger stand on culturally relevant science teaching.

By considering science through a critical multicultural framework, Ahlquist and Kailin provide a strong argument for the inclusion of an expanded sociocultural focus in science curricula in Chapter 3. They use this framework to demonstrate the importance of students having a more global perspective on science with an eye toward increasing civic responsibility.

Atwater and Crockett examine how worldview and self-identity can influence science teaching by studying culturally diverse preservice science teachers in Chapter 4. They also provide an excellent overview of how cultural diversity impacts science education internationally.

Chapter 5 by Gholston Key employs the research on multicultural education and Science Technology and Society curriculum to frame her argument that African American student interest in science is enhanced by employing culturally inclusive science pedagogy. She also explains the development of her own cultural inclusion model.

In Chapter 6, Rowland and Adkins invite us to consider the unique challenges of educating Native American students of science. While they offer specific research-based prescriptives for teaching these students, they also discuss these prescriptives in relation to the within-group variations among Native American students.

Simmons's work describes a case study of a university-based enrichment program for urban secondary students in Chapter 7. The study clearly demonstrates that with persistence, it is possible to increase student achievement in science in one of the most challenging urban settings.

Through the study of culturally relevant curriculum, Loving and Ortiz de Montellano admonish us not to sacrifice quality science education for "feel good" science curriculum in Chapter 8. Their use of specific examples demonstrates what curriculum developers should be wary of when selecting and developing culturally relevant science curricula.

color and immigration patterns, it has been estimated that early in the 21st century, both Hispanic and Asian American populations will increase by an additional 20% (*African American Education Data Book,* 1997; Estrada, 1993) while the African American population will increase by 12%. For decades, demographers predicted that persons of color would constitute one-third of the population of the United States by the year 2000, a prediction that became a reality. It has also been predicted that people of color will constitute more than half of the American population by the middle of the 21st century (Bishop, 1992; Murdock, Hogue, & White, 1997).

The demographic population in schools has made major shifts. For example, people of European decent made up 73% of the nation's student population in 1982; since 1990, the largest 25 school districts have had a minority European decent population. In addition to the largest school districts, in states such as California, Texas, and New Mexico, children of color are the majority of the school-age population (Carter & Larke, 1995). In 50 of the nation's largest urban public school systems, African Americans, Hispanics, Asian Americans, and Native Americans made up 76.5% of the student population in 1992 (Council of Great City Schools, 1994). These numbers are expected to increase in cities such as Chicago, Los Angeles, Washington, DC, New York, Seattle, San Francisco, Dallas, and Houston, where again, half or more of the public school students are children of color. It has been predicted that by the year 2020 students of European decent will make up only 54.5% of the nation's student population and students of color about 45.5% (Pallas, Natriello, & McDill, 1989).

The population of the nation's schools is becoming increasingly low income. The number of children in poverty is growing in the United States and this trend is expected to continue. The percentage of children in poverty increased from 14.9% in 1970 to 21.1% in 1991 (Estrada, 1993). About one of every five children below the age of 18 was living below the poverty level in 1991 (U.S. Bureau of the Census, 1993, p. 469).

In contrast, 88% of public and private school teachers were White in 1990; 8% were African American, and 68% of the total were female (Carter & Larke, 1995). It is apparent that teachers in the United States are predominantly White and female. The typical science teacher is 40 years old with 13 years in the classroom, and 90% of high school science teachers are White, of whom 50 % are male (Atwater, 1993; Weiss &

Boyd, 1990). While the teaching force is predominantly White, the student population is becoming increasingly diverse. This dynamic has created a challenge for teachers who do not share the social and cultural background of their students.

In addition, the workplace in general is becoming increasingly diverse, with 85% of entering workers being females or people of color during the beginning of the 21st century (Clark, 1996; Nobles & Larke, 1998). Despite this fact, females and people of color are underrepresented in science-related professions. An American Association of University Women Educational Foundation (1992) study of how girls are treated in schools found the gender gap in science increasing, and more than eight years later, the evidence still supports the study. Even girls who are highly competent in science are much less likely to pursue scientific or technological careers than their male classmates (Gollnick & Chinn, 1998).

The Task Force on Women, Minorities and the Handicapped in Science and Technology estimates that a shortage of 560,000 scientists and engineers may develop by the year 2010 if present trends continue (Parsons, 1997). Hart (1977) states that "despite the faith of underrepresented people of color in the American educational system as a means for social and economic advancement, equal education has not assured culturally diverse individuals equal access to opportunity" (p. 2) especially in science and related computer technology fields. African Americans, Hispanics/Latinos, Native Americans, and other culturally diverse individuals comprise approximately 27% to 30% of the population but only 2.2% of our technical workforce. Recent literature has attributed the underrepresentation of people of color and White females in science fields to several variables (Eide & Heikkinen, 1998; Grubbs, Rosenthal, & Lee, 1998; Noordhoff & Kleinfeld, 1993; Santos & Larke, 1998). They are:

1. Lack of student interest in science;
2. Science anxiety;
3. White-male-dominated images of science;
4. Lack of minority role models in science and related technology careers;
5. Socioeconomic barriers;
6. Improper counseling regarding academic track coursework at the high school level;
7. Teacher attitudes and expectations; and
8. Lack of proper academic preparation.

In the professional arena, culturally diverse individuals have made significant gains in their participation rates in business and industry sectors during the past three decades but have not made gains in science and related technology fields.

The educational system reveals that people of color are also underrepresented in science at every academic level, from graduate school to elementary school (Clark, 1996). For example, in 1992–1993 the number of total doctorates awarded in engineering, life sciences, and physical sciences and science technologies were 4,961, 2,620, and 3,429 respectively. Only 6 Black females were awarded doctorates in engineering, 23 in life sciences, and 8 in the physical sciences and science technology (Snyder & Hoffman, 1995, as cited in Parsons, 1997).

The number of people of color enrolled in mathematics, science, computer science, and computer engineering courses remains low, despite the supposed removal of many social and legal barriers to the full participation of these students in science careers. Some cite the fact that colleges and universities in our country are still experiencing an underrepresentation of culturally diverse applicants who are capable of meeting entry standards in science and mathematics majors. Others state that many high-ability or high-potential culturally and/or linguistically diverse students face educational and economic barriers to their pursuit of training for highly technological jobs.

People of color, especially those who speak a first language other than English, consistently perform more poorly overall on standard measures of academic achievement (e.g., SAT, GRE, MAT) than do their English-speaking peers. In addition, high school attrition (dropout) rates at all socioeconomic levels in this nation are higher for people of color than for European students and some Asian students (U.S. Bureau of the Census, 1993). Although many states have made concerted efforts to improve the participation, persistence, and graduation rates of students of color, they continue to lag far behind the number of European student enrollments.

CRITICAL ISSUES IN TRADITIONAL SCIENCE EDUCATION

The problem of the underrepresentation of people of color in science careers does not begin at the university or high school level but rather at the elementary school level, where there are basic flaws in instruction for many children. When science is taught in the elementary school, often it is taught from textbooks rather than as a hands-on, inquiry-based learning experience. While ethnic groups are represented adequately in science textbooks, teachers' manuals are lacking in multicultural content (Eide & Heikkinen, 1998) that includes suggestions for activities like reports, posters, plays, debates, and experiments.

Studies show that many elementary teachers rely heavily on expository teaching methods and textbooks as the primary means for instructing children in science. One survey indicated that 75% of lower elementary (K–3) and 90% of upper elementary (4–6) science instruction involves lecture and discussion teaching methods (Hashweh, 1987; Yager, 1983, 1989). Elementary science is taught by many teachers as if science learning consisted of memorizing facts, definitions, and rules. Ninety percent of American science teachers use classroom textbooks 95% of the time, and, for those with less knowledge of science, the textbook is followed very closely (Yager, 1989). In most elementary classrooms, children are expected to assume a passive role when science is taught. Added to this concern is the amount of time that has been committed to science. On average, across the United States, elementary students spend less than 20 minutes a day studying science (Weiss, 1987).

While there are basic issues that deal with science education and science in general, the need to prepare the culturally diverse learner is particularly acute. Researchers and educators across the nation are re-thinking science education, because there is powerful evidence that traditional ways of teaching are not increasing the number of students of color who are interested in science and science-related careers. Equally troublesome is the loss of students of color who could, through science, gain knowledge and a sense of empowerment that could provide untold benefits to their lives and the lives of others. Various studies characterize teachers in general who are unable to meet the needs of culturally diverse students as those who are under-prepared to deal with the needs of diverse learners, lack understanding and skills in designing meaningful lessons, and lack a knowledge base to fully understand the needs of various ethnic groups (Eide & Heikkinen, 1998; Grubbs et al., 1998; Noordhoff & Kleinfeld, 1993; Santos & Larke, 1998).

There are a growing number of researchers who see these points as issues but also believe that major reform of science education is needed likewise. They state the urgency to change traditional Western science education into multicultural science education, if the nation is going to be effective in the 21st century.

Field-sensitive students, for example, must be taught to conceptualize abstract representations and relate them to real objects, actions, and experiences. Research suggests that bilingual individuals can do this, that is, move back and forth between global and analytical orientations, better than monolinguists (Bennett, 1995). Students can learn to construct their own understanding, but it will be filtered through their specific cultural experiences. It is important for science educators to realize that one's culture does affect the way science is perceived and that a person's worldview serves as a basis for what one can accept as knowledge worth learning (Ogawa, 1995).

The deficit model is another factor that has paralyzed the learning process of poor students and students of color. The deficit model refers to the assumption that some students, because of genetic, cultural, or experiential differences, are inferior to other children; that is, they have a deficit (Nieto, 1996). Teachers in most cases have been trained to identify the weaknesses of their students in order to develop an instructional plan. Often, teachers view students who live in poverty, come from homes with problems, and/or live in communities with social ills (neighborhoods noted for gangs, drugs, etc.) as possessing deficits that cannot be overcome in the classroom.

The deficit model has an impact on teacher expectations for students, and more importantly, it impacts the teacher's sense of efficacy about learning. Teacher efficacy is the extent to which a teacher believes he/she can affect student learning in the science classroom (Gibson & Dembo, 1984). Teacher efficacy is intricately tied into the teacher's belief system about students and the learning process. The deficit model paralyzes many teachers, because they believe that circumstances in the student's life prevent learning. Teachers who have low efficacy believe that factors beyond their control cause student outcomes. Teachers who have low efficacy believe that trying makes little difference and that situational factors in the lives of students will cause success or failure in the classroom. If situational factors are favorable, meaning the students come from two-parent homes, display middle-class values, and live in neighborhoods that reflect middle-class incomes or better, then success will follow. If situational factors are not favorable, that is, students come from one-parent families and live in poverty-stricken neighborhoods, failure is inevitable. Ultimately, the teacher with low efficacy will not take responsibility for teaching all children.

It is imperative that teachers shed the deficit model and begin to embrace models of resilience that build on the strengths of students and focus on high expectations for all learners. Teachers who possess a high sense of efficacy believe that effort causes outcomes, rather than factors that are outside of the classroom. The efficacious teacher believes that trying hard will bring success and that those teachers who do not try hard will fail. They take full responsibility for teaching all learners in their classroom. Teachers and schools cannot alleviate poverty and other social ills in society that some students face every day. It is necessary to address the challenges they can resolve in the form of policies, practices, and provisions for educational environments that encourage all students to learn to the best of their ability (Nieto, 1996).

Another factor that is significant is culturally relevant teaching in diverse classrooms. Ladson-Billings (1995) defines culturally relevant teaching as a pedagogy of opposition that includes collective and individual empowerment. It is collective because we must all work together as human beings in order to empower our nation. It is individual empowerment because students must experience personal academic success in their science classes. If students have been discouraged from previous learning experiences, it is especially important not to allow them to fail. A successful teacher of multicultural science believes that all students can learn. Allowing students to sit in the back of the class and not take an interest in the class is a decision that, unfortunately, some teachers make. Teachers should not adopt a "sink or swim" mentality; they must realize that not all students learn in the same manner and therefore should not all be treated the same. The more teachers are able to realize each student's needs, the more all students will have an equal opportunity to achieve.

This type of teaching also represents individual empowerment because students must develop and maintain their cultural identities (Nelson-Barber & Estrin, 1995). If we accept the metaphor that the United States is a "tossed salad" of diverse groups, the curriculum and teacher should facilitate understanding and appreciation of the distinctiveness of individuals and their contributions to American society (Bryant, 1996).

APPROACHES FOR ATTAINING MULTICULTURAL SCIENCE EDUCATION

Atwater (1993) defined multicultural science as "a construct, a process, and an educational reform movement with the goal of providing equitable opportunities for culturally diverse student populations to learn quality science in schools, colleges and universities" (p. 32). Furthermore, Hodson (1993) described to multicultural science education as the education of students of diverse ethnic backgrounds, achieved through a culture- and society-oriented curriculum aimed at preparing students to live in and contribute to a diverse society.

There have been various approaches to attaining multicultural science education. Many have been related to the work of Banks and Banks (1997), who developed four levels that describe how multicultural content has been integrated into curriculum since the 1960s. The first level is the contributions approach. It is described as an approach that inserts ethnic heroes, holidays, and cultural elements into the curriculum. Scientists of color, for example, would be discussed during ethnic months, celebrations, or special events. Baptiste and Key (1996) wrote specifically about science and developed a three-level typology that illustrates the development of the multicultural science classroom. The first level, the product, is characterized by elements similar to those of Banks and Banks, namely, the isolated, tack-on addition of multicultural material to a traditional curriculum. A key factor of the contributions approach and the Level I typology is that mainstream curriculum does not change in its structure, goals, and underlying characteristics (Banks & Banks, 1997). Students at this level do not get a healthy view of the pluralistic nature of American society. Instead, they see ethnic and cultural groups as outsiders who are given token recognition that may or may not be deserved. Students also get the impression that White males are the nucleus of all significant science activity worldwide. Unfortunately, this is the most popular method among teachers who want to make their classrooms culturally inclusive.

The second level is the additive approach. It is described as an approach that adds "content, concepts, themes and perspectives to the curriculum without changing its basic structure, purposes and characteristics" (Banks & Banks, p. 235). It is similar to Level II, process/product, of the Baptiste and Key typology (1996). Scientists of color and women would be infused into curriculum through the addition of a book, unit, or course, and attention could be given to the various learning styles of students. The limitation of this approach is the fact that science and its ethnic content are viewed through the lens of White, middle-class, mainstream Americans. This occurs because the curriculum has not been restructured. This approach does not help students to understand how science is interrelated with ethnic and mainstream cultures.

The third level of Banks and Banks is the transformation approach. It is described as an approach in which "the structure of the curriculum is changed to enable students to view concepts, issues, events and themes from the perspectives of diverse ethic and cultural groups" (p. 233). This approach is significant because science should be viewed from more than one traditional perspective, and it promotes the idea of a shared culture.

The fourth level of Banks and Banks is the social action approach. It includes all the ingredients of the transformation approach but requires students to make decisions on important social issues and take actions to help solve them. It has similar ideals when compared to Level III, the process/philosophical orientation, of the Baptiste and Key typology. In the typology, science teachers would become social activists, and in addition, they would help their science students promote equality in the school and their community. The goal is for teachers to design, develop, or seek out science programs that are antiracist and multicultural. Atwater (1999, p. 47) states that "students must develop critical consciousness through which they can challenge the status quo of the current social order with their scientific knowledge and skills." Western science education has been criticized internationally for not teaching students how science affects the global economy and the environment, and how people use science to promote causes that can be noble or destructive. A key factor of the social action approach and the Level III typology is that students will be taught how to engage in activities that will resolve social issues in science and ultimately in society.

The transformation of Western science education is a complex, if not daunting, task for teachers, who may see more than 180 students pass through their classrooms each day. Certainly, national reform efforts such as those created by the American Association for the Advancement of Science, the National Research Council, and the National Science Teachers Association all promote equal opportunity for all students and give helpful strategies for addressing the needs of female and minority students.

In 1991, the National Science Teachers Association (NSTA) issued a position statement on multicultural science education describing eight goals that would lead to achievement of international leadership in science education (NSTA, 1991). Four directly addressed curriculum and instruction:

> Quality science education must be accessible and provide knowledge and opportunities that will enable people of color to become successful participants in our democratic society.
> Cultural diversity must be reflected in the curricular content and instructional strategies.
> Science teachers must be aware of culturally related learning styles and preferences.
> Science teachers have the responsibility to present all children the opportunity to explore career opportunities in science. (p. 1)

Still, these reform efforts have fallen short when it comes to giving the inexperienced teacher a way to "make that first step" toward change.

Multicultural science approaches are for a classroom in which the teacher is willing to depart from the traditional approach in which he or she is the sole source of information and controls a classroom where students sit at their desks doing "busywork." These approaches are intended for a teacher who acts, as Aikenhead (1996) describes, as a "tour guide" allowing students to explore unfamiliar areas as they relate what they learn to their everyday lives.

Teachers need to base their class on the values of an inclusive approach, realizing that diverse perspectives of nature offered by different worldviews can make positive contributions to science (Atwater, 1993). Thus, it is of utmost importance to relate the subject matter to students' everyday lives. This can be done through learning contracts and/or portfolios. A learning contract is developed by both teacher and student and outlines a program of activities and projects tailored to the student's interests and background (Hodson, 1993). A portfolio is essentially a learning contract, and emphasizes giving students a sense of ownership over what they have learned over time. Both of these approaches allow students to take an active part in their instruction and will ultimately give them the satisfaction of completing a set of goals they have set for themselves (Rakow & Bermudez, 1993).

A teacher should also inquire if students would like to make changes to the physical setting of the classroom (Versey, 1990). For instance, do students find the lab coats, goggles, and general decor of the laboratory setting particularly drab? Because appearance is important to many students, a teacher may need to engage in discussions, especially if attire keeps some students from participating fully in the lab because they don't like the way they look when they wear a pair of "standard-issue" goggles. Some students of color do not like the idea of dressing or "acting White," which can be a real issue with some cultural groups and must be addressed in the classroom (Fordham, 1993). Some items can be changed, while others cannot, but all concerns should be discussed. The input of the students should be respected and changes made, if possible.

Of particular concern in a learner-oriented classroom are the needs of English as a second language (ESL) students. Rakow and Bermudez (1993) have suggested that using the Latin roots to explain some scientific terms has been helpful in instructing Hispanic ESL students. In addition, working collaboratively enhances language development when interactions between group members can take place in both English and the student's native language (Hodson, 1993). It may also be helpful for a teacher to simplify scientific terms and avoid overuse of complex terminology. The use of simpler terms, however, does not imply the delivery of lesser content.

Another approach is aimed at getting the community involved in the science classroom. It is important that students see how the class relates to other people's lives in the adult world. One suggestion by Rakow and Bermudez (1993) is to have former students come and visit the class. This way, students get to know someone who "made it through the class" and are able to gain some insight as to life after school.

The importance of same-race mentors cannot be overstated, as students see that others like themselves can do science. Teachers should make a point to locate people of color who can bring students closer to the subject matter. A teacher can seek role models from local hospitals, universities, and public and private laboratories.

As part of creating a multicultural atmosphere and taking part in social activism, a teacher should also contact local advocacy groups and organizations that represent the interests of minority groups (Allen-Somerville, 1996). These groups can act as a strong center of community support for the multicultural science classroom by providing an additional source of role models and opportunities to raise funds for lab equipment, student projects, and activities.

Specific class activities, lessons, and projects promote a multicultural classroom as well. Cobern (1994) suggests that teachers begin their instruction by creating an atmosphere in which students are more important than the subject matter and in which serious, positive dialogue can take place. By emphasizing the humanistic side of science, the classroom can become a place where students can learn from each other and express their beliefs and opinions. Multicultural dialogue can take place in classes other than language arts and history. In order to establish a classroom environment that is conducive to dialogue, Cobern (1994) suggests that teachers begin by asking their class to comment on metaphysical topics, such as the essence of nature, the existence of life, the meaning of being human, and the definition of society. These are questions that can be asked on the first day of class. Teachers must clearly communicate from the first day that science is a human activity and that it is acceptable to ask questions that concern everyone. Students should be aware that the science classroom can be a place where a multicultural dialogue can take place.

Dorough and Bonner (1996) describe two classroom activities that promote multicultural dialogue. In the first activity, "The Egg Drop," students try to construct a vehicle for a raw egg such that it will not break when dropped. Instead of allowing students to choose whatever materials they want, the teacher makes up several different kits for each team of students. For example, one kit may have plastic straws and masking tape, another may have Styrofoam cups and glue, while still another kit has only a few sheets of aluminum foil. After the students build their egg-drop vehicles and the most successful team is selected, teachers facilitate a discussion among the students. Students should discuss how they felt about some groups having an unfair advantage. This activity allows students to demonstrate their creativity and discuss issues of inequality and oppression in a science-related context.

The second activity that Dorough and Bonner (1996) describe, "Cross-Cultural chemicals," emphasizes unfamiliar student-to-student interaction. Students are each given 15 trading cards, with each card labeled C, N, O, H, or Cl, corresponding to one atom of the respective element. Students then trade cards with each other with the goal of assembling molecules with different point values. For example, CCl_4 is worth 4 points while CH_4 is worth 3 points. Some students will have more Cl cards than others will, making the initial distribution of points intentionally unequal. Students are not allowed to talk except while trading and must also shake hands during a trade. After 10 minutes of trading, the student with the most points wins, and the teacher engages the class in a discussion. Like "The Egg Drop," this activity promotes a discussion of equality among students, while alerting them to their own tendencies to associate with particular people. Most importantly, this activity challenges their feelings about coming into physical contact with people they do not interact with in their social environment.

While the methods for these activities should be kept intact, these lessons can be modified to fit other science-related activities. Virtually any experiment that requires students to construct something can be aligned with these antiracist activities.

When conducting antiracist activities, it is important to give a clear definition of what antiracism means. Hodson (1993) defines antiracism as revealing and combating inflexible attitudes that place minority groups at a disadvantage in society. Antiracist education, therefore, takes a critical look at the existing power structures within our society.

In taking a critical look at society, students should investigate the ways in which the term *race* has been misused to perpetuate racism and how science has been used by the dominant culture to classify people as inferior (Hodson, 1993). Also, a teacher needs to show how industry and modern warfare use science for moneymaking and destruction. Most importantly, students should realize that they have the power to change the way science is used in our society and how scientific knowledge can be applied to the advancement of people as a whole.

Students can research specific topics such as how technological advancements perpetuate classism or how the greed of Western nations has depleted natural resources and lowered the standard of living in countries around the world. Students should be able to find ways that they can change the manner in which science is used by our society. Research projects such as these should be added to a student's portfolio.

While it is important for a teacher to evaluate his or her materials from a multicultural perspective, students can also benefit from taking part in this process (Hodson, 1993). Students can work collaboratively, scanning science textbooks, videos, filmstrips, etc., for material that reinforces prejudice. A list of criteria can be used to evaluate material on the basis of linguistics, stereotyping, and other criteria. By applying these criteria to various sources of information, students will learn how important it is to evaluate everything with a critical eye.

CONCLUSION/SUMMARY

Our nation desperately needs to reform the way it teaches science; not just in order to attract more people of color into science-related fields, but to create a learning environment that promotes and nurtures the principles of democracy and social justice. The process of multicultural science is a complex path that every science educator should consider. Having a multicultural science program is a necessity if science educators are interested in addressing the needs of a culturally, linguistically, ethnically, and economically diverse student population.

REFERENCES

African American Education Data Book, Volume I: Higher and Adult Education. (1997). Fairfax, VA: Fredrick D. Patterson Research Institute.

Aikenhead, G. S. (1996). Toward a first nations cross-cultural science and technology curriculum. *Science Education, 81*(2), 217–238.

Allen-Sommerville, L. (1996). Capitalizing on diversity: Strategies for customizing your curriculum to meet the needs of all students. *Science Teacher, 63*(2), 20–23.

American Association of University Women (1992). *How schools short-change girls.* Washington, DC: American Association of University Women Educational Foundation.

Atwater, M. M. (1993). Multicultural science education: Assumptions and alternative views. *Science Teacher, 60*(3), 32–37.

Atwater, M. M., & Brown, M. (1999). Inclusive Reform. *Science Teacher, 66*(3), 44–48.

Banks, J. & Banks, C. (1997). *Multicultural Education: Issues and Perspectives* (3rd ed.). Boston: Allyn and Bacon.

Baptiste, P. H., & Key, S. G. (1996). Cultural inclusion: Where does your program stand? *Science Teacher, 63*(2), 32–35.

Bennett, C. I. (1995). *Comprehensive Multicultural Education: Theory and Practice* (3rd ed.). Boston: Allyn and Bacon.

Bennett, C. I. (1990). *Comprehensive Multicultural Education: Theory and Practice* (2nd ed.). Boston: Allyn and Bacon.

Bishop, R. S. (1992). Extending multicultural understanding. In B. Cullinan (Ed.), *Invitation to read: More children's literature in the reading program* (pp. 80–91). Newark, DE: International Reading Association.

Bryant, N., Jr. (1996). Make the curriculum multicultural. *Science Teacher, 63*(2): 28–31.

Carter, N. P., & Larke, P. J. (1995). Preparing the urban teacher: Reconceptualizing the experience. In O'Hair and Dell (Eds.), *Teacher education yearbook II* (pp. 77–95). Thousand Oaks, CA: Corwin.

Clark, J. V. (1996). *Redirecting science education: Reform for a culturally diverse classroom.* Thousand Oaks, CA: Corwin.

Cobb, P. (1994). Constructivism in mathematics and science education. *Educational Researcher, 23*(7), 4.

Cobern, W. (1994). Point: Belief, understanding, and the teaching of evolution. *Journal of Research in Science Teaching, 31*(5), 583–590.

The Council of Great City Schools. (1994). *Dropouts in great city schools.* Washington, DC: Author.

Dorough, D. K., & Bonner, R. C. (1996). Incorporating multicultural dialogue: How to encourage open discourse in the classroom. *Science Teacher, 63*(2), 50–52.

Eide, K. Y., & Heikkinen, M. W. (1998). The inclusion of multicultural material in middle school science teachers' resource materials. *Science Education, 82*(2), 181–195.

Estrada, L. F. (1993). The dynamic of demographic mosaic called America: Implications for education. *Education and Urban Society, 25*(3), 231–245.

Fordham, S. (1993). Those loud Black girls: (Black) women, silence, and gender "passing" in the academy. *Anthropology and Education Quarterly, 24*(1), 3–33.

Gibson, S., & Dembo, M. H. (1984). Teacher efficacy: A construct validation. *Journal of Educational Psychology, 76*(4), 569–582.

Gollnick, D. M. & Chinn, P. C. (1998). *Multicultural education in a pluralistic society* (5th ed.). Upper Saddle River, NJ: Prentice-Hall.

Grubbs, A. M., Rosenthal, D., & Lee, J. A. (1998, April). *Formative evaluation within a program to increase minority participation in science teaching and learning.* Paper presented at the annual meeting of the National Association for Research in Science Teaching, Anaheim, CA.

Hart, D. (1977). Enlarging the American dream. *American Education, 13*(4), 10–17.

Hashweh, M. (1987). Effects of subject-matter knowledge in the teaching of biology and physics. *Teaching and Teacher Education, 3*(2), 109–120.

Hodson, D. (1993). In search of a rationale for multicultural science education. *Science Education, 77*(6), 685–711.

Ladson-Billings, G. (1995). But that's just good teaching! The case for culturally relevant pedagogy. *Theory into Practice, 34*(3), 159–165.

Murdock, S., Hogue, M., & White, P. (1997). *The Texas challenge: Population change and the future of Texas.* College Station, TX: Texas A&M University.

National Science Teachers Association Board of Directors (1991). *A NSTA position statement: Multicultural science education.* Washington, DC: National Science Teachers Association.

Nelson-Barber, S. & Estrin, E. (1995). Bringing Native American perspectives to mathematics and science teaching. *Theory into Practice, 34*(3), 174–185.

Nieto, S. (1996). *Affirming diversity: The sociopolitical context of multicultural education* (2nd ed.). White Plains, NY: Longman.

Nobles, C., & Larke, P. (1998, October). *Embracing diversity in the workplace.* Paper presented at the annual meeting of the National Association of Multicultural Education, St. Louis, MO.

Noordhoff, K., & Kleinfeld, J. (1993). Preparing teachers for multicultural classrooms. *Teaching and Teacher Education, 9*(1), 27–39.

Ogawa, M. (1995). Science education in a multiscience perspective. *Science Education, 79*(5), 583–593.

Pallas, A. M., Natriello, G., & McDill, E. L. (1989). The changing nature of disadvantaged population: Dimensions and future trends. *Educational Researcher, 18*(5), 16–22.

Parsons, E. C. (1997). Black high school females' images of the scientist: Expression of culture. *Journal of Research in Science Teaching, 34*(7), 745–768.

Rakow, S. J., & Bermudez, A. B. (1993). Science is "ciencia": Meeting the needs of Hispanic American students. *Science Education, 77*(6), 669–683.

Ramirez, M., & Castaneda, A. (1974). *Cultural democracy: Bicognitive development and education.* New York: Academic Press.

Santos, E. & Larke, P. (1998, October). *What can I do in my science class tomorrow? A primer for teaching science that is multicultural.* Paper presented at the annual meeting of the National Association of Multicultural Education, St. Louis, MO.

Stanley, W. B. & Brickhouse, N. W. (1994). Multiculturalism, universalism and science education. *Science Education, 78*(4), 387–398.

U.S. Bureau of the Census. (1993). *Statistical Abstract of the United States* (113th ed.). Washington, DC: U.S. Government Printing Office.

Versey, J. (1990). Taking action on gender issues in science education. *School Science Review, 71*(256), 9–14.

Weiss, I. S. (1987). *Report of the 1985–1986 national survey of science and mathematics education.* National Science Foundation. SPE-8317070. Washington, DC: U.S. Government Printing Office.

Weiss, I. & Boyd, S. (1990). *Where are they now? A follow-up study of 1985–86 science and mathematics teaching force.* Chapel Hill, NC: Horizon Research.

The World Almanac and Book of Facts 1997. (1996). Mahwah, NJ: World Almanac Books.

Yager, R. E. (1989). What science should contribute to cultural literacy. *Clearing House, 62*(7), 297–302.

Yager, R. E. (1983). The importance of terminology in teaching K–12 science. *Journal of Research in Science Teaching, 78*(6), 577–588.

CHAPTER 2

"Science for All" and Invisible
Ethnicities: How the Discourse of
Power and Good Intentions
Undermine the National Science
Education Standards

Alberto J. Rodriguez

INTRODUCTION

Our conclusions were these: more than ever we must take care to ignore color. We must *only* look at behavior, and since a black child will
be more prominent in a white classroom, we must bend over backward
to see no color, hear no color, speak no color. (p. 7, emphasis in the
original)

These are well-intentioned, yet misguided, words from Vivian Paley's
compelling book *White Teacher* (1979). In her book, Paley explained
how after five years of keen observation and introspection, she learned to
celebrate the cultural diversity of her classroom, and to avoid making her
students' cultural differences (their color) invisible. In fact, for the last
two decades, multicultural education as a field of inquiry has advanced
our understanding of how cultural differences can be used as powerful
resources for enhancing learning, participation, and collaboration in the
classroom (Atwater 1995, 1993; Banks, 1995, 1993; Grant & Sleeter,
1986). Despite the progress made in recent years, the current "standards
craze" sweeping the country threatens the educational opportunities of
already disadvantaged students by making invisible the social inequities
that gave rise to the calls for education reform and standards in the first

place. A good example of this problem is reflected in the National Research Council's influential *National Science Education Standards* (1996). In this chapter, I argue that the Science Education Standards are written with the same kind of "cultural color-blindness" that Paley urged us to avoid almost 20 years ago. The *discourse of invisibility* used in the Science Standards dangerously compromises their well-intended goals by not directly addressing the ethnic, socioeconomic, gender, and pedagogical issues that afflict science education today. This prevents the Standards from having the desired impact on curriculum and teacher professional development that could lead to higher achievement and participation of traditionally underrepresented students (i.e., women, the poor, and students from Latino/a, African, First Nations [Native American], and Asian ethnic backgrounds).

I begin this critique with a discussion of how the Standards make ethnicity invisible, and how this invisibility contradicts one of the Standards' main goals—to make science accessible to "all Americans." This will be followed by an analysis of how preservice and established teachers resist learning to teach for diversity and for understanding. Sometimes this resistance is grounded on ideological and/or pedagogical differences between what teachers perceive to be good teaching and what reform documents dictate. For beginning teachers, however, sometimes resistance to change may mean having to reluctantly comply with what their school advisors dictate in order to do well in ("survive") their student teaching experience. It is argued that the complexity of implementing sweeping structural and cultural changes in the teaching profession must be acknowledged in the Standards document as a first step to establishing intellectually honest and meaningful dialogues.

In the last section of this chapter, one of the vignettes or illustrations of exemplary practice in the Standards document will be discussed. My goal is to describe how the example provided by the Standards is another case of ethnocentric, hands-on, minds-off teaching and learning that prevents students from understanding the contributions to science made by men and women from diverse backgrounds.

(IN)VISIBLE FACES

There are 44 photographs in the National Science Standards (1996) document. Fifty-eight percent of all the individuals shown in the photographs are from ethnic groups traditionally underrepresented in science.

In fact, most of the photographs depict minority boys (28 in total) and girls (25 in total) actively engaged in hands-on science. Another traditionally marginalized group in the sciences, females, is the second largest group (55%) of individuals included in the photographs. Some may think that such an effort to make minority students and women so visible in the National Science Education Standards should be cause for celebration. I would agree if it were not for how the same underrepresented groups were made invisible within the text of the Standards.

The discourse of invisibility used in the Standards takes many forms, and some forms are subtler than others. For example, words commonly used to describe ethnic groups such as Latinas/Latinos (Hispanics), African Americans, Asian Americans, and/or First Nations Peoples (Native Americans), are not even used once in the entire 262-page document. These ethnic groups are made invisible within general statements such as: "The National Science Education Standards are standards for all Americans: Equity is an underlying principle for the Standards and should pervade all aspects of science education" (p. 16). This stance unequivocally points in the direction of much needed social change. But the Standards fail to explain equity for whom and why. Are there historical, institutional, and social reasons why we should be so concerned with equity today?

Answers to these questions are not found anywhere in the Standards document, and this absence damages the potential of the Standards to foster equity "for all Americans." I do find, however, tentative yet ambiguous language every time reference is made to equity issues. For instance, "[The Standards] emphatically reject any situation in science education where some people, for example members of certain populations, are discouraged from pursuing science and excluded from opportunities to learn science" (p. 20). Therefore, all those concerned with equity issues must ask, who are these "members of certain populations"? Why are they made invisible in the document? Why are they not named directly?

It is this rendering invisible of women, the poor, and students of African, Latino/a, and First Nations ethnic backgrounds that raises critical questions about the ability of the Science Education Standards to provide a road map for education reform. In their present form, the only map the Standards provide is a map that leads to cultural color blindness.

How can the Standards be improved? What is needed is a well-articulated rationale as to *why* equity has taken such a prominent place in the Standards. A good place to start would be to make readers aware of the persistent achievement gap between students of middle- and upper-class Anglo-European and Asian descent and traditionally underserved students in science (Blank & Gruebel, 1995; Mullis et al., 1994; Rodriguez, 1998a; Smith, et. al., 1995). For instance, the National Assessment of Educational Progress (NAEP) is probably the most comprehensive tool for assessing students' cognitive achievement in science. NAEP draws from a representative sample of the U.S. student population in grades 4 (age 9), 8 (age 13), and 12 (age 17). When one observes the NAEP trends in student achievement for the last 20 years, the gap in science performance scores of students of African, Latino/a, and Anglo–European descent closed modestly from 1977 to 1986 (Mullis et al., 1994). From 1986 to 1992, however, the achievement gains of underserved students seem to have stalled. Furthermore, despite the improvement in the last 10 years, the gaps and differences in scores among Anglo-European students and traditionally underserved students are still quite large for all three age groups considered. A more detailed discussion of trends in student achievement by gender within ethnic groups, and of the adverse effects of unequal access to educational opportunities, is presented elsewhere (Rodriguez, 1998a).[1]

The differences in student dropout (pushout) rates can also be used as powerful indicators of the need for reform in education. For example, in 1972, about 21% of African Americans between the ages of 16 and 24 had dropped out of school. The rate for the same ethnic group dropped 9 points to 12.6% in 1994. In contrast, the dropout rate of U.S. Anglo students changed from 12.5% in 1972 to 7.7% in 1994. At the other extreme, the dropout rate of 16-to 24-year-old Latina/o students has consistently remained between 30 and 35% for over two decades! (McMillen & Kaufman, 1994; Secada et. al., 1998). Despite some improvement in the dropout rates of students from African and Anglo-European backgrounds, the dropout rate of Latinos/as has stayed virtually the same for the last 26 years (McMillen & Kaufman, 1994).

How can calls for science education reform be made without explaining why the fastest growing ethnic groups in the country continue to be underrepresented in science, mathematics, engineering, and technology-related fields? Reformers should make good use of available information in support of equity. For example, we know that in 1991, just over 6% of all science and engineering degrees awarded to U.S. citizens were conferred to African Americans (National Science Foundation,

1996). Similarly, Latinos/as attained only 5% of all science and engineering degrees.

In addition to making readers aware of how current trends in student achievement affect our collective future, the Science Education Standards should have provided a more intellectually honest dialogue with regard to the challenges associated in bringing about change in today's schools. It is naive to expect that teachers and administrators who already are overworked will be willing and/or will have the time to take the challenges associated with transforming their traditional practices in substantial ways. An increasing body of research (Ahlquist, 1991; Gomez, 1994; Haberman, 1991; Tatum, 1992; Zeichner, 1992) indicates that preservice and inservice teachers demand and deserve a lot more than "well-intended" policies to help them change their traditional practices. Some teacher educators (Grant, 1991; Sleeter, 1994) point to institutional racism as one of the main causes preventing teachers from learning to teach for diversity (i.e., implementing socially relevant and culturally inclusive pedagogical strategies for the benefit of all children). Sleeter (1994) explains that institutional racism (taken-for-granted institutional practices such as standardized testing, tracking, heavy teaching loads, large classes, etc.) discriminates against underserved students and serves to reproduce the status quo. Similarly, King (1991) states that dysconscious racism (a subtle and unconscious form of discrimination) is deeply embedded in an individual's belief and values system and conspires against the individual's opportunities to see the social world in new and inclusive ways. My research work with preservice secondary science teachers supports these claims.

(IN)VISIBLE RESISTANCE TO CHANGE

In my secondary science methods class, I am usually the only member of an underrepresented ethnic group, and in this class some students strongly resist the multicultural science focus of the course. They perceive teaching for diversity as something that "should be discussed in other classes, not in a science classroom" (Rodriguez, 1998b). Some feel that they do not have to worry about diversity issues because they "do not want to teach in urban schools." Other students, during classroom discussions on the nature of science, have declared that "if women and minorities want to be successful in science then they are just going to have to work as hard as White males" (Rodriguez, 1998b). These comments come from deeply ingrained belief systems preservice teachers bring with them (Grossman & Richert, 1988; Lortie, 1975). Therefore, these preservice teachers are essentially demanding to know *why* they should change the same competitive system that has worked well for them so far. It is at this intersection that the Standards miss their mark. The Standards miss the opportunity to provide strong arguments in support of *why* we should teach for "all Americans" and not just for the traditionally privileged few.

Similarly, while the Standards suggest that teachers should use student-centered and collaborative styles of teaching, some researchers have indicated how reluctant some teachers can be to change their ways. Some established teachers may also oppose beginning teachers' attempts to teach against the grain; to teach in ways different from the accepted norm in their school. In recent studies, Erickson, Mayer-Smith, Rodriguez, Chin, and Mitchell (1994) and Rodriguez (1995) explain that even preservice teachers who were originally interested in moving away from traditional, teacher-centered roles found themselves copying their cooperating teachers as a strategy to "do what works" and get through the content-laden curriculum.

By following six preservice teachers during their teacher preparation program, Rodriguez (1995, 1993) found that despite efforts to enhance communication and collaboration with school and university advisors through monthly meetings and frequent school visits, social factors such as trust, power, school culture, and institutional issues such as curriculum demands, time constraints, university expectations, pupil ability, and others, worked against some of the preservice teachers' desire to implement innovative or constructivist approaches in their classrooms. Rodriguez explained that due to these tensions, some preservice teachers implemented a series of strategies to guarantee the successful completion of their student teaching experience. These strategies are in direct opposition to what the Professional Development Standards suggest in the NRC Standards, but these strategies are what some of the preservice teachers felt they needed to do to "survive" their student teaching experience. This type of finding is not by any means new. Research on teacher socialization has made this clear (Britzman, 1986; Lacey, 1977; McNeil, 1986; Zeichner & Gore, 1990; Zeichner & Tabachnick, 1981). However, what we need to explore more fully and what the NRC Standards should make more visible are specific suggestions for managing the factors working against beginning teachers' efforts to teach in student-centered ways. For instance, Colin Lacey (1977) explains that teachers engage in *strategic compliance* when they feel they *must* follow given directives and expectations despite their strong reservations on the usefulness or benefits of such directives. Similarly, preservice teachers enact various forms of verbal and nonverbal strategic compliance to manage the contradictions and dilemmas they encounter in learning to teach in borrowed classrooms (Rodriguez, 1995, 1993).

Ellen, one of the preservice teachers in Rodriguez's (1995, 1993) study, provides a good example of strategic compliance below:

> I guess before the practicum I kind of had ideas of what [my faculty advisor] expected or wanted. That sort of thing, so she really hasn't changed my views all that much. I listen to what she has to say, and if it's different I may try it out, but I'm more to the point that I'll try out my sponsor teacher's stuff before hers. Except for when she comes [to observe my class]. I mean, because everybody plays the game that when the sponsor teacher comes—or the faculty advisor comes you give them what they want. And I think that's just because they're only there four or five times and everybody believe that you have to do well for them. (Interview mid-point of student teaching placement, MP3)

In other words, if the university supervisor (who was also involved in the research project) expected the student to implement a constructivist and student-centered approach, then the preservice teacher performed what the supervisor wanted to see. On the other hand, if the cooperating teacher came in to observe and he or she found constructivist teaching to be "too time-consuming," unmanageable or "airy-fairy,"[2] the preservice teacher would lecture and follow a more rigid classroom interaction. This complex performance of whatever approach to teaching and learning the supervisor who came to observe their classes favored the most has very little to do with learning to teach. It has to do only with making sense of perceived contradictory information between the ideal (well-intended policies, teacher education program goals, etc.), and the actual demands of learning to become a member of a profession so resistant to change.

Another factor that the Standards fail to acknowledge is the difficulties teachers often encounter when attempting to change the content-laden science curriculum. While I wholeheartedly agree with the spirit behind the Standards' maxim of "less is more," my work with preservice and inservice teachers again points out the need to provide teachers with more than powerful slogans. Alfred, another preservice teacher participating in the collaborative project mentioned above, explains the strategy he used to cope with curriculum demands during student teaching:

> Alfred: I found out, and heard people talked about this summer, that when you are out there [during student teaching] you want to try this activity, or that activity because it's fun, it's innovative [constructivist], but you would burn yourself out. There is no one in the world that would have all the time and energy to do all those things. Someone said that you sort of have to step back and go into the "old way of teaching," and once you get into the swing of things, then you can start pulling things and do demos, and stuff. You should try some things, but you just can't start full out from the beginning of the year.

> AR: Did you find that you were trying a lot of these activities and that you were getting burnt out?

> Alfred: Not burnt out, but I did things to prevent getting burnt out. Like my school advisor said that I spent too much time behind the overhead projector, but that was my way of surviving; my way of keeping from burning out.

> AR: By the "old-fashioned way of teaching" you mean—

> Alfred: Teacher-directed, lecturing, blabbing on and on. Simply because there wasn't enough time. (Interview at the end of the student teaching, EP4)

Note that Alfred was very interested in the project's focus on student-centered, constructivist teaching, which is the same focus as the Standards, but he felt that the demands of teaching in the school context took precedence over what he believed to be "good teaching." In other words, the curriculum ends driving the teacher instead of the teacher driving the curriculum to meet the needs of his/her students in their specific contexts. This is a common issue in education today that the Standards should acknowledge and directly address.

In the end, three of the six preservice teachers participating in Rodriguez's study felt that they spent more time learning how to be "good" preservice teachers (i.e., avoiding conflicts with their supervisors and pupils), while their original intentions were to learn how to be effective science teachers (Rodriguez, 1995, 1993). The other three preservice teachers who developed more collaborative relationships with their school advisors in this study indicated that they felt more confident in taking risks and trying new pedagogical approaches in the classroom because their advisors created a genuine environment of trust and support.

I believe that for the Standards to have the kind of meaningful and lasting impact they wish to have on science teaching and learning, they must first engage readers in an intellectually honest dialogue. Just as the Standards provide vignettes as examples for implementation, they should provide vignettes describing the dilemmas and difficulties preservice and inservice teachers encounter when attempting to teach against the grain. In this way, the Standards could provide research-based arguments and compelling evidence that would urge teachers and administrators to critically reflect on how well their students are learning, how socially relevant the prescribed curriculum is, how ethnically and gender-diverse their advanced science courses are, and how all of us are affected by not having diverse learners pursue science-related careers.

It is going to take a great deal more than what the present Standards offer to encourage established teachers and administrators to transform their traditional practices. By acknowledging, making visible, the social, structural, theoretical, or/and ideological factors encouraging teachers to resist change, all concerned can begin to work collectively to counter this resistance.

AN (IN)VISIBLE STANDARD EXAMPLE OF ETHNOCENTRIC PRACTICE IN THE STANDARDS

Throughout the Science Standards document, a variety of vignettes are presented to illustrate more concretely how some of the goals of the Standards could be implemented. However, from the perspective of a Latino science educator engaged in multicultural science education, the most disappointing part of the Science Standards begins in the vignette found on page 215. This example is meant to illustrate how mathematics and science can be integrated, how teachers from different disciplines can collaborate to enhance student learning, how pupils can be engaged in scientific inquiry, and how "men and women have made a variety of contributions throughout the history of science and technology" (p. 141), the latter point being one of the Standards' main goals, equity. However, in this example, as in others, we are presented with a nameless teacher (Ms. B.), who has an invisible ethnic background and who is teaching in an ethnically and culturally invisible Grade 8 classroom. In this example, students are to figure out how to determine the circumference of the

earth. This activity "was designed to allow students to think like astronomers did 500 years ago" (p. 215). The teacher set the stage by
asking kids to speculate how something as large as the circumference of
the earth could be measured. After getting some expected responses, Ms.
B. declared that they "were going to try to find out for themselves" in a
way similar to how "astronomers learned new things" (p. 215). She went
on to explain that students could calculate the circumference of the earth
by using the North Star. After a few late-night observations and some basic instruction in geometry, Ms. B. helped students "discover" how in
"Columbus's day" it was known from ground travel that the distance
between a town in Scandinavia (where the North Star angle was 67 degrees from the horizon) and another town in Italy (where the North Star
angle was 43 degrees from the horizon) was about 3,000 miles. This activity yields a crude, yet pretty close, approximation of the actual
circumference of the earth. Many students no doubt would enjoy the
problem-solving aspect of the activity. So what is wrong with this example, and how does it contradict the suggested Standards?

To start, this example certainly appears hands-on, but how is it
minds-on and how is it multiculturally inclusive? If students are guided
to "discover" (replicate) something that they know the teacher knows in
the first place, and if the students realize that they are supposed to discover the answer to the given problem(s) by using the given tools and by
following the given procedures, where does creative scientific inquiry
enter into this equation? Furthermore, I would argue that students who
for one reason or another are not interested in science may not feel motivated to discover anything, because they know that there is always going
to eventually be one right answer, the teacher's answer. Second, students
in the example given above are robbed of an excellent opportunity to
celebrate the ingenuity of peoples from other cultures and hence accom-
plish one of the main goals of the Standards. The example provided on
page 215 never gives credit to Eratosthenes, the first scientist from antiquity to measure the circumference of the earth (Newman, 1956). Even
worse, the example was Westernized to include only Western cities (in
Scandinavia and Italy), only Western measurements (miles), and only
Western timelines ("500 years ago" and "Columbus's day").

A multicultural and minds-on scientific inquiry approach in this vignette would have been an excellent way to demonstrate how the
Standards could provide some leadership in transforming today's classroom. For instance, a different way of presenting this vignette would be

to engage students in a role-playing activity by which each one of them is a member of the great University of Alexandria. There, they are involved in scientific inquiry with Eratosthenes (played by the teacher or a student). In reality, Eratosthenes was born in Libya around 274 B.C. and was educated in the city of Athens, a thriving center of arts and science at the time. He then taught at the University of Alexandria (Egypt), and there he was given charge of the most important library in the known Western world. Students usually find it fascinating to figure out how over 2,000 years ago Eratosthenes calculated the circumference of the earth by measuring the angle of the shadow the sun cast on sun dials in two different cities in North Africa. He knew that on June 21, at noon, the sun cast no shadows in Syene; hence, he concluded that the sun must be directly overhead. In the city of Alexandria, on the other hand, the sun did cast shadows. Hence, Eratosthenes concluded that the sun's rays striking the earth must be parallel. Using some basic geometry, he determined the angle of the sun's rays falling on Alexandria by using the length of the sun dial pointer and the length of the pointer's shadow. Since the distance between Alexandria and Syene was known to be 5,000 *stadia*,[3] Eratosthenes used a simple proportion calculation to estimate the circumference of the earth, and his estimate was off only by about 16% of the actual value! (Multiculturalism in mathematics, science and technology, 1993; Newman, 1956). There are many ways a teacher could facilitate learning in this activity, and the role-playing format encourages students to immerse themselves in the social context of how scientists from ancient times lived and carried out their work.

Another important difference between this approach and the one given in the Standards is intellectual honesty. In the role-playing activity, students are aware that they are not expected to discover how Eratosthenes calculated the circumference of the earth (because they know that Eratosthenes already did that), they are instead expected to figure out how he did it and find alternate ways to solve the problem if possible. They are also expected to use materials and construct models to collaboratively arrive at reasonable explanation(s). Furthermore, they are later encouraged to apply the newly acquired knowledge by solving related problems, such as how to calculate the length of South America and so on. I could revisit other examples/vignettes provided in the Standards document, but this is not the focus of the essay. Hopefully, it is clear that the example provided on page 215 fails to demonstrate what is meant by "Themes and topics chosen for curricula should support the premise that men and women of diverse backgrounds engage in and participate in science and have done so throughout history" (p. 222).

To close, the Standards do have many positive aspects. Perhaps the most important is that the existence of a nationwide set of science education standards opens a focal point for dialogue about what constitutes good teaching and what science knowledges and processes are of most value. The Standards also provide many bold suggestions on the roles policy makers and administrators should take in order to implement any kind of long-lasting and significant change at the systemic level. Despite these strengths, I argue that the science education standards on teaching, on professional development, and on content are framed in a discourse of invisibility that primarily undermines the Standards' principle of equity and excellence. Those who believe that the Standards provide a starting point for much needed social change at all school levels will be inclined to demand that the Standards be strengthened by making *visible* more arguments and evidence in support of equity and excellence as everybody's concern. These arguments must also be supported with specific suggestions for how to enact the necessary structural and cultural changes that could sustain an inclusive and student-centered science curriculum. In this way, equity could eventually become an act of social conscience, rather than a set of well-intended written or spoken words. Excellence in education can only be measured when equity has been established first.

NOTES

[1]This study also includes an analysis of the problems and stereotypes associated with reporting the academic achievement in science of students of color under generic ethnic groups such as "Asian" or "Latino/a."

[2]Some of the cooperating teachers upheld this term throughout the project. They believed that a constructivist approach was unrealistic in terms of the demands to cover the content-laden high school curriculum and in terms of the demands to manage the pupils' behavior.

[3]During this time, one *stadium* (plural: *stadia*) was the distance from one end of a stadium to the other.

REFERENCES

Ahlquist, R. (1991). Position and imposition: Power relations in a multicultural foundations class. *Journal of Negro Education, 60*(2), 158–169.

Atwater, M. (1995). The multicultural science classroom. *Science Teacher, 62*(2), 21–23.

Atwater, M. (1993). Multicultural science education: Perspectives, definitions, and research agenda. *Science Education, 77*(6), 661–668.

Banks, J. (1995). The historical reconstruction of knowledge about race: Implications for transformative teaching. *Educational Researcher, 24*(2), 15–25.

Banks, J. (1993). *Multicultural education: Historical development, dimensions and practice. Review of Research in Education, 19,* 3–49.

Blank, R. K., & Gruebel, D. (1995). *State indicators of science and mathematics education 1995: State-by-state trends and new indicators from the 1993–94 school year.* Washington, DC: Council of Chief of State School Officers.

Britzman, D. P. (1986). Cultural myths in the making of a teacher: Biography and social structure in teacher education. *Harvard Educational Review, 56*(4), 442–456.

Erickson, G., Mayer-Smith, J., Rodriguez, A. J., Chin, P., & Mitchell, I. (1994). Perspectives on learning to teach science: Insights and dilemmas from a collaborative practicum project. *International Journal of Science Education, 16,* 585–597.

Gomez, M. L. (1994). Teacher education reform and prospective teachers' perspectives on teaching "other people's" children. *Teaching and Teacher Education, 10*(3), 319–334.

Grant, C. (1991). Culture and teaching: What do teachers need to know? In M. Kennedy (Ed.), *Teaching academic subjects to diverse learners* (pp. 237–256). New York: Teachers College.

Grant, C., & Sleeter, C. (1986). *Turning on learning: Five approaches for multicultural teaching plans for race, class, gender and disability.* New York: Merrill.

Grossman, P. L., & Richert, A. E. (1988). Unacknowledged knowledge growth: A re-examination of the effects of teacher education. *Teaching & Teacher Education, 4*(1), 53–62.

Haberman, M. (1991). Can cultural awareness be taught in teacher education programs? *Teaching Education, 4*(1), 25–32.

King, J. (1991). Dysconscious racism: Ideology, identity, and the miseducation of teachers. *The Journal of Negro Education, 60*(2), 133–146.

Lacey, C. (1977). *The socialization of teachers.* London: Methuen.

Lortie, D. (1975). *School teacher.* Chicago: University of Chicago.

McMillen, M. M., & Kaufman, P. A. (1994). *Dropout rates in the United States: 1994 (NCES 96-863)*. Washington, DC: National Center for Educational Statistics.

McNeil, L. M. (1986). *Contradictions of control: School structure and school knowledge*. New York: Routledge.

Mullis, I. V. S., Dossey, J. A., Campbell, J. R., Gentile, C. A., O'Sullivan, C., & Latham, A. (1994). *NAEP 1992 trends in academic progress: Achievement of U.S. students in science, 1969 to 1992; mathematics, 1973 to 1992; reading, 1971 to 1992 and writing, 1984 to 1992* (23-TR01). Washington, DC: National Center for Education Statistics.

Multiculturalism in mathematics, science and technology. (1993). *Multiculturalism in mathematics, science and technology: Readings and activities*. Menlo Park, CA: Addison-Wesley.

National Research Council (1996). *National science education standards*. Washington, DC: National Academy Press.

National Science Foundation. (1996). *Indicators of science and mathematics education 1995*. Arlington: Author.

Newman, J. (1956). *The world of mathematics*. New York: Simon & Schuster.

Paley, V. G. (1979). *White teacher*. Cambridge, MA: Harvard University.

Rodriguez, A. J. (1998a). Busting open the meritocracy myth: Rethinking equity and student achievement in science. *Journal of Women and Minorities in Science and Engineering, 4*(2&3), 195–216.

Rodriguez, A. J. (1998b). Strategies for counterresistance: Toward sociotransformative constructivism and learning to teach science for diversity and for understanding. *Journal of Research in Science Teaching, 36*(6), 589–622.

Rodriguez, A. J. (1995). *"I'm just performing": Playing roles, resistance and managing the dilemmas of learning to teach science*. Paper presented at the Annual Meeting of the American Research Association, San Francisco, CA.

Rodriguez, A. J. (1993). "A dose of reality": Understanding the origin of the theory/practice dichotomy in teacher education from the students' point of view. *Journal of Teacher Education, 44*(3), 213–222.

Secada, W., Chavez-Chavez, R., Garcia, E., Munoz, C., Oakes, J., Santiago-Santiago, I., & Slavin, R. (1998). *No more excuses: The final report of the Hispanic dropout project*. Washington, DC: U.S. Department of Education.

Sleeter, C. (1994). White racism. *Multicultural Education, 1*(4), 5–8, 39.

Smith, T. M., Perie, M., Asalam, N., Mahoney, R. P., Bae, Y., & Young, B. A. (1995). *The condition of education 1995* (NCES 95-273). Washington, DC: National Center for Education Statistics.

Tatum, B. D. (1992). Talking about race, learning about racism: The application of racial identity development theory in the classroom. *Harvard Educational Review, 62*(1), 1–24.

Zeichner, K. M. (1992). *Educating teachers for cultural diversity.* East Lansing, MI: National Center for Research on Teacher Education.

Zeichner, K. M., & Gore, J. M. (1990). Teacher socialization. In W. R. Houston (Ed.), *Handbook of research on teaching education* (pp. 329–348). New York: Macmillan.

Zeichner, K. M., & Tabachnick, B. R. (1981). Are the effects of university teacher education "washed out" by school experience? *Journal of Teacher Education, 23*(3), 7–11.

CHAPTER 3

Teaching Science from a Critical Multicultural Perspective

Roberta Ahlquist and Julie Kailin

In this chapter, we discuss the need to examine science education from a critical multicultural perspective. By critical multiculturalism we refer to a theoretical framework that goes beyond the typical cultural pluralist models of multicultural education. Such models advocate that we celebrate the contributions of all, but they neglect to acknowledge the systemic reasons why there is even a struggle for inclusion in the first place (Kailin, 1994). Often what are considered "multicultural" strategies do not confront the structural or the social and economic contexts of global corporate capitalism. By ignoring this social/political context, the awareness of stratification in society along race, class, and gender lines is minimized or even unrecognized. It is these oppressive divisions that help maintain the status quo, hence we believe it necessary to examine the social context of these divisions from a critical multicultural perspective. What we would like to focus on here are not the particulars of any branch of science, but rather on the necessity of helping our students consider science, in theory and practice, from a global, macro, socioeconomic, and historical context. This discussion does not concern the content of the curriculum *per se* but rather the need to incorporate into the curriculum a consideration of the social and political context of the development and application of science and technology.

Science, because of its elevated status in society, has always played a pivotal role in maintaining the status quo. But science can also be used to contest the status quo. We believe that science education should be an avenue of opportunity through which we can help our students critically analyze the functions that science and technology play in our society.

Such a critical perspective can help our students build concrete ideas about how science might help them more clearly define their potential roles in contributing to a more just, livable, and equitable world. This requires that science curriculum, just as much as the curriculum in the social sciences, can be used to help students understand in theory and practice the way our world "works."

Some kinds of knowledge in society have more cultural capital than others. In the United States in particular, and in the Western[1] capitalist world in general, science as a discipline traditionally holds an elevated and elitist status. Since the 17th century, Western capitalist sciences have had a monopoly on what is legitimated as scientific knowledge and whose knowledge gets known (Harding, 1998; O'Brien, 1993). Western science has been presented to most students in public schools as "neutral" or "value-free." Yet we know that the paradigms for science have and continue to be generated from Western colonial perspectives that represent certain interests of the ruling class and are hardly value-free (Harding, 1998). This is why it is important to demystify and dismantle the myth of superiority that Western capitalist science promotes. It is a dangerous myth because it disrespects and disregards the vast contributions of other peoples and civilizations on this earth. It is dangerous not only for the misreading of history, but for the arrogance that persists and manifests itself in the present moment, reinforcing the White supremacist assumption that the United States must be the number one superpower, world cop, accountable to no one. This myth of Western scientific superiority negates the vast Afro-Asiatic roots of science and so-called Western civilization (Bernal 1987; Weatherford, 1988). It also masks the fact of the appropriation of and reliance on scientists throughout the rest of the world by U.S. government and corporate interests. For example, a large number of the recent Ph.D.s in the sciences in the United States are from China and India, which contributes to a serious brain drain of scientists from many developing countries. These scientists are exploited in part because they are young and in the process of completing graduate work, and are therefore hired much more cheaply than American scientists.

Addressing science from a critical multicultural perspective means that we must situate science historically in time, circumstance, and place, and be critical, global, and inclusive. The development of modern science needs to be understood within the context of the global contributions to its development. All cultures of the world have made contributions to science and scientific methods and have exchanged or borrowed scientific ideas from other cultures, in their own particular histories (Bernal, 1987; Harding, 1998; Rodney, 1972; Shiva, 1997). For example, the teaching of mathematics would be incomplete without an appreciation and examination of the Arabic and Persian contributions to numbers theory (Ahlquist, 1998).

The historically significant scientific contributions of people from "developing" or more accurately, "super-exploited countries," those countries that have been grossly exploited by colonial and imperialist powers, must be included in the study of science. We must confront the historical amnesia that motivated "forgetting" or masking of, for example, the pivotal contributions and inventions of so-called "pre–Columbian" peoples in the "Western" world. As Weatherford (1988) and Bernal (1987) remind us, much of what we consider as "Western" in origin or invention, such as developments in agronomy and agriculture, astronomy and physics, comes from indigenous peoples in the Americas, Africa, and Asia. We must challenge the "West is best" prejudice that ignores or denies the values of different scientific paradigms and ways of seeing and knowing, and ways of being in different cultures. One aspect of the globalization of knowledge, and particularly of science, is that European science has been valorized while indigenous science, and science from developing countries, has been even more marginalized and essentialized, or reduced to simplistic explanations, by the Western science tradition (Harding, 1998; Malcolm, 1993). Harding describes Eurocentric science:

> Central among the presuppositions of Eurocentric discourses are that peoples of European descent, their institutions, practices, and favored conceptual schemes, express the unique heights of human development. Moreover, peoples of European descent and their civilization are presumed to be fundamentally self-generated, owing little or nothing to the institutions, practices, conceptual schemes, or peoples of other parts of the world. (p. 57)

How can science education be used to counter such an arrogant worldview? How can educators open their students' eyes to the larger social context of scientific and technological development? In the area of medicine, for example, a study of Western medicine is incomplete without a comparison and contrast among the many significant contributions of Eastern medicine, indigenous medical practices, and the development of "alternative" forms of healing and wellness, such as acupuncture, moxibustion, acupressure, massage, and herbal treatments from all over the world. Yet medical education does not require nor even provide an opportunity for an examination of alternative models of health, healing, disease, and proper nutrition. The one dimensional paradigm adopted by our powerful American medical establishment has not only ignored and de-legitimized the perspectives and practices of people of color, but it has robbed that historical knowledge from members of the dominant White cultures as well. After all, "folk" medicines have been used by all "folk" throughout human history.

We cannot afford to ignore the negative impact of racism, sexism, and patriarchy on the development of medicine and healing in general. For example, until very recently, heart research has historically been the domain of research on primarily White male patients, not females. Funding for male medical research has had priority over female research; for example, breast cancer only recently is getting the funding it deserves as a result of intensive lobbying by women, funding by women's organizations, and public criticism of the White male medical model of treatment (NOW Report on Women's Health, 1997). Other forms of cancer seem to affect certain racial minorities and ethnic groups disproportionately. For example, the incidence of lung cancer, the nation's number one cancer killer, is two and one-half times greater for African Americans than for Latinos. African Americans have also had the highest rates of lung, prostate, colon, and rectal cancer (Brown, 1999).

Our students should be required to take nothing for granted. They must examine the hard "objective" data from a social context. While we may not have the answers, for answers never are simplistic, nevertheless we must have the questions. For example, we must ask why the cancer rate for men is declining both in incidence and mortality at a higher rate than it is for women (Centers for Disease Control and Prevention, National Cancer Institute, and American Cancer Society, 1996). What are the ethnic, cultural, economic, or social factors that scientists should consider? What is the role of stress in contributing to disease? What is the effect of racism and sexism on contributing to stress? What are the physical and spiritual effects of stress on the body and soul? What is the role of social relations in producing stress? Nutrition, diet, social stress, and access to and quality of medical care play a significant role in differences in rates and treatment of disease as well as in scientific efforts to eradicate them.

Not only are race and gender often ignored in discussions of scientific progress, but research shows that U.S. government statistics often obscure social class in this country as well. In fact, it appears that the powers that be would just as soon not address social/economic status or class in statistics on health, safety, and other critical indicators of society. Social class is the key factor in determining whether someone has access to the best health care, in terms of diagnosis and treatment. Yet frequently there is a denial or absence of discussion of the socioeconomic context of capitalism. Navarro (1991) points out that in the majority of developed capitalist countries, social class is used to collect mortality statistics. But in the United States, the government collects statistics about mortality rates and causes of death by race, gender, and region, and not by socioeconomic class. This refusal to include class and the structural context of capitalism in an analysis of illness and disease distracts the focus on the *causes* of inequality in an inherently unjust system.

CORPORATE CAPITALISM AND THE ABUSE OF SCIENTIFIC "PROGRESS"

A critical science education should examine not only the extraordinary inventions and discoveries of science from all over the world but also the social impact of the application of science and technology on the daily life of the ordinary citizen and of those who have been disfranchised and marginalized. While science has indeed been applied to enhance the quality of life in many respects, the reckless application and use of science may lead to the deterioration of the quality of life for some, particularly for those who do not have a voice.

Students should critically examine the application/misapplication of science and technology. A recent example was in 1997 in Indonesia. Large plantation companies, many of these multinational conglomerates, set hundreds of acres of forest on fire in Indonesia, to quickly and cheaply clear wooded areas to replace the natural forest with fast-growing trees, such as rubber, eucalyptus, and oil palms. The resulting deadly haze over Malaysia and Indonesia has been described as the worst environmental crisis ever (*Time for Kids*, Malaysia, 1998). The air pollution index hit a record of 839 in Sarawak, Malaysia, on September 23, 1997. Even though in 1994 the Indonesian government banned forest burning, these fires continue and the law is being ignored. These multinational companies destroy peoples' health in that entire region of the world, as well as the existing environment of valuable tropical hardwood and lush tropical rain forests. Thousands of children and adults in Southeast Asia suffer today from respiratory ailments as a result of this disregard for human life.

This reckless use of scientific "progress" has also resulted in serious cases of environmental racism, where poor and minority communities have been used as toxic waste dumps. Taiwan companies recently tried to dump nuclear wastes first in Malaysia, and then in Thailand, before environmental groups became aware of their actions. Subsequently these toxic wastes were forced back onto the Taiwanese corporations to dispose of in a more responsible, less hazardous way. American and European corporations have been able to "sell" their nuclear and toxic wastes to countries in Africa and Asia, which often accept such waste as the only productive capacity they have because their own economies have been destroyed by colonialism and neocolonial policies. But who monitors these events such that powerless citizens in developing countries can be assured that they are not being subjected to such socially irresponsible actions? It is important for our students to understand the role that capitalist exploitation plays and not simply examine the role of development as a neutral enterprise. Industrialization and technology under capitalism have developed in ways that have often wreaked havoc on the environment as well as on the customs and the quality of daily life for working people. This environmental racism gets exported to the developing world, whose health safety has been disregarded by multinational corporations. Another classic example of multinational corporate disregard for the environments of others is the 1984 case of the Union Carbide Corporation in Bhopal, India, where the company knowingly built a substandard pesticide plant resulting in a deadly explosion that killed over 10,000 people and injured 200,000.

Such disregard also affects those in advanced capitalist countries. In the United States as well, those without power often find themselves working in the most dangerous and toxic environments. For example, Korean, Filipino, and Vietnamese women, working as programmers and technicians, who were exposed to chemicals in the computer chip industry in Silicon Valley in California, had a 33% higher incidence of miscarriage than women workers not exposed to these chemicals working in similar jobs (Silicon Valley Toxics Coalition, 1998). There is much documentation to show that the rate of cancers among California farm workers and their children who work in pesticide-sprayed fields is far higher than for farm workers not exposed to such pesticides. Because of the pressure and power of multinational corporations and their refusal to seriously address health and safety standards and to safely dispose of their toxic wastes, some corporations in the United States have managed to get the laws changed so that toxic wastes can now be classified as fertilizers, which will enter the food chain of future generations (Stauber & Rampton, 1995). Yet another blatant example of global capitalist abuse is that the rate for lung cancer is on the rise in developing and poor countries, in direct relation to the marketing of tobacco products around the world. In the United States some doctors and non-profit medical organizations have been successful in restricting the advertising campaigns of tobacco companies such that lung cancer rates have declined. As a result the tobacco industry has increased its marketing in other countries, contributing to the higher rates of lung cancer in the Soviet Union and Eastern Europe ("Lung Cancer," 1999).

SOCIAL AND CIVIC RESPONSIBILITY

From the above discussion it should be obvious that one cannot talk about science or progress without talking about social responsibility. Scientific developments are not without human consequences. A quick look at the local newspapers provides a litany of examples of socially irresponsible science. Genetic engineering is occurring so rapidly that laws have not kept up with the experiments. Recently it was discovered that genetically engineered corn kills Monarch butterflies and may have a devastating ecological impact. This corn amounts to 25% of the total acreage of corn planted in the United States in 1998 ("Genetically altered corn," 1999). Scientists have yet to determine what other unseen damage it may be doing to the food chain. Biotech firms are now being challenged by the Internet flight of money from the stock market, which funds research to bring new products to doctors and patients. The results of biotech work are often blindly transferred to developing countries, if it is profitable. In fact, transferring Eurowestern science to developing nations has often had a devastatingly negative or destructive effect on the people who live in those countries (McClellan, 1992; Rodney, 1972).

Besides providing theoretical knowledge, science education should help us develop the skills to weigh and assess the socioeconomic and human implications of the role that science has played under capitalism in order to determine the future role that scientific progress can or should play for all people in the world. In this current world order, dominated by only one world capitalist system, we need to give our students the analytical tools to demystify how the system works and to help them see themselves as agents of constructive change and improvement for all the people on the globe. Therefore, it is important to help our students critique and understand the impact of multinational corporate capitalism.

By and large however, we are doing just the opposite. Most scientists, science teachers, and students in the United States, and other industrialized nations have been educated and socialized from a decidedly Euro or Anglocentric scientific bias. Other ways of knowing of other cultures and racial minority groups are viewed as inadequate, inferior in status, archaic, or superseded by Western scientific knowledge. The influence of White supremacy persists in the school curriculum in the United States and elsewhere (Kailin, 2000). As Ninnes (1999) illustrates in his examination of secondary science texts in Australia, less powerful groups have been essentialized or described in overly simplistic ways. Representations of alternative ways of knowing the world are undertaken in such a way as to present them as inferior to "scientific" methods, or as outdated or historical relics of the past.

SCIENTIFIC RESEARCH AND FUNDING

Scientific innovation and invention are promoted and supported by the ruling class of any given society. The particular feature of capitalism, however, which is for capital to reproduce itself, means that there is an inherent contradiction in the use of science for humanitarian needs if these needs conflict with the accumulation of profit. Shiva (1997) warns about this tendency:

> Once priorities shift from social need to potential return on investment, which is the main criterion for commercially guided research, entire streams of knowledge and learning will be forgotten and become extinct. While these diverse fields might not be commercially profitable, they are socially necessary. As a society facing ecological problems, we need epidemiology, ecology, and evolutionary and developmental biology. We need experts on particular taxonomic groups, such as microbes, insects, and plants, to respond to the crisis of biodiversity erosion. The moment we ignore the useful and the necessary, and concentrate only on the profitable, we are destroying the social conditions for the creation of intellectual diversity. (p. 17)

This is not to say that the application of science is uncontested. Scientists may and often do work toward the progressive and socially responsible use of science. Science and technological advancements may indeed be applied toward the betterment of humanity. But the problem of innovation and progress being outside of the range of control of the inventors is very real indeed. Applied research done within corporations is obviously done for profit. But the university also operates like a corporation when it is dependent on corporate funding for research. Therefore scientific research may actually reflect not what scientists are interested in researching but rather what the corporate sponsors want the universities to support. In general, scientists can only carry out research for which they are funded, so although they may be interested in carrying out socially responsible research, they may be unable to do so due to a lack of funding (Stauber & Rampton, 1995). An understanding of this situation is important, otherwise one can place too much blame on individual scientists and not enough on government, military, and corporate policies.

In addition to examining the issue of the application and development of scientific research, there are other problems concerning the marginalized status of science in the school curriculum, which is seen as attainable only by the few. In terms of careers, the findings from the study the *Condition of Education* (National Center for Education Statistics, 1997) show that only 5% of high school seniors expect to have a career in engineering and just 1% plan to have a career in science or math. Only the most "successful" students ever make it to the more advanced levels beyond the basics of science and mathematics. Students of color and females in general suffer from a lack of representation in the science classroom. Rather than focusing on ways to include women and racial minorities in science, we are importing and appropriating the "best and brightest" scientists and engineers, from developing countries, as well as from some of the former socialist countries. As previously stated, this creates a serious "brain drain" from other countries already under economic duress, while our own racial minorities, working class students, and women in general continue to be marginalized in the field of science at home. Although White women, Native Americans, Blacks and Hispanics comprise the majority of the U.S. population, they represent only 14.5% of all employed scientists and engineers (Changing America: The New Face of Science and Engineering, 1988). While there have been some advances in the inclusion of females in science, they are still in the minority. At the level of advanced high school science courses, females are still more likely than males to be advised against taking the "hard" advanced courses in chemistry or physics (National Center for Education Statistics, 1997). At the postsecondary level, while there has been some narrowing of the gender gap between men and women who earned degrees in computer sciences and engineering, the gap between women and men who earned degrees in physics and chemistry increased (National Center for Education Statistics, 1997, p.17). Men are five times more likely to earn an advanced degree in computer science and engineering and two times more likely to earn master's degrees in mathematics than are women (National Center for Education Statistics, 1997). The racial disparity is also extremely problematic, with students of color being largely left out of advanced science courses in high school. In one study of one of the most highly regarded school districts in the United States, with 25% or more students of color, racially oppressed minority groups were almost totally absent in any of the advanced courses in computer robotics, physics, or chemistry (Kailin, 1999). In terms of social class, science continues to be an elitist, high status endeavor, and it serves to draw in generally privileged White students from upper-middle-class and upper-class backgrounds. Clearly, this pattern serves to perpetuate inequality of access and opportunity to the field of science for a significant portion of our population. These inequities, and particularly the gross underrepresentation of minority groups, need to be addressed.

THE MYSTIFICATION OF SCIENCE AND THE MYTH OF SCIENTIFIC NEUTRALITY

Yet another major obstacle pervades the teaching of science. It is more in the form of attitudes about what science is and is not. There is an assumption on the part of students, and even a few teachers, that somehow science as a field is without "heart." The stereotypes portray scientists as White males with glasses, wearing white coats. Scientists must be cold, unemotional, aloof, calculating, and neutral; further, they seldom take a position, follow procedures exactly, and seldom if ever debate the controversies inherent in the field, especially those revolving around the moral and ethical questions of who decides what area or topic is worthy of research and funding, or which research is ethical. What are the origins of these stereotypes? What impact do they have on the general public, and more specifically on students thinking about careers in science? The interaction between student and teacher, in the process of learning a new idea or concept, involves both intellectual and affective learning. Students respond positively to teachers who are willing to take the time to help them comprehend a difficult concept. Perhaps they would be more drawn into science if they see its application to socially responsible ends.

Science needs to be taught so that students see it as a life-affirming research field that can contribute to overcoming human oppression around the world. Currently in science classes there is too little discussion about socially responsible science for global survival and democratization. Science has also been made "frightening" to most students, who believe that it is out of their range of possibility. Many high school students, especially from underrepresented groups such as students of color, poor students, and females, are reticent to take science classes because they have the reputation of being too difficult. In fact they are often boring, because they are abstract and taught in a vacuum, try to cover too much material in a superficial manner, and are seldom related to the real social problems and solutions in people's daily life.

Because there is actually little time in the school curriculum devoted to science, early introductions to the subject may lend themselves towards rote memory rather than critical reflection, which is so necessary for complex concepts. We must find ways to counter the trend to focus on teaching students for "right answers." If students speak only a total of seven minutes a day in a typical classroom, and teachers do the rest of the talking, how can we expect our students to become articulate in any subject, let alone science? Finally, teachers lack the time to discuss with each other ways to collaborate on socially, politically, and environmentally relevant research projects, which if done with a group of science teachers might yield a more comprehensive, integrated approach to solving problems of the savage inequities in society. Teachers must argue for school time in which to share materials and compare results.

BIG BUSINESS IN THE CLASSROOM

Some science teachers do attempt to teach a curriculum that demystifies science and makes connections between science, scientific study, and people's daily life experiences. But there are many obstacles to this approach. One of the more serious obstacles comes in the lack of available relevant science curricula that address contemporary and global issues and controversies in science and make it possible to develop experiments that speak to local solutions to problems in our communities. Much of the science curricula from textbooks is outdated, poorly written, and abstract. More often it is void of any historical or political context, with solutions developed in isolation, if solutions to pressing science issues are addressed at all. And the content in both texts and supplemental "educational materials," which are often supplied by industry, are clearly not value-free. In fact, corporate investment and therefore influence over science curricula is on the increase, as school budgets for instructional materials dwindle. For example, industry has a clear self-interest in maintaining some control over what and how content is taught in the area of energy and environmental science. Thus Edison Electric Institute developed some pronuclear propaganda called the "Energy-Environment Game." This "learning tool" pits environmentalists against utility executives, who claim to remain neutral in their efforts to balance the needs of people against the environment. A consumer research group sponsored by people working with Ralph Nader has analyzed it as one of the better games among a barrage of corporate-developed teaching materials. Ford Motor, American Iron and Steel, and Westinghouse Electric are only a few of the corporations infiltrating the schools with such biased curricula. Recently, in response to outcries from concerned citizens, guidelines and standards have been developed by a California citizens' group citing that big business is indoctrinating our children to create a lifestyle around the consumption of gadgets and environmentally unsafe projects.

WHAT DO INSERVICE AND PRESERVICE TEACHERS HAVE TO SAY ABOUT MAKING SCIENCE MORE INCLUSIVE AND RELEVANT TO STUDENTS' LIVES?

Discussions with some of our preservice science education students as well as inservice teachers indicate that they would like to learn and teach science from a more culturally engaged perspective. In a recent informal survey of prospective biology teachers, we asked them what they would change about the way high school biology is taught. The following list is a sample of the typical responses:

1. More crucial issues in the field of biology and environmental issues in science need to be addressed: the social construction of race and gender; ecology; the state of the environment; air, water, and ground pollution; the conservation of dwindling natural global resources on our

planet; more equitable food distribution; alternative forms of energy; the effects of toxins and pesticides on our bodies and the planet; gender differences and how they affect how we relate to each other; human sexuality; the ethical implications of gene cloning; the role of drugs, legal and illegal, in a drug culture.

2. Develop science for the majority of citizens, including working class and poor citizens. Let students define, design, and carry out their own experiments in which they can relate or connect to some social, biological, or environmental issue or problem that needs to be addressed in the local community and contrasted against events in the world. Let students become the scientists instead of always having them do lab work that is defined and set up for them by the teacher. By investigating their own experiments, the students can do their own questioning, thinking, and problem solving. Students should be encouraged to become researchers in their own right. They can take more responsibility over their learning if they present their research to each other. This encourages students to take a more active role in their own learning. The solutions could be developed for real, concrete situations that societies face today or in the future. Teachers should be encouraged to make science applicable to the real-world scientific problems we face globally and locally.

3. Classroom sizes need to be smaller. A lab class of 30 limits the type and depth of experimentation. People need to work together in smaller groups. We need to spend time critiquing our experiments to understand them more deeply. We need to learn how to apply our research to daily life situations. It is too hard to do when classes are so large.

In summary, if we are going to teach science from a critical multicultural perspective, we should:

1. Actively develop an ongoing program to recruit and support those who have historically and traditionally been left out of science, i.e., students of color, females, disabled students. This involves also providing meaningful support and mentors so these students will succeed.

2. Teach the sciences from historical/cultural/political perspectives, including the scientific contributions of non-Western peoples. This means we must decenter the Anglocentric and Western science perspective and examine the discoveries from people of color, indigenous cultures, Afro-Asian countries and non-Western science and scientific developments.

3. Demystify science by showing how it is related to and impacts everyday life, by teaching the social context of what/how science is produced and who produces it. Discuss Western science in contrast to non-Western paradigms.

4. Examine the question of socially responsible science, which will reveal which sciences get funded and why. This means we must also critique corporate capitalism and its impact on funding, support, and knowledge bases in the development and application of science.

5. Challenge science textbooks that are Anglocentric and Eurocentric. Write to publishers seeking more globally inclusive science curricula.

6. Teach for equity and social justice. Help students become activists for equity. Global, multicultural science challenges racism and other forms of oppression.

While the educational system (including the media) have tended to depoliticize science for public consumption, Sandra Harding (1998) reminds us that science is deeply political:

> Scientific and technological change are inherently political, since they redistribute costs and benefits of access to nature's resources in new ways. They tend to widen any pre-existing gaps between the haves and the have-nots unless issues of just distribution are directly addressed. Under current development policies, the inequitable distribution of such costs and benefits are visible for all to see—at least among those who wish to see them. (pp. 50–51)

In this chapter we have argued about the need to take issue with some of the predominant assumptions about Anglocentric science; we have posed critical questions about what a science curriculum that is critically multicultural would consider; and we have urged that science education speak to the demystification and decommodification of science, as well as to the dismantling of the elitist status of science and scientists. If we want to promote the teaching of science in a way that addresses science from a critical multicultural and antiracist perspective, and which addresses the issues of power and knowledge in a corporate capitalist world order, we need to broaden and deepen our current science curricula. Science education should offer not only multiple views of science, but scientific solutions to the critical and pressing daily life science issues that currently face global society, such as hunger and poverty, food production and distribution, exportation of pesticides, genetic engineering, the uses and abuses of energy, and the increasing forms of environmental pollution. An important aspect of this project involves making science teaching more inclusive for all students so that science education does not reproduce and reinforce relations of domination.

NOTES

[1]We acknowledge here that even using the term "Western" carries with it the implicit assumption that we are referring to Europe, and North and South America. But one might ask why in particular is this western? West of what? The very geography and drawing of boundaries, directions, and time is itself a social construction and in this case refers to the legacy of colonialism and imperialism of the various European and American empires.

REFERENCES

Ahlquist, R. (1998). Critical multicultural mathematics curriculum: Multiple connections through the lenses of race, ethnicity, gender and social class. In National Council of Teachers of Mathematics Perspectives on Gender Series, Vol. 1.

American Cancer Society. 1996.

Bernal, M. (1987). *Black Athena: The Afro Asiatic roots of classical civilization*. New Brunswick, NJ: Rutgers University Press.

Brown, D. (1999, April, 21). U. S. Cancer Cases, deaths declining but report says news isn't as good for women, Some Ethnic Groups. *San Francisco Chronicle*.

Centers for Disease Control and Prevention, National Cancer Institute and American Cancer Society, 1996.

Changing America: The new face of science and engineering. Final Report (1988). (ERIC Document Reproduction Service No. ED 317 386).

Genetically altered corn found to kill butterflies. (1999, May 20). *The Orange County (CA) Register, p. 16.*

Harding, S. (1998). *Is science multicultural?* Bloomington: Indiana University Press.

Harding, S. (Ed.). (1993). *The "racial" economy of science: Towards a democratic future*. Bloomington: Indiana University Press.

Kailin, J. (2000). *Anti-racist education*. Mahwah, NJ: Lawrence Erlbaum Associates.

Kailin, J. (1999). How White teachers perceive the problem of racism in their schools: A case study in "liberal" Lakeview. *Teachers College Record, 100*(4), 169-84.

Kailin, J. (1994). Anti-racist staff development for teachers: Considerations of race, class and gender. *Teaching and Teacher Education, 10*, 1--15.

Lung cancer now world's deadliest cancer. (1999, May 20). *USA Today*, section D, p. 1.

Malcolm, S. (1993). Increasing the participation of black women in science and technology. In S. Harding (Ed.), *The "racial" economy of science: Towards a democratic future*. Bloomington: Indiana University Press.

McClellan, J. E. (1992). *Colonialism and science: Saint Dominique in the old regime*. Baltimore: John Hopkins University Press.

National Center for Education Statistics (1997). *The Condition of Education, 1997*. Washington, DC: Office of Educational Research and Improvement, U.S. Dept. of Education.

National Organization of Women (1997). *Report on Women's Health*, Washington, DC: .

Navarro, V. (1991). Class and race: Life and death situations. *Monthly Review, 43*(4), 1.

Ninnes, P. (1999, April). *Representations of ways of knowing in junior high school science texts in plural societies*. Paper presented at the annual meeting of the American Educational Research Association, Montreal, Canada.

O'Brien, E. M. (1993). Without more minorities, women, disabled, U.S. scientific failure certain, federal study says. *The "racial" economy of science*. In S. Harding, (Ed.), Bloomington: Indiana University Press.

Rodney, W. (1972). *How Europe underdeveloped Africa*. Washington, DC: Howard University Press.

Shiva, V. (1997). *Biopiracy: The plunder of nature and knowledge*. Boston: South End Press.

Silicon Valley Toxics Coalition (Spring, 1999). *Action, XVII*(1).

Stauber, J., & Rampton, S. (1995). *Toxic sludge is good for you! Lies, damn lies and the public relations industry*. Monroe, Maine: Common Courage.

Time for Kids (1998). Kuala Lumpur, Malaysia: Office of Education.

Weatherford, J. (1988). *The Indian givers: How the Indians of the Americas transformed the world.* New York: Fawcett Columbine.

CHAPTER 4

Prospective Teachers' Education
World View and Teacher Education
Programs: Through the Eyes of
Culture, Ethnicity, and Class

Mary M. Atwater and Denise Crockett

INTRODUCTION

The availability of prepared teachers to instruct diversifying science classrooms is a critical element for quality science instruction (Atwater, 1995). In 1985 in the United States, 86% of the public and private school teachers were White, another 10% were African Americans, and 68% were females (*The Condition of Education,* 1987). In 1989 in the United States, the typical science teacher was 40 years old with 13 years of teaching experience; 90% of high school science teachers were White and 50% of these high school teachers were males (Weiss & Boyd, 1990). According to the most recent data available, in 1994, 7.4% of U.S. public school teachers were African Americans (*Mini-Digest of Education Statistics 1997*) with a severe underrepresentation of science teachers—5.5% (Hawkins, 1997). Many teachers have experienced few situations in teaching students from different class, cultural, ethnic, language, and racial backgrounds than their own.

The problems related to diversity are not unique to the United States. Other countries have similar dilemmas. For instance, in Nigeria, there are seven ethnic groups: Hausa, Fulani, Ibo, Kanuri, Ibibio, Tiv, and Ijain. Fifty percent of the population is Muslim, 40% is Christian, and the other 10% practice indigenous beliefs (Mbendi Information for Africa, 1999). In South Africa, the apartheid government recognized four ethnic groups: Whites (12.6%), who hold most of the wealth in the country.

Blacks/Africans (76.3%), who had no citizenship rights and lived in either urban townships and rural homelands until the dismantling of apartheid; "Coloured" (8.5%); and "Indians/Asians" (2.5%), who had limited rights of self-governing legislative chambers, but were second-class citizens (IDASA Democracy in S.A., 1999). The four major ethnic groups among Black South Africans are the Nguni, Sotho, Shangaan-Tsonga, and Venda (*Reference: People*, 1999). Black South Africans come from a variety of different ethnic groups with distinct languages: isiZula (22.4%), isiXhosa (17.5%), Sepedi (9.8%), Setswana (7.2%), Sesotho (6.9%), Xitsonga (4.2%), Siswati (2.6%), Tshivenda (1.7%), and isiNdebele (1.5%). There are two distinct White South Africans: descendants of Dutch and French Huguenot invaders, who speak Afrikaans (15.1%), and the descents of British invaders who speak English (9.1%) (IDASA Democracy in S.A., 1999). The largest Nguni-speaking language group is the Zulus, who comprise 300 tribes. Not one of South Africa's major languages is spoken by a majority of its people (*Reference: People*, 1999). Questions such as what should the teaching of science do for African countries and how can the sociocultural and cosmological backgrounds of the teachers and learners be integrated into science education continue to be asked by African scholars such as Jegede (1989). In Australia, Aborigines and recent immigrants from the United Kingdom, Hong Kong, Southeast Asia, and India have added to this country's diversity (Allan & Hill, 1995). Consequently, many teachers and schools are not equipped to handle the ever increasing student diversity in schools in many parts of the world.

People interpret the world and their experiences differently. Their world views are explicit culturally dependent internal models found in their cognitive structures and are the result of their life experiences (Borden, 1991). World view is described by Cobern (1991) as "the foundational belief, i.e., presuppositions, about the world that support both common sense and scientific theories" (p. 7). Each person has a fundamental, epistemological macrostructure that forms the panorama of his or her reality (Cobern, 1991). Therefore, the views of people about reality are socioculturally constructed and are given personal meaning by their sociocultural experiences. Their world views are the very skeletons of concrete cognitive assumptions on which their decisions and actions are founded (Kearney, 1984; Wallace, 1970). The significance of world view is seen in peoples' religion and their ideas about death, suffering, their place in nature and the universe, education, and reality (Skow, Samovar, & Heilweg, 1990).

In this socioconstructed world lies the agency of schooling. An important part of people's world view is how formal education connects to this grand schema. This constructed world view permeates through every aspect of formal education. Not only is this true of world view but of cultures as well.

Interpretations of experiences are influenced by culture, "the knowledge, ideas, and skills that enable a group to survive in and adapt to its environment" (Bullivant, 1989, p. 28). Culture encompasses "speech, knowledge, beliefs, customs, arts and technologies, ideals, and rules what we learn from other [people], from our elders or the past, plus what we may add to it" (Kroeber, 1948, p. 253). Culture provides people "a frame of reference in which to function and has a strong role in formation of values, attitudes, and communication styles." (Newmark & Asante, 1974, p. 55). According to Kluckhohn (1954), "culture is those historically created meanings of situations which individuals gain by virtue of participation in or contact with groups of people; consequently, people within the same culture usually interpret the meaning of symbols, artifacts, and behaviors in the same or similar ways" (Newmark & Asante, 1974, p. 8). Many sociocultural researchers begin with the assumption that people "are construed as inhabitants of language-carried traditions" (Preston, 1997, p. 27). However, culture is not static, but is ever changing within a group of people (Preston, 1997).

According to Brock and Tulasiewicz (1985), cultural identity is the "internalized cultural consciousness" (p. 4). It is an identification with a distinct concept of reality, accepted by participation in a pattern of life with its political, economic, educational, and social structures. According to Preston (1997), cultural identity is shaped by (a) the way individuals construe their relationship to the community in which they operate, (b) the manner in which people lodge themselves in dispersed groups and how these groups understand their relation to other groups in the wider collectivity, and (c) the ways in which individuals, groups, and society secure their understanding and legitimation of power. Cultural differences arise when the mental images of at least two individuals from different cultures conflict (Borden, 1991). In any society, there are variations within a culture (Timm, 1996). Some call these distinct variations microcultures. Microcultures "mediate, interpret, re-interpret, perceive and experience these over-arching national values differently" (Banks,

1994, p. 84). Gollnick and Chinn (1994) believe that some of these microcultures in the United States are characterized by age, class, ethnicity, gender, geographical region, race, and religion. The word *ethnicity* is derived from the Greek word *ethnos*, meaning a nation or race (Petersen, Novak, & Gleason, 1982). It was originally used in England to denote non-Christian or non-Jewish origins and to describe people as pagans or heathens (Petersen, Novak & Gleason, 1982). Today, researchers use the word ethnicity to describe "a complex and dynamic [social] concept that refers to how members of a group perceive themselves, and how, in turn, they are perceived by others" (Baruth & Manning, 1992, p. 11). An ethnic group is characterized by its shared "image and sense of identity derived from cultural patterns (e.g., values, behaviors, perspectives, language) and a sense of history; shared political and economic interests; and membership that is involuntary, although individual identification with the group may be optional" (Baruth & Manning, 1992, p. 11). According to Pusch (1979), ethnic membership in the United States is determined by birth; however, Rothenberg (1995) believes that ethnicity has a social and not biological origin. According to Cashmore (1988), ethnic identity is a response to the marginalization that the group feels from the dominant society because of shared experiences.

Ethnic identity is a set of self ideas about the individual's own socially defined membership and the knowledge, understanding, values, and feelings that are the direct results of that ownership (Grant & Ladson–Billings, 1997; Knight, Bernal, Cota, Garza, & Ocampo, 1993). Ethnic identity is composed of five components: ethnic self-identification, ethnic constancy, ethnic role behaviors, ethnic knowledge, and ethnic preferences and feelings (Knight et al., 1993). Ethnic identity differs from racial identity. Race has been delineated as "a determined category that is related to physical characteristics in a complex way. Two individuals with nearly identical physical characteristics or phenotypes can be classified as members of two different races in two different countries" (Banks, 1989, p. 17). Consequently, race is a social and political construction and not a scientific or biological category (Gould, 1994; Grant & Ladson-Billings, 1997; Rothenberg, 1995; Shreeve, 1994). Racial identity is a collective identity based on a person's perception that he or she shares with a common heritage with a particular group based on physical criteria (Grant & Ladson-Billings, 1997; Helms, 1990). People can identify themselves based on an ethnic group, such as Irish American, and not think they belong to a racial group such as White and members of the microculture–White Americans. On the other hand, Black Haitians believe they are members of a microculture–Haitians, but are many times forced by the dominant group in the United States to consider their racial identity as Black and their ethnic group as African American.

Class refers to a stratum of individuals within a society who share basic, economic, political, cultural, or social characteristics; for example, wealth or its absence. Nieto (1992) further elaborates on class to include the values associated with the group of people. Working-class people differ from middle-class people not only in their economic resources but in particular values and practices. Class membership may provide "access to power and privilege or other benefits within a social, economic or political structure" (Pusch, 1979, p. 3). In many countries, class is determined by both economics and politics. In other countries, economics alone may determine class. Class relationships reflect the constraints and limitations people and groups experience in the area of income level, occupation, place of residence, and other indicators of status and social rank. The study of class relations deals with social distribution of power and its structural allocations (McLauren, 1994).

Research findings support the thesis that both teacher attitudes and beliefs drive classroom actions (Nespor, 1987; Peck & Tucker, 1973; Richardson, 1996). Personal experiences of teachers help form their educational world views; intellectual and ethical dispositions; beliefs about self in relation to others; understandings of the relationship of schooling to society; and other forms of personal, familial, and cultural understandings (Richardson, 1996). In addition, ethnic, racial, and social backgrounds, along with gender, geographic location, religious upbringing, and life decisions, affect learning to teach and teaching (Richardson, 1996). Many times, teachers' reflections on personal and classroom events are filtered through the lens of world views, beliefs, attitudes, and images (Bullough & Knowles, 1991; Clandinin, 1986; Mundy & Russell, 1992; Richardson, 1996); consequently, it is essential that science teacher educators and researchers examine these influences on science learning and teaching.

Many scholars study culture, class, ethnicity, and gender separately; however, few attempt to examine these concepts in a holistic manner in educational research. People's interpretations of their experiences are products of their cultures and hence, culture is influenced by race, ethnicity, class, geographical region, politics, religion, and gender.

Teachers' knowledge about learning, teaching, and their students usually
fits their experiences (Brickhouse & Bodner, 1992). Therefore, we now
discuss the influence of ethnicity, ethnic identification, culture, cultural
identification, and class on the educational world views of science education graduate students at an Eastern university.

THEORETICAL FRAMEWORKS

Self-identity is a crucial and major concept in modern society, especially
in the United States except in some countries where the population is
homogeneous and stable (Banks, 1989; Hoffman, 1996; Kitano, 1985). A
hegemonic society such as that found in the United States and South Africa demands that marginalized people discard their ancestral and
national identities and adopt newer ones based on the image of the self-
made individual in order to be "successful" and makes it difficult for its
marginalized members to establish their own identity (Rothenberg, 1995;
Seller & Weiss, 1997). Identity is a "way in which [a person] more or
less self-consciously locates [herself or himself] in [her or his] social position (Preston, 1997). Some researchers believe that the American
identity in the United States is shaped by race, religion, national origin,
and social and political class (Kitano, 1985; Taylor, 1994). Self-identity,
especially ethnic and cultural identity, and its influence on the interpretation of educational experiences of prospective science teachers and
science teacher educators compel us to use the interpretive theoretical
approach, in which three male participants disclose their life stories or
oral histories (Casey, 1993; deMarrais & LeCompte, 1995; Denzin &
Lincoln, 1994). The investigators focus on the construction of cultural
and ethnic self, changes in cultural and ethnic self, and meanings of ethnicity and culture, along with the interpretation of participants' reality in
their interaction with others in their families, communities, and schooling
setting as these interactions influence their world view about their educational experiences. This kind of inquiry analyzes the issues of the ways
in which people are lodged in and relegated to ongoing traditions (Preston, 1997). Life histories are appropriate for both the micro-level of
analysis and the macro-level linkages to class, culture, ethnicity, race,
and politics (Denzin & Lincoln, 1994; LeCompte & Preissle, 1993),
since the identity of a person can be unpacked in terms of locale (a particular place, the sphere of activities and interactions that is richly
suffused with meanings), network (the people and places with whom the

individual interacts at a distance from her or his familiar locality), and memory (what is remembered and what is presently demanded) (Preston, 1997).

Our intent is to provide a vehicle for the voice of participants and interpretations of both the participants and investigator. The following research ideas guided the study: (a) a description of the participants' perspectives about ethnicity, their own ethnic identification, culture, and their own cultural identity; (b) a delineation of the graduate students' past experiences that formed their ideas about ethnicity, ethnic identification, culture, and cultural identity; and (c) the influence of their ethnicity, ethnic identification, culture, and cultural identity on their "big picture," or world view, about their own educational experiences.

METHODOLOGY

Qualitative studies usually occur when researchers want to examine in–depth complex social phenomena for which many of the relevant variables have not been identified (Marshall & Rossman, 1989). The purpose of this study was to chronicle events through interviews in participants' lives as they related to culture, class, and ethnicity and to characterize these experiences in relation to their life histories and teacher education. These life histories allow the participants' perspectives to be shared as well as the interpretations of both the participants and investigators, since teacher education is a complex enterprise (Lee & Yarger, 1996). Since life stories have the potential for the exploration of identities (Gray, 1997), cultural analysis was utilized in studying the interview data. According to Geertz (1973), cultural analysis is "guessing at meanings, assessing the guesses, and drawing exploratory conclusions from the better guesses" (p. 20). Researchers using cultural analysis not only arrive at explanations but must also account for the ways in which the "known" is understood by the participants in the study (Murdock, 1997). The researchers use cultural analyses to identify some major patterns, since this approach recognizes the importance of variation within and between cultural experiences. This methodological strategy allows the research using a dialogic approach to explicitly explain the ways in which participants in an investigation fashion sense of their respective worlds and the various exchanges between these worlds (Preston, 1997). According to Smith (1994), "the sequence of events as an individual passes through a culture during the course of a life is one view of that culture. And the resulting kind of person and his or her outlook on life [world view] are related additional ways of viewing culture" (p. 296). By reading and rereading the participants' transcripts of their interviews, these readings offer a solid basis for creative interpretation with rich descriptions, since there has been continual interchange between the interviewer and the interviewee (Murdock, 1997).

Site and Participation Selection

This study includes the interviews of three male students pursuing master's degrees in science education who were participants in a much larger study. The larger qualitative study included interviews from 14 students enrolled in a graduate course on theory and methods of education. The first author of this chapter was a visiting professor at the university for a semester. She was there to rethink her research focus and to conduct research in the area of multicultural science teacher education. In addition, the first author assisted two faculty members in their teaching.

Description of Participants and Researchers

The three participants whose life histories are reported in this chapter were selected because (a) their majors were science education, (b) their sex was the same; therefore, gender would not be a confounding variable, (c) their citizenship varied, therefore providing the researchers a glimpse of intercultural influences, and (d) the two U.S. citizens had different class backgrounds. Two of the three participants, Robert and Thomas (pseudonyms), are U.S. citizens; the third, David (pseudonym) is a citizen of South Africa. The three participants in this study are enrolled in a MAT program that leads to state certification and one (Robert) was already accepted into a Ph.D. program; however, none of the teachers were certified to teach in their countries during the study. One of the participants, Thomas, had previous science teaching experience in a high school setting. The researcher decided to focus on three students with bachelor's degrees in science enrolled in a master's program because the university offered only graduate-level education. No undergraduate education programs leading to certification were available at this institution; however, most of the students enrolled in the master's program planned to obtain certification and teach science or mathematics in public high schools in their countries.

David, a Black South African, grew up in South Africa during the time of apartheid in what he called a "developed area." There was one elementary and high school in the "village." The village is organized in such a way that the husbands, who are the breadwinners for the family, work somewhere else to support their families. The women plow the fields and care for the crops. Decisions are made when the men return, usually during Christmas time. Currently in South Africa, many women and children do not follow the men to the town in which they are employed. David considers home to be where his father lives. His father owns two houses in the area. David graduated from the village high school, which was a boarding school. He attended a predominantly White university in Johannesburg and graduated with majors in microbiology and botany. David plans to return to South Africa and teach high school science upon completion of his master's degree program.

Robert, a White male, grew up in a town in the northeastern part of the United States. His entire extended family lived on the same street that he did for the first five years of Robert's life. His paternal grandparents lived upstairs in a two-family home. Next door were his maternal grandparents, with his aunt, uncle, and cousins on the second floor. Originally, the home was located in a rural area with all dirt roads. Over the years, the place became a residential suburb of a major city. His neighbors were "lower middle class, working blue collar." Before the residential development of the area, children played a lot of outdoor activities. This area was a place where everyone knew each other, even the different generations. Middle-class families moved into the neighborhood because of its friendly, close atmosphere. Robert's parents supported his decision to attend college. Presently, he and his wife live in a house they are buying in a residential area that is two miles from the university. Many children live in this "friendly" neighborhood because many of the residents live in multifamily housing and are also graduate students. Robert describes himself as a Ph.D. science education student at the university and plans to enter the field of science education at a university.

Thomas, a White male with a Spanish surname, grew up in an upper-middle-class area in a northeastern state in the United States. His family lived in a suburban area whose residents were "civil servants," "teachers," "sanitation managers," and "people with good jobs." This area was very racially segregated, with no Black families. (Thomas had no "Black friends" until he came to the university as an undergraduate student. He believes this was unfortunate.) The residents of this neighborhood were mostly Irish Americans, Italian Americans, and Jewish. Hispanic people, most Puerto Ricans, lived in the projects, which were far away from his

family's neighborhood. His "Caucasian" parents still live in the neighborhood, which remains segregated because of "real estate" reasons. He
currently lives in a graduate "dormitory" with "very nice room, nice size,
and a very diverse place." He has friends from Australia, France, Spain,
and Japan. This university dormitory has a "United Nations feel." Thomas had been a science teacher and plans to return to high school science
teaching upon completion of his master's degree with state certification.

According to Firth (1965), some account of the relationship between
the researcher and the participants is relevant to the nature of the results
of the investigation. Hence, we provide information about both of the
authors of this chapter, since the first author was the interviewer and the
second author also analyzed the transcripts of the interviews. The first
author is an African American female professor at a Research I institution in the southeastern part of the United States. When she undertook
this study, she was a visiting professor at an Eastern Research I university. She assisted in teaching two graduate courses as a visiting professor.
The three participants were students in the classes in which she taught.
She actively participated in all discussions and became an integral member of the classes. Hence, she was the designer of this study and
interviewer for this qualitative investigation. Each participant understood
the purpose of the study and had interacted with her for many weeks
prior to the interviews.

The second author is a White female who was a graduate student at
the same university as the first author. She had taught high school science for several years prior to her admission into a doctoral program. Her
research interest included culture and ethnicity. By the time she began
analyzing the transcripts, she had completed all of her doctoral work and
most of her data collection for the dissertation.

Data Collection and Analysis

The conceptualization of the research plan for this study was facilitated
by the employment of a Vee diagram (Gowin, 1981; Novak & Gowin,
1984). The three interviews took place at an eastern university. The
amount of time for each interview varied because the interviewer wanted
each participant to answer all the focus questions. The interviewer also
asked probing questions when the participants' answers were incomplete
or needed further elaboration. A semistructured interview protocol was
developed and consisted of 12 focus questions. Examples of questions
include: Where did you grow up? Describe the place; What do you think

culture is?; What is your ethnic identification?; How has your cul-tural/ethnic identification affected your K–12 schooling?; How has your cultural/ethnic identification affected your schooling at this institution? Most questions were open-ended to discover important categories, di-mensions, and interrelationships. Interview focus questions and emergent questions allow researchers to discuss culture, cultural identification, ethnicity, ethnic identification, and class and to determine their impact on the participants' educational experiences (Gowin,1981; Novak & Gowin, 1984).

Each interview was transcribed by a professional transcriber. The transcriptions were read by the interviewer and any missing words or lines were entered by the interviewer. At the onset of the study, a few guiding hypotheses were generated:

(1) Cultural and ethnic identities are initially formed at home and these identities formed at home may have a lasting impact on people's interpretations of their experiences;

(2) Cultural and ethnic perspectives of students are important in under-standing the influence of ethnic/cultural identification on schooling experiences;

(3) Mental representations are textually constructed within a social tra-dition or culture;

(4) Ethnic identification is a part of one's culture and social traditions;

(5) Peoples' ethnic and cultural identities can influence their percep-tions of home, schooling, and educational experiences; and,

(6) Ethnic and cultural identification can influence the quality of schooling at both the precollege and university levels.

Interview data were analyzed line by line using inductive analysis, which means that categories, themes, and patterns come from the data (Jane-sick, 1994; Straus, 1987). Event, situation, relationship, and social structure codes were identified to organize the data into phrases, partici-pants' ways of thinking, and repeated experiences (Bogdan & Biklen, 1992). A detailed, thick description with direct quotations captures the science education students' perspectives and experiences. The research-ers' personal experiences and insights were a significant part of the study and are critical to the data analysis, since both of the U. S. participants consider themselves to be White Americans. The first author was the in-terviewer; the second author read the transcripts of each interview and also analyzed the data and determined the assertions advanced in this study. The two authors spent many hours discussing the transcripts, ask-

ing each other questions, and challenging each other about what assertions were warranted by the data. Hence, the second author was a major
player in analyzing the transcript data.

Efforts were made to stay close to the data; therefore, the participants' stories could be told. The researchers used Husserl's conception of
bracketing as described by Denzin (1989) in analyzing the interview
data. The following steps were then employed: (a) locating within the life
story key phrases and statements that speak to culture, ethnicity, cultural
identity, ethnic identity, self-identity, and life experiences that allude to
the participants' world view of education; (b) interpreting the meanings
of these phrases as an informed reader; (c) inspecting these meanings for
what they disclose about the essential, recurring features of ethnicity,
culture, cultural identify, ethnic identity, self-identity, and life experiences; and (d) advancing tentative assertions about investigated
phenomena (Denzin, 1989).

LIMITATIONS OF THE STUDY

There were several limitations to this study. First, the participants were
all students in two classes at an Eastern university. Therefore, diversity
in participants' lives was limited by time and place. The interview technique itself has its own limitations and weaknesses. An interviewer and a
participant must establish a rapport with each other so that the participant
is willing to share information with the interviewer (Bogdan & Biklen,
1992; Whyte, 1984). One of the authors was a participant observer in the
class; she was viewed by the students not as a student but as a visiting
faculty member who had an interest in multicultural science education
research. The African American interviewer had no difficulty establishing rapport with the three participants in this study, since she had become
an integral part of the participants' classes and developed a rapport with
the students prior to the interviews, which were conducted near the end
of the first semester. Research has found that similar ethnicities, same
gender, and similar ages between interviewer and interviewee establish a
cooperative and truthful atmosphere during the interview (Bogdan &
Biklen, 1992; Fine & Sandstrom, 1988; Warren, 1988; Wax, 1979). Dissimilar ethnicities and gender did not appear to be a problem with these
three students, even though two of the male students were White citizens
of the United States; the other one was a Black South African. The participants were told that all of the information they shared with the

interviewer would be kept confidential and they would not be identifiable in any publication.

Researchers can have their own biases that they can interject into the interviewing process; consequently, the first author and interviewer made great attempts to listen to the participants' stories and ask them follow-up questions related to their stories. However, the interviewer became aware of one bias. At the beginning of the larger study, she believed that students would be comfortable discussing and would be knowledgeable about both culture and ethnicity. She soon discovered that many White students from the United States did not feel comfortable discussing ethnicity and believed they did not belong to an ethnic group. Thus, she began to ask students about both their cultural and ethnic identifications. The interviewer found one article related to cultural identity in her review of literature, but there was no discussion about cultural identification versus ethnic identification (Whaley, 1993). Consequently, in this chapter, there is an in-depth discussion of both cultural and ethnic identification since a function of case studies is to refine theories, to suggest complexities for further research studies, and to help establish the limits of generalizability (Stake, 1994).

Triangulation has been espoused by many qualitative researchers as a strategy for making qualitative research more rigorous, valid, and reliable (Brewer & Hunter, 1989; Denzin & Lincoln, 1994; Fielding & Fielding, 1986; Flick, 1992). However, there are several types of triangulation: data triangulation, investigator triangulation, theory triangulation, methodological triangulation, interdisciplinary triangulation (Janesick, 1994). The authors utilized two different types of triangulation. First, conversations, formally and informally, were conducted between the professors and the researcher. Background information given by the professors provided a rich background necessary to carry out initial nonparticipant observations, to allow entrée, and to develop the trust of all research subjects. Participants who were pursuing graduate-level teacher education degrees were then invited by the first author. The other approach was that two different researchers analyzed the transcripts.

Finally, qualitative researchers do pass along to readers some of their own personal meanings about occurrences and ideas and fail to pass along others (Stake, 1994). Hopefully, it is understood by the readers of this chapter that they too will reconstruct the findings found in this study in ways that will make them more personal. An attempt has been made to describe in detail the interpretative life histories so that the reader can make fitting conclusions.

DESCRIPTION, ANALYSIS, AND INTERPRETATIONS

The following narratives provide evidence for the three assertions generated by the investigators. The first assertion focuses on the participants' perceptions of who they are within the domains of culture, ethnicity, and class. The second assertion explores self-identity, and the third assertion describes and interprets the participants' educational world view as seen through self-identity, family, community, and schooling. The third assertion identifies some components of the educational world views of the three participants.

Notions of ethnicity and culture are different; however, ethnicity includes culture

Thomas finds ethnicity to be a difficult concept to define and personalizes the concept in the following manner:

> Ethnicity, it's uh... difficult... uh... concept. I could say that I'm many different *many different ethnic groups* [italics added] within me. Cause I am... I am part Spanish, Irish- German, uh... Polish, English... I mean I have these different ethnic groups, that I mean, are sort of my *heritage* [italics added].

He continues to provide personal examples by saying, "But yet, I have some how become... and my family, we've all become American. I don't really think of myself as an Irish American or Spanish American or Polish American, but I think of myself as American." Thomas acknowledges that he is an "American" and that is different from being an ethnic American in the United States.

David, the Black South African, describes ethnicity as:

> descriptive or a description of [long pause] yeah, a group of people ah who are of the same. I would say that is an ethnic group. A group of people with the same language, same culture, same history, and ah same living... *who have a history of living together* [italics added].

For Thomas and David, ethnicity is rooted in the tangible and concrete. Ethnicity can be detected by the use of the human senses such as hearing words or living in a particular place and is grounded in realities and space. On the other hand, culture is more abstract and elusive. Thomas delineates culture in the following manner:

> Culture to me, is huh...the things that...make...me...uh like who I am, like the kinds of things I do, maybe... traditions that my family and I have... things that we do that...that we think are part of like the good life.

He further explains that culture is part of his faith and religion, both which are intangible and abstract. David describes culture as "the way people are.... The way people you know people are." It includes your "particular society or community" with its "practices and ways of thinking, communicating, and expressing yourself," "ways of ...celebrating and working for cooperation and building community spirit. You know, it's a world of things." Many researchers view culture as more encompassing than ethnicity; however, two of the participants see ethnicity as more definitive and separate from culture and based on ancestry.

Self-identity is textually bound by cultural, ethnic, and class experiences

According to Blasi and Glodis (1995), identity is a distinct experience of self characterized by perception of one's own person, "the realization of what is true, real, genuine about oneself, and the subjective experience of unity produced by such a realization" (p. 406). Self-identity is arrived by realistically appraising oneself and one's past, one's culture, and the epectations that society has for oneself (Blasi & Glodis, 1995). In addition, exchanges with one's society and culture and the synthesizing with self are crucial to self-identity (Blasi & Glodis, 1995). For example, Robert says the following about himself.

> [W]hen people see my last name, they say [says surname], that's a very unusual name. Where did it come from? I say it's sort of an ethnic identity, [however] people ask you what nationality. Sometimes I think about that and I want to say well my ancestors came from Italy, but really *I* am an American and I don't know any other way [emphasis added]. I can't speak Italian, my family does a lot Italian cooking....

Robert identifies himself as an American, but not an Italian American. He further explains what it means to be an American:

There is a certain history that most Americans share as far as social, political and economic structures... their ethnicities hasn't completely gone away and that's something that's American.

He relates an incident about Americanism with a young Swedish female, who cared for his 14-month-old daughter, and her friend. Their baby–sitter and her friend are interested in American traditions and practices.

I told them that well, it's quite variable, um, because since most people in America trace their roots to somewhere else, that they bring parts of those cultures and those societies with them and they are perpetuated within a family....my grandparents were Italian immigrants, so many of the traditions that we have on the holidays center around Italian traditions, which are quite different from the traditions in my wife's family, who can trace her roots back to the beginning of this country.

Thomas discusses his thoughts on ethnic identity:

We've [referring to his family] become, which in a sense I think... it's become in itself an ethnic in a sense...uh...an identification and I'm not...I don't really think of myself, at all, as an Irish American or a Spanish American or Polish American, etc. but I think of myself as an American American and I've become an American and I think that is part of my...uh...ethnicity...I mean, that...that is my ethnic background now. I'm an American. But, there ...I acknowledge it, I'm also a White American and that has become part too.

For Thomas, ethnicity is a different concept. He stumbles through ethnic groups to sort through the process of discovering his heritage and finally describes himself as White American. Thomas further elaborates his thoughts about ethnic identity.

Certainly that has affected my... identification that I feel I guess, I mean...uh...you know how I would describe myself and I mean in that, I think, if I had born... been born an African American I think my...my...I would have different, you know different feelings, I guess and different ways of thinking about all kinds of things because...which is...its a different...uh...in a sense. ...a White American and a Black American, while both Americans are...are...grouped in two different ethnic groups within the American...uh...uh...city...while they are both Americans they...there are these many different things about them because of the groups that they've been part of...

Thomas understands that there can be different ethnic groups in the United States, even though he doesn't claim to be "Hispanic." He has a Spanish surname, but Thomas describes himself as White and says that his ancestors came from Spain. Thomas describes his cultural identity in the following manner: "But in many senses it is the... it's a middle class... uh... Roman-Catholic... uh.... I'd say... uh.... White culture.... uh... that, you know, I... I've grown up in...

Thomas easily gets confused with the terms cultural identity and ethnic identity. He says, "It overlaps you. I find them a bit confusing." He considers himself a member of the American culture, middle class, Roman Catholic, and a member of the White culture.

David never discusses ethnic identification. When the researcher asked him:

And are you much more comfortable with the word culture or ethnicity? And that's going to determine the rest of the questions. Do you feel more comfortable using the word culture or do you feel more comfortable using the word ethnicity—in your particular case?

He responds by saying: "I wouldn't care really because... I think they all go together."
David discusses cultural identity.

I grew up in an area where it is difficult to make a living... and historically I am also [names his cultural affiliation]. My parents and forefathers are [names their cultural affiliation] who moved from the south to [names his land] and they settled there and now my cultural identification is mainly historically developed. But taken more into... culture. The historical part is not strong anymore, but I know where it comes from. I know where I come from. You understand?. ...but it is what I would say my cultural identification is.

He goes on further to say, "But I lost everything about [names his cultural affiliation]. I just don't know. I don't even speak the language. But I still have pride as [names his cultural affiliation]."

The participants appear to have difficulty in delineating ethnic and cultural identification. For David, ethnicity is a "description" of a group of people "who are the same." However, culture is much more complex.

To David, it is a "way of living for people." These definitions strongly contribute to his world view. David says, "I grew up in a particular culture and that defines me." Just like Robert, he more easily identifies his cultural identity than his ethnic identity. Robert and Thomas continually describe themselves as Americans, but White Americans. They see their Whiteness as the norm culture in the United States; however, Robert is very conscious of class.

Educational world view is created from family, community, and schooling experiences and through the lens of identity

Interpretations of educational experiences are shaped by self-identity, community, and schooling experiences. Robert talks about prior experiences and how they shaped his educational accomplishments. He says:

> [Y]ou are shaped by your experiences. Experiences that you have had in the past I would use part yourself as my family...coming from the background that I did since at the time only one other person in my extended family has been to college, my mother's brother. He went on to get a Ph.D. I have always been interested in the biological sciences growing up. I can say [I] always had a strong interest in that discipline from kindergarten.... Actually, one of the things [his ethnic identification], it did have a marked influence on me is that since I came from really a working-class background and working family. It [work] is very important to my family and it is a value to be instilled on all of us. Ah, my parents who are very adamant about us using some type of work activities (tape slips). So we had a lot of things to do around the house, a lot of chores that we had to deal with. Then when we became of working age we were expected to go out and get a job and earn some money, and go to school at the same time, I think of the consequence... particularly when I turned sixteen, from that point on I suffered because I was expected to work a part time job. I thank my family that I was working doing something and that, I have... Right now I have mixed feelings about that [working]. On the other hand, I thought it was a very good experience. On the other hand, my parents were more interested in developing that work ethic, employment versus academics.... Even in my extended family, that's the way it was; that's part of my ethnic heritage.

For Robert, prior experiences, either positive or negative, helped to create his world view. One of the main components in shaping Robert's interpretation of his educational achievements is that of "family." He sees his family as having a negative impact on his schooling. He believes that his class status is a main factor contributing to his educational world view. For Robert's family, the work ethic is a very important value. At a young age, he was working at the insistence of his family. Robert even comments that he had "mixed feelings" about his parents "developing that work ethic, employment versus academics." Even in his graduate studies, he feels their influence. He says:

> I think that when I first came here, I was enrolled in a Ph.D. program in plant pathology. I always feel inadequate being there and it was a completely... different world, definitely. My first course was with [names a professor]. *Sometimes* [italics added] I [did] feel like I am on the same intellectual level with other graduate students.

He continues by discussing his experience in a graduate class:

> Think of what it's like to be a graduate student here and your very busy schedule and going home, the only time but at the same time studying after, or very much so. My wife is involved you know by doing a lot of thinking and reflection. Other than that, it would be like growing up in my own family....
>
> My first inclination would be to say that it [the graduate course in which he is currently enrolled] is in conflict with my ethnic background. I don't see many of my family members either engaging in or [having an] interest in constructing knowledge, and trying to make sense of their experiences in the world around them. [They are] getting up in the morning, going to work, coming home, working, whether it be in the house or in the yard or... without really seeing whether they have any intellectual goals or anything like that. Basically they work to survive, [to have enough] food, and [to] put clothes on their backs. It's gotten easier through the generations, my grandparents were poor... and my dad, I've asked him what it was like growing up for him. He said they were poor. But things have gotten better you know, now I consider my parents to be not lower middle class, but you know maybe mid to upper middle class because they have worked their way. I have a difficult time talking to them about it [his graduate level educational experiences]. How things are going.

Robert relates the way his graduate school learning experience is very different from his learning experiences at home.

> What I am learning is it's.... My father, I think my father... does engage. He has been interested in history and he has read a lot. I can think

of other family members, particularly female family members, like my grandmother, and to a certain extent upon roles in the household and I... guess knowing the different levels of how a woman comes to know what she knows and I see many of the females in my family as very low level...

Robert states that he has "conflict" with his class background. He also talks of his family's constant struggle with their class status; however, Robert has an understanding of female roles in society from his experiences with his grandmother "knowing the different levels of how a woman comes to know" (Belenky, Clinchy, Goldberger, & Tarule, 1986). He has an on-going internal battle, sorting through this "conflict." Robert says:

> I see their way of life as my way of life, and what I perceive is my future way of life to be. Sometimes I think that, I get the feeling that they don't understand what all this is that I am going through.

He believes that his class status has affected his education at the graduate level "both at the psychological and emotional level. Sometimes, I feel like I didn't have the same opportunities as many other students who are attending [names the university]. Sometimes, I think of myself as being behind and having to try to catch up." His parents had a "casual approach to education." They had an interest in grades, but they "were very detached" to the "profit of learning and the subject matter of what I was learning." Therefore, he "did enough to get by in high school."

Robert's parents were not involved in reading and thinking, especially reflective thinking. Instead, they were involved in working to support their families. Robert does not recall his parents being engaged in thinking, especially reflective thinking. His family's values conflict with Robert's educational experiences. This conflict continues to influence his academic self-worth and his relationship with his parents.

Thomas, also, speaks to the issues of how his prior high school experiences contributed to his self-identity and educational experiences. Thomas says:

> [M]y classes were so very homogeneous in racial composition. Well, I guess, as a White male, I didn't understand much about what it was like *not* to be a White male because everyone I knew was also a White male or female.... I knew very few Black students.... I think there were

1,200 students in... my whole high school and there were maybe four or five [Black] students and that was all.

Thomas is aware that schooling is an important component of his cultural identification. He shares the following:

> I'd say it [education] becomes, in a sense, a part of my culture in a sense that... I have gone on to graduate school. I have a sense of academia, [it] has become a part of my culture. In many ways, my education is [part of my] cultural identification.

Unlike Robert, the educational values of Thomas's family are consistent with his own. Thomas's interactions with people of different backgrounds from his own are very limited. Even though he lives in an international resident hall, his memories about his interactions with international students demonstrate his cultural insensitivity. For instance, he shares this story:

> I remember one day we were sitting in the kitchen at [names the residence hall] and we're all eating and there was a student from Japan who was cooking his spaghetti and we had a great time sort of making fun of his spaghetti which really, now that I look at it, we were all laughing and he was laughing with us... maybe he was laughing [but] he may not have enjoyed that. And I didn't really think of it until later.... He was cooking spaghetti but then he was putting, uh, he was putting seaweed on it and dried fish and these little noodles... start squirming—they looked like worms. So we were making... we know Japanese people eat sushi, but... these worms. ...I hope it was in good taste. I certainly wasn't trying to be mean.

Thomas does not experience dissonance, even when he has cultural experiences because his values are parallel to those of his family and friends.

Thomas does admit that his experiences with "homogeneity" affected his science teaching in public school and his other educational experiences. "I was shortchanged in a sense as a student in that I was surrounded by homogeneity all the time" since he attended a predominantly White Catholic high school. "There's something missing in my education"; "my teachers could have done more to make me aware, make us aware"; "they could have maybe [done] some multicultural-type things, but it never really happened." He believes that "integration" is very important because it teachers White students "firsthand about people from other groups." However, when he had the opportunity in his "United Nations" residence hall, he learned very little from that experience about diversity or multiculturalism.

David speaks about his family's influence on his education:

> Parents told you to go to school and everyone knew you, you wanted to go to school and meet your friends and get all of this good learning so you could get a good job and so on and so forth. They tell you lies when you go to school and that's how I went to school. That's how schooling has been like. I had a concept of schooling—more of somewhere, you know, where you go and do things and that will pay you later in life. And you get good appraisals for doing some school work—homework—doing well in school and so on.

David continues his ideas about culture and education:

> Oh, I would say culture has been affected by school, mainly by the political setup in South Africa. We have gone through schooling that is mainly meant for keeping the African people in South Africa subservient to the White masters. ...It was clearly conceptualized by the Whites of the government, they couldn't in a way conquer our forefathers.... The way I see it, it has been really used as a vehicle to keep African children in school—to promise them good things in the future and those good things don't come.

David sees political class as a significant factor in his education because of apartheid in South Africa. Apartheid controlled his chances of fulfilling his educational dreams. He interprets his educational accomplishments through the lens of oppression. David sees not only the school system being controlled, but also "labor, security, and finances." He states: "But you have teachers, a few people, inspectors, who determine what goes on in the school. The department says this is based on what they think is right and it doesn't concern the people. Nobody, no one is there to question."

The participants in this study talked about the microcultures of class, ethnicity, race, religion, and geographical origin. The interpretations of their educational experiences are seen through these lenses. For two of the participants (Thomas and Robert) class, religion, and American self-identity are key elements for their educational world view. On the other hand, for David, ethnicity, geographical origin, politics, and race are the primary lenses through which he views his educational experience.

DISCUSSION AND IMPLICATIONS

Participants' cultural identity appears to be very important to self-identification and more important than ethnic identification. Culture and ethnicity are used interchangeably to describe unique behavioral characteristics, even in scholarly publications (Slonim, 1991). Even though culture deals with symbolic generalities and universals and ethnicity deals with a person's sense of identification to a reference group, ethnicity is demonstrated by the values, attitudes, lifestyles, customs, rituals, and personality types of people who identify with a particular ethnic group (Slonim, 1991). Our participants are better able to articulate their ideas about culture than ethnicity. All of them see themselves belonging to a cultural group. Thomas and Robert see themselves as Americans, while David sees himself as a Black South African with geographical roots in South Africa.

Ethnic identification is described as having many components: ethnic self, ethnic constancy, ethnic role behavior, ethnic knowledge, and ethnic preference and feelings (Knight et al., 1993). We propose that cultural identification probably has components similar to ethnic identification. However, sometimes the cultural identification of a person focuses on one or more of the microcultures: class, race, religion, language, and geographic region. Thomas talks about his cultural identification in terms of religion (Roman Catholic), race (White), culture (American), and class (middle-class). On the other hand, Robert focuses more on economic class (white collar). David, however, has named geographic family origin, political class, and language. Thus, their cultural identity remains fixed.

There are expected cultural role behaviors, such as educational pursuit for Thomas, working for Robert, and "staying in your place" for David. Cultural knowledge is a critical factor in cultural identification. For David, language and his geographical origin are important. Robert's knowledge of his Italian ancestry is not as important as Thomas's understanding that he is an "American American." Cultural preferences and feelings are also keys to understanding cultural identification. Robert discusses eating Italian foods and his inability to relate to his parents because of their inadequate understanding of the role education plays in his graduate experience. Thomas states that to be a middle-class American, he has a sense of academics, while Robert believes his preparation has been inadequate compared to other graduate students at his university.

David appears to be still bound to the political class issue in South Africa.

Cultural identification serves as a powerful filter in the participants' lives and their educational world views. Thomas has little change in his educational world view even with his few different cultural experiences. On the other hand, Robert's educational experiences have alienated him from his parents. He feels he is struggling with a graduate education because of his parents' work ethic. Work is more important than learning. David finds that his experiences with White South Africans did change his perceptions of Whites. He used his undergraduate experiences to observe and, learn the rules, and he is involved in activities against apartheid. He is having a similar experience in his current graduate program—very little interaction with Whites.

Culture shapes the world views of students, and consequently impacts their learning, interests, and epistemologies. Nevertheless, when students' lives change, their culture changes with them. Variability, flexibility, and contradictions are as much a part of culture as they are a part of human beings. Educational experiences have an impact on individuals to such degree that their world views can change or remain fairly stable depending on the kinds of experiences they have, as demonstrated by Robert, Thomas, and David. These three participants are enrolled in the same teacher education program; however, each participant's experiences in the graduate program will be interpreted differently. Their teaching success is influenced not only by their education world view, but also by their cultural and ethnic identities and how well their program has taught them to interact and instruct all the students in their countries.

Implications for Science Teacher Education Programs. Science teachers and science teacher educators need to understand the nature, history, and philosophy of science in the countries where they teach (Atwater, 1995; Jegede, 1989; Urevbu, 1987). McDaniel (1995) found that prospective science teachers' ideas about culture and ethnicity had little influence on their perceptions of how their students learned during a practicum experience. She recommends that science teacher education programs provide students the opportunity to experience cultural bumps in both their courses and field experiences. Does Thomas need cultural bumps for him to understand his privileged position? (He has not understood it, at this point.)   Some of his students might not have his privileged position. How can Robert be assisted to come to feel better about his "science" self?   Some of his students might have similar dilemmas. How can David begin to be less skeptical of Whites? How can he overcome his political class experiences to believe that education in South Africa can fulfill its promises to all Black South Africans? The answers to these questions are important because most science teacher education programs in the United States have students with similar dilemmas.

Creating cultural bumps for teacher education students might assist them in their further development as multicultural teachers. However, research findings indicate that the bump is not the only essential element (King & Ladson-Billings, 1990; Spindler & Spindler, 1993; Young, 1993). Science teacher educators and cooperating teachers must possess the knowledge and skills to assist their students' reinterpretation of their cultural experiences (McIntyre, 1997; Narode, Rennie-Hill, & Peterson, 1994; Ross, Johnson, & Smith, 1991; Zeichner & Hoeft, 1996).

Would it help Thomas to read articles related to White privilege and to discuss his readings with other White students, students of color, and a science teacher educator who is skilled in this discussion strategy? Over time, Robert's success in teaching science might be enough for him to become more comfortable with his "science" self. David's skepticism about Whites might be dissolved when he is forced to work with Whites in a cooperative setting where the participants are dependent on each other for success. One encounter will not be enough for David. His professors must be cognizant of David's ideas and scrutinize the group's interactions. If David is not an integral part of that group, his beliefs and attitude about Whites will be reinforced.

Science teachers are crucial activists and reformers in the struggle for science education reform. They are the ones who will be measuring student science learning, transforming and constructing science curriculum, and thinking through issues of equality and equity. Consequently, it is important that teachers, whether they are science teachers or science teacher educators, possess the cultural knowledge and skills to teach *all* students in their classrooms. For this goal to be accomplished, teacher education programs must be reformed so that prospective science teachers are encouraged to take risks, to look into the future and imagine a schooling world where *all* students are successful. To realize this goal, multicultural science teacher education programs must include (a) a social justice agenda; (b) a "cradle-to-grave" approach to science teacher education programs; (c) collaborations across institutions and communities; (d) a focus on professional development school reform in science classrooms, and on reinventing the university's role in K–12 science schooling; (e) a blending of science education research and practice; (f) a serious and sustained engagement in science learning and teaching by focusing on science knowledge, powerful pedagogies, and school culture; and (g) a self-renewing organizational structure.

Implications for Future Research. Cultural identification and cultural experiences appear to have a profound effect on participants' interpretations and their educational identities. If cultural identification is such an integral part of self-identity, then further research is needed on this construct. How strong is this idea among and within societies and microsocieties?

Finally, how important are the microcultures of race, class, religion, language, gender, and geographical region on the cultural identification of science teachers? What impact do these factors have separately and collectively on the interpretations and educational world views of teachers? Under what conditions do these microcultures influence teachers' interpretations of education? Lastly, how do culture, ethnicity, race, gender, and geographical region affect science teachers' actions in their classrooms? These research questions need further investigation if science education reforms are to address the needs of all students.

REFERENCES

Allan, R., & Hill, B. (1995). Multicultural education in Australia: Historical development and current status. In J. A. Banks (Ed.), *Handbook of research on multicultural education* (pp. 763–777). New York: Macmillan.

Atwater, M. M. (1995). The multicultural science classrooms, part III: Preparing science teachers to meet the challenges of multicultural education. *The Science Teacher, 62*(5), 26–30.

Banks, J. A. (1994). *Multiethnic education: Theory and practice.* Needham Heights, MA: Allyn and Bacon.

Banks, J. A. (1989). Multicultural education: characteristics and goals. In J. A. Banks & C. A. McGee Banks (Eds.), *Multicultural education: Issues and perspectives* (pp. 2–25). Needham Heights, MA: Allyn and Bacon.

Baruth, L. G. & Manning, M. L. (1992). *Multicultural education of children and adolescents.* Needham Heights, MA: Allyn and Bacon.

Belenky, M., Clinchy, B., Goldberger, N., & Tarule, J. (1986). *Women's ways of knowing: The development of self, voice, and mind*. New York: Baine.

Blasi, A., & Glodis, A. (1995). The development of identity: A critical analysis from the perspective of the self as subject. *Development Review, 15*, 204–433.

Bogdan, R. C., & Biklen, S. K. (1992). *Qualitative research for education: An introduction to theory and methods*. Boston: Allyn and Bacon.

Borden, G. A. (1991). *Cultural orientation: An approach to understanding intercultural communication*. Englewood Cliffs, NJ: Prentice Hall.

Brewer, J., & Hunter, A. (1989). *Multimethod research: A synthesis of style*. Newbury Park, CA: Sage.

Brickhouse, N., & Bodner, G. M. (1992). The beginning science teacher: Narratives of convictions and constraints. *Journal of Research in Science Teaching, 29*(5), 471–485.

Brock, C., & Tulasiewicz, W. (Eds.). (1985). *Cultural identity and educational policy*. New York: St. Martin's Press.

Bullivant, B. M. (1989). Culture: Its nature and meaning for educators. In J. A. Banks, & C. A. McGee Banks (Eds.), *Multicultural education: Issues and perspectives* (pp. 27–48). Needham Heights, MA: Allyn and Bacon.

Bullough, R., & Knowles, J. (1991). Teaching and nurturing: Changing conceptions of self as teacher in a case study of becoming a teacher. *Qualitative Studies in Education, 4*, 121–140.

Casey, K. (1993). *Theory, methodology, and politics in discourse collection and analysis. I answer with my life: Histories of female teachers working for social change*. New York: Routledge.

Cashmore, E. E. (1988). *Dictionary of race and ethnic relations*. London: Routledge.

Cobern, W. W. (1991). *World view theory and science education theory*. Monograph of the National Association for Research in Science Teaching (No. 3). National Association for Research in Science Teaching, Kansas State University, Manhattan.

Clandinin, D. J. (1986). *Classroom practice: Teacher images in action*. London: Falmer.

The Condition of Education (1987). Washington, DC: Office of Educational Research and Improvement, U.S. Department of Education.

deMarrais, K. B., & LeCompte, M. D. (1995). *The way schools work: A sociological analysis of education.* White Plains, NY: Longman.

Denzin, N. K. (1989). *Interpretive interactionism.* Newbury Park, CA: Sage.

Denzin, N. K., & Lincoln, Y. S. (1994). Introduction: Entering the field of qualitative research. In N. K. Denzin & Y. S. Lincoln (Eds.), *Handbook of qualitative research* (pp. 1–17). Thousand Oaks, CA: Sage.

Fielding, N. G., & Fielding, J. L. (1986). *Linking data.* Beverly Hills, CA: Sage.

Fine, G. A., & Sandstrom, K. L. (1988). *Knowing children: Participant observations with minors.* Newbury, CA: Sage.

Firth, R. (1965). *We the Tikopia.* Boston: Beacon.

Flick, U. (1992). Triangulation revisited: Strategy of validation or alternative? *Journal for the Theory of Social Behavior, 22,* 175–198.

Geertz, C. (1973). Thick descriptions toward an interpretive theory of culture. In C. Geertz (Ed.), *The interpretations of cultures: Selected essays.* New York: Basic Books.

Gollnick, D. M., & Chinn, D. C. (1994). *Multicultural education in a pluralistic society.* Columbus, OH: Merrill.

Gould, S. J. (1994). The geometer of race. *Discover, 15*(11), 65–69.

Gowin, D. B. (1981). *Educating.* Ithaca, NY: Cornell University.

Grant, C.A., & Ladson-Billings, G. (1997). *Dictionary of multicultural education.* Phoenix, AZ: Oryx Press.

Gray, A. (1997). Learning from experience: Cultural studies and feminism. In J. McGuigan (Ed.), *Cultural methodologies* (pp. 87–105). Thousand Oaks, CA: Sage.

Hawkins, B. D. (1997). UNCF databook provides statistical look at K–12 education. *Black Issues in Higher Education, 14*(9), 14–16.

Helms, J. (Ed.). (1990). *Black and White racial identity: Theory, research, and practice.* Westport, CT: Greenwood Press.

Hoffman, D. M. (1996). Culture and self in multicultural education: Reflections on discourse, text, and practice. *American Educational Research Journal, 33*(3), 545–569.

IDASA Democracy in S. A. (1999). Our citizens. [On-line]. http://www.idasa.org.za/democracy/citizens.htm.

Janesick, V. J. (1994). The dance of qualitative research design: Metaphor, methodolatry, and meaning. In N. K. Denzin & Y. S. Lincoln (Eds.), *Handbook of qualitative research* (pp. 209–219). Thousand Oaks, CA: Sage.

Jegede, O. (1989). Toward a philosophical basis for science education of the 1990s: An African view-point. In D. E. Herget (Ed.), *The history and philosophy of science in science teaching* (pp. 185–198). Tallahassee, FL: Science Education and Department of Philosophy, Florida State University.

Kearney, M. (1984). *World view*. Novate, CA: Chandler and Sharp.

King, J., & Ladson-Billings, G. (1990). The teacher education challenge in elite university settings: Developing critical perspectives for teaching in a democratic and multicultural society. *European Journal of Intercultural Studies, 1*(2), 15–30.

Kitano, H. H. L. (1985). *Race relations*. Englewood Cliffs, NJ: Prentice-Hall.

Kluckhohn, C. (1954). *Culture and behavior*. New York: Free Press.

Knight, G. P., Bernal, M. E., Cota, M. K., Garza, C. A., & Ocampo, K. (1993). Family socialization and Mexican American identity and behavior. In M. Bernal and G. P. Knight (Eds.), *Ethnic identity: Formation and transmission among Hispanics and other minorities* (pp. 105–130). Albany: State University of New York Press.

Kroeber, A. (1948). *Anthropology*. New York: Harcourt, Brace.

LeCompte, M. D., & Preissle, J. (1993). *Ethnography and qualitative design in educational research*. San Diego, CA: Academic Press.

Lee, O., & Yarger, S. (1996). Modes of inquiry in research on teacher education. In J. Sikula, T. J. Buttery, and E. Guyton (Eds.), *Handbook of research on teacher education* (pp. 14–37). New York: Macmillan.

Marshall, C., & Rossman, G. B. (1989). *Designing qualitative research*. Newbury Park, CA: Sage.

Mbendi Information for Africa. (1999). Country Profile South Africa. [On-line]. http://www.mbendi.co.za/cysacy.htm#basic.

McDaniel, P. (1995). *Preservice secondary science teachers' ideas about culture, ethnicity, and learning of marginalized students*. Unpublished master's thesis, University of Georgia, Athens.

McIntyre, A. (1997). *Making meaning of Whiteness*. Albany: State University of New York Press.

McLauren, P. (1994). *Life in schools: An introduction to critical pedagogy in the foundations of education*. New York: Longman.

Mini-Digest of Education Statistics 1997 (1997). [On-line]. http://nces.gov/pubs98/MiniDigest97/980203-3.html.

Mundy, H., & Russell, T. (1992). Transforming chemistry research into chemistry teaching: The complexities of adopting new frames for experience. In T. Russell & H. Munby (Eds.), *Teachers and teaching: From classroom to reflection* (pp. 90–123). London: Falmer.

Murdock, G. (1997). Thin descriptions: Questions of method in cultural analysis. In J. McGuigan (Ed.), *Cultural analysis* (pp. 178–192). Thousand Oaks, CA: Sage.

Narode, R., Rennie-Hill, L., & Peterson, K. (1994). Urban community study by prospective teachers. *Urban Education, 29*(1), 5–21.

Nespor, J. (1987). The role of beliefs in the practice of teaching. *Journal of Curriculum Studies, 19*(4), 317–328.

Newmark, E., & Asante, M. K. (1974). Perception of self and others: An approach to intercultural communication. In F. L. Casmir (Ed.), *The international and intercultural communication annual* (pp. 54–61). Falls Church, VA: Speech Communication Association.

Nieto, S. (1992). *Affirming diversity: The sociopolitical context of multicultural education.* New York: Longman.

Novak, J. D., & Gowin, D. B. (1984). *Learning how to learn.* New York: Cambridge University Press.

Peck, R. F., & Tucker, J. A. (1973). Research on teacher education. In R. M. Travers (Ed.), *Second handbook of research on teaching* (pp. 940–978). Chicago: Rand McNally.

Petersen, W., Novak, M., & Gleason, P. (1982). *Concepts of ethnicity.* Cambridge: Harvard University Press.

Preston, P. W. (1997). *Political/cultural identity: Citizens and nations in a global era.* Thousand Oaks, CA: Sage.

Pusch, M. (1979). *A cross cultural training approach.* La Grange, IL: Intercultural Press.

Reference: People. (1999). [On-line] http://South Africa.net/reference/people.html.

Richardson, V. (1996). The role of attitudes and beliefs in learning to teach. In J. Sikula, T. J. Buttery, & E. Guyton (Eds.), *Handbook of research on teacher education* (pp. 102–119). New York: Macmillan.

Ross, D., Johnson, M., & Smith, W. (1991). *Helping preservice teachers to confront issues related to educational equity: Assessing revisions in coursework and fieldwork.* Paper presented at the annual meeting of the American Educational Research Association, Chicago.

Rothenberg, P. S. (1995). *Race, class, and gender in the United States.* New York: St. Martin's Press.

Seller, M., & Weiss, L. (Eds.) (1997). *Beyond Black and White: New faces and voices in U.S. schools*. Albany: State University of New York Press.

Shreeve, J. (1994). Terms of estrangement. *Discover, 15*(11), 57–63.

Skow, L., Samovar, L. A., & Heilweg, S. A. (1990, February). *World view: The second hidden dimension*. Paper presented at the meeting of the Intercultural Communication Interest Group of the Western Speech Communication Association Conference, Sacramento, CA.

Slonim, M. B. (1991). *Children, culture, and ethnicity: Evaluating and understanding the impact*. New York: Garland.

Smith, L. M. (1994). Biographical method. In N. K. Denzin & Y. S. Lincoln (Eds.), *Handbook of qualitative research* (pp. 286–305). Thousand Oaks, CA: Sage.

Spindler, G., & Spindler, L. (1993). The process of culture and person: Cultural therapy and culturally diverse schools. In P. Phelan & A. L. Davidson (Eds.), *Renegotiating cultural diversity in American schools* (pp. 27–51). New York: Teachers College Press.

Stake, R. E. (1994). A brief history and some advice. In N. K. Denzin & Y. S. Lincoln (Eds.), *Handbook of qualitative research* (pp. 200–215). Thousand Oaks, CA: Sage.

Straus, A. L. (1987). *Qualitative analysis for social sciences*. New York: Cambridge University Press.

Taylor, C. (1994). The politics of recognition. In D. T. Goldberg (Ed.), *Multiculturalism: A critical reader* (pp. 75–106). Cambridge, MA: Blackwell.

Timm, J. T. (1996). *Four perspectives in multicultural education*. Belmont, CA: Wadsworth.

Urevbu, O. (1987). Cross-cultural teaching of the interactions of science: An African perspective. In I. Lowe (Ed.), *Teaching the interactions of science, technology, and society* (pp. 283–293). Melbourne, Australia: Longman Cheshire.

Wallace, A. F. C. (1970). *Culture and personality*. New York: Random House.

Warren, C. A. B. (1988). *Gender in field research*. Newbury, CA: Sage.

Wax, R. (1979). Gender and age in fieldwork and fieldwork education: No good thing is done by any man alone. *Social Problems, 25*, 509–523.

Weiss, I. R. & Boyd, S. E. (1990). *Where are they now? A follow-up study of 1985–86 science and mathematics teaching force*. Chapel Hill, NC: Horizon Research, Inc.

Whaley, A. L. (1993). Self-esteem, cultural identity, and psychosocial adjustment in African American children. *Journal of Black Psychology, 19*, 406–422.

Whyte, W. F. (1984). *Learning from the field*. Beverly Hills, CA: Sage.

Young, L. (1993, February). *Learning about me, learning about them: Pluralism in a preservice education classroom*. Paper presented at the annual meeting of the Association of Teacher Educators, Los Angeles.

Zeichner, K. M., & Hoeft, K. (1996). Teacher socialization for cultural diversity. In J. Sikula (ed.), *Handbook of research on teacher education* (pp. 525–547). New York: Macmillan.

CHAPTER 5

Enhancing the Science Interest of African American Students Using Cultural Inclusion

Shirley Gholston Key

Science educators have examined certain factors that interact and affect science achievement in order to facilitate American students' improvement, global ranking in science achievement, and success in mastering science competencies before leaving grades four, eight, and twelve. In order to reach this goal, much research has been done on factors such as students' interests, attitudes, and motivation in science education. Educators have researched different curricula, curricular topics, and the relevancy of these topics. Recently the TIMSS (Third International Mathematics and Science Study) yielded data on the U.S. global ranking, science achievement, and science curricular topics (Forgione, 1998; Valverde & Schmidt, 1998). Yet there is still a prevailing problem in science education today. Many African American students are not achieving successfully in science. Not only do they perform poorly in the science classroom, but this failure trend also impacts entry into science careers. The lack of success in science affects not only African American students and other culturally diverse populations but the country as a whole. Unless equity and access to knowledge is facilitated as described in many national standards and TIMSS countries, a segment of the U.S. population will always be underachievers in science (Valverde & Schmidt, 1998). So there is an urgent need to find out why African American students and other students of color consistently perform poorly in science. Each group of students warrants being studied separately to identify unique problems that hinder their science achievement.

Science achievement is influenced by many factors, such as student attitudes, interests, motivation, type of curricula, relevancy of materials, and the culture of the students. The investigation of these factors was found to have been rare, and the investigation of these factors in reference to African American culture is even less. Neither has the interaction of these factors with the culture of African American students been studied. How these factors affect African American students' view of science and their science achievement is a major concern, for science is viewed as something foreign to many African American students, who study science for years before reading about a scientist or inventor of their own ethnic group.

Even though science processes are generic or "culture-free," if students cannot and do not identify with those who are "processing," they may internalize the notion that they cannot perform science or are not expected to process scientific information and thus negate the content being taught. Validating and/or correcting perceived notions is a process that depends on one's culture. Using African American students' culture to perform these processes in science learning is both constructivistic and culturally inclusive, which could possibly increase their interest and achievement in science. Multicultural science or culturally inclusive science is believed to be an enhancement for African American and other students of color.

There are five dimensions of multicultural education: content integration, knowledge construction process, prejudice reduction, an equity pedagogy, and an empowering school culture and social structure (Banks & Banks, 1995). *Content integration* encompasses the extent to which teachers use culturally relevant examples, data, and information from a variety of cultures and groups to illustrate key concepts, principles, generalizations, and theories in their subject areas or disciplines. The *knowledge construction process* involves the procedure by which social, behavioral, and natural scientists create knowledge and the manner in which the implicit cultural assumption, frames of reference, perspective, and biases influence the ways that knowledge is constructed within each discipline. *Prejudice reduction* describes the characteristics of children's racial attitudes and suggests strategies that can help students develop more democratic attitudes and values. *Equity pedagogy* consists of using techniques and methods that facilitate the academic achievement of students from diverse racial, ethnic, and social class groups. *Empowering school culture and social structure* is used to describe the process of restructuring the school's culture and organization so that students from diverse racial, ethnic, and social class groups will experience educational equality (Banks & Banks, 1995).

These dimensions of multicultural education are not usually addressed in traditional curricula. Nor do curricular topics directly address the dimensions of multicultural education and the general interest of African American students; rather, they focus on specific bodies of knowledge selected by discipline specialists. Traditional science curricula and curricular topics usually employ the expository method of teaching science, with the instructor dominating the discussion. This method also includes laboratory activities and topics that reinforce known facts and theories expounded by the teacher.

Contrary to the traditional curriculum, Science-Technology-Society (STS) curriculum is structured to integrate science, technology, and society. Thus, it encourages the development of students' interest, disseminates relevant information, crosses ability levels, promotes cultural relevancy, and solicits solutions to societal issues. In general, STS topics are usually social and environmental issues that not only integrate science, technology, and society but also enhance citizenship participation. This curriculum can be equitable and allow African American students the opportunity to integrate their culture more readily than the traditional curriculum. STS also enhances the inclusion of African Americans in higher level science courses and increases achievement in science disciplines for African American students.

Both traditional and STS science curricula can be made more relevant for African American students by incorporating the equity pedagogy and the content integration dimensions described by Banks & Banks (1995). These two dimensions possess those characteristics essential for cultural inclusion (Key & Kline-Cherry, 1998). For this study, these two dimensions will be used to help define and describe the cultural inclusion model.

The culturally inclusive model demonstrates that the equity pedagogy and the content integration dimensions are not mutually exclusive. They should be used in conjunction with each other to allow instructors to address the needs of all students and especially students of color. Cultural inclusion emphasizes the pedagogy and exemplars that invite students of color to participate in the learning process.

Equity pedagogy exists when teachers use techniques and methods that facilitate the academic achievement of students from diverse racial, ethnic, and social class groups. It is supported by the culture difference theorists Cummins (1986) and Ogbu (1990), who believe that students are not having academic success because they experience serious cultural conflicts in school. The students have rich cultures and values, but the school's culture usually conflicts seriously with cultures of students from low income and ethnic minority groups. Equity pedagogy makes use of ethnic culture, devotes little attention to social class, and lists cultural characteristics (e.g., learning styles, teaching styles, and language) to help teachers build on the cultural strengths of ethnic students. Content integration allows teachers to use culturally relevant examples, data, and elaborations with their pedagogy (Banks & Banks, 1995). As these dimensions are integrated into classrooms and curricula, cultural values are shared in the learning process.

Cultural inclusion is a type of equity pedagogy because it is defined as the knowledge about or relating to a student's culture that supports the learner's academic environment while showing that the learner is valued as a responsible participant in a culturally diverse society (Hollins & Spencer, 1990). Culturally inclusive science is the integration of the learner's culture into the academic and social context of the science classroom to aid and support science learning and includes learning styles, teaching styles, and language (Baptiste & Key, 1996).

This study uses the contributionist and the additive approaches (Banks & Banks, 1995) to evaluate how African American students perceive culturally inclusive topics. Since the integration of cultures in science curricula is nonexistent, this study approached it from students' perception and not actual viewpoint. Banks and Banks (1989) indicated that students of color many times did not know about their culture because of the lack of exposure in the traditional classroom and texts. Why? Don't all students deserve to know all the facts about science concepts, inventions, inventors, and issues related to the inventions? This knowledge will benefit not only African American students but all students. Therefore, for this study traditional science curricular concepts, topics, and issues were used and made culturally inclusive by adding contributions, scientists, or various examples from the African American culture to them.

The two curricula in this study were made culturally inclusive by introducing culturally relevant elements, examples, and data from African American culture into the traditional science topics and the nontraditional, STS science topics. For example, the *traditional* and non–culturally inclusive statement about the topic of *scientists* read:

> "I would like to study about different scientists and their contribution to science."

To make this statement a *culturally inclusive* statement, it was rewritten to read:

> "I would like to study about African American scientists and their contributions to science."

> "I would like to study about Charles Drew, an African American scientist, and his work on blood plasma."

Culturally inclusive items were evaluated by African American students in this study. The study was designed to assess the perceived interest of eighth-grade science students concerning culturally inclusive science topics.

REVIEW OF RELATED LITERATURE

Cultural inclusion is a factor that influences the learning of African American students (Banks & Banks, 1995; Banks & Banks, 1989; Hollins & Spencer, 1990; Ladson-Billings, 1994). Cultural inclusive science is defined as the integrating of the learner's culture into the academic and social context of the science classroom to aid and support science learning for all students (Key, 1995). It is a combination of content integration and equity pedagogy. It can be included throughout the science curriculum on a daily basis. The science content or science processes being taught or discussed can be taught and discussed from the culture of all students inclusively. Cultural inclusion does not need a new scope and sequence, new equipment, or a national mandate; it only needs to be integrated into the science curriculum and all aspects of the science learning environment on a daily basis. It stresses changing science classrooms to make them culturally consistent, relevant, and meaningful to diverse populations.

Achievement is increased and failure is reduced in science when cultural inclusion is addressed in the curriculum. Researchers have found that students of color were more successful in science when the classes were integrated and showed respect for their cultures (Hewson & Hewson, 1983; Jegede & Okebukola, 1991; Johnson, Collins, Dupuis, & Johansen, 1988). Native American students, for example, taught using culturally relevant materials, achieved at a significantly higher rate and showed a significantly more positive attitude toward science (Matthews & Smith, 1991). Other Native American students who used similar materials without the culturally relevant inclusions did not fare as well (Matthews & Smith, 1991). African American and Hispanic students demonstrated higher achievement and more positive attitudes when taught using a culturally inclusive science curriculum (Key, 1998; Key & Kline-Cherry, 1998).

Students learn best and are motivated when the school curriculum reflects their cultures, experiences, and perspectives (Banks & Banks, 1989; Baptiste, 1991; Bennett, 1989; Hollins, 1990a, 1990b). The Joint Center for Political Studies (1989) recommended that curricula be expanded to reflect the lives and interests of African American and other students of color for all students need to see people like themselves and to be symbolically represented in the classroom.

Some students of color can operate effectively even when cultural inclusion is lacking. However, many African American students find this barrier hard to overcome. Ogbu (1990) believes that trying to learn in a culturally different and linguistically different environment helps explain the difficulty in school adjustment and poor academic performance of students of color.

This study has indicated that the African American students responded positively to science topics that related to them and their culture. It also showed that they were not significantly interested in either of the curricular topics when they did not relate to their culture. This study supports others that found that respect for culture and integration of the culture were major factors affecting interests in science (Jegede & Okebukola, 1991; Johnson, Mitchell & Kean, 1991; Matthews & Smith, 1991). Barba (1995) states, "Culturally familiar elaborations, which use culturally familiar objects, environments or contexts, examples, and analogies function as powerful variables in terms of students of color's concept acquisition" (p. 17).

Cultural inclusion can be used with any type of curriculum, science concept, or science discipline. It has been shown in this study that traditional and nontraditional science topics were more interesting to the African American students only when they were integrated with their culture. This fact may help to explain Graham's (1994) study, Kahle's

(1982) study, and a chart in *Education Week* (Dimensions, 1993) on attitudes about school subjects. Graham (1994) found that African American students considered themselves successful even though their grades indicated otherwise. Kunjufu (1988) explained that some very capable African American students do not perform well in school as a result of "choice" rather than a lack of ability. Through daily and personal experiences they have formed conclusions that have led them to believe that American society does not value them personally or members of their race as a group of people. They know that if they perform as the system (teachers, educational system, economic systems, etc.) would like them to, they could be successful and accepted by the White, dominant culture. To many African American students, this is "selling out" or disrespecting your race. So many students do not participate in the educational system in classrooms across America because of this ethnic peer pressure and the belief that they are not recognized in the curricula in these classrooms. Instead they choose to barely pass or even fail and drop out of school (Kunjufu, 1988; Atwater, 1994).

In a middle school faculty meeting, A. Rison, author of Rison's TAAS (Texas Assessment of Academic Skills) Preparation Booklet (Faculty meeting presentation, November, 1994), contended that African American students in many schools and school districts that used his booklets were successful. He also contended that the successful achievements were a result of the cultural inclusive review books. The books' contents referred to cultural elements, elaborations, data, examples, and so on that the African American students identified with and were familiar with in math, language arts, and reading exercises. Culture, again, has been shown to help increase the achievement of African American students.

Daponte's (1992) study found that African American students' achievement increased when they studied physical science concepts couched within sports-related vignettes. This increase in achievement was believed to have been associated with African American students' interest in sports. After reviewing this sample of African American students' responses to topics, Barba's (1995) comment on cultural elaboration, Kunjufu's (1988) analysis of failure in the African American teenage group, and Rison's (Faculty meeting presentation, November, 1994), comments about successful TAAS scores with a culturally inclusive preparation booklet, one may question whether sports were as important as the image, race, and success of the athlete or participants.

The sports personalities or heroes could be the cultural tie the students are relating to in the vignettes and other instances. One cannot speak or write about basketball and football without mentioning African Americans who are well known to African American students. A case in point is the increasing interest of African American youths in golf due to Tiger Woods's success in this sport. These studies indicate that there is a common factor involved, the inclusion of African American students' culture.

Several studies found that African American students express positive attitudes about science and their science classes, but these students do not perform successfully in science classes and on standardized science tests (Dimensions, 1993; Graham, 1994; Kahle, 1982). This study seeks to add some information to the field of science education by proposing and demonstrating statistically that culture is another important determinant in the learning process of science for African American students. Specifically, the African American students' responses were statistically significant for science topics from the two curricula that integrated their culture. Their responses were not statistically significant for topics that did not integrate their culture.

THE SETTING OF THE STUDY

This study was conducted in a suburban school district, Fort Bend Independent, located southwest of Houston, Texas. The ethnicity of the school district was 57% Caucasian students and 43% students of color. The 1994 sample for this study consisted of 131 African American eighth-grade science students from three middle schools. There were 64 males and 66 females.

The three middle schools, Christa McAuliffe Middle School, Missouri City Middle School, and Quail Valley Middle School, had the highest African American middle school population in the district. The majority of the African American population lived within the Houston city limits. Christa McAuliffe Middle School was located within Houston's city limits and the other two schools were located in Missouri City, Texas, a suburb of Houston. Missouri City Middle School was near the Houston city limits. Because of their location, the two schools are referred to as "urban-suburban" schools. The third school, Quail Valley Middle School, was in the middle of an affluent suburban neighborhood.

All of the classes at all three schools were heterogeneously mixed regarding academic ability.

The student population of Quail Valley Middle School consists of 57% White Americans, 38% African Americans, and 5% Hispanic Americans and Asian Americans. The majority of the African American population lived within the Houston city limits and not in the immediate neighborhood of the school. According to the principal, "the socioeconomic status (SES) of the students ranges from average to median at this school" (Leach, Interview, November, 1994). Fewer than 10% of the school's population is on free or reduced lunch.

The second school, Christa McAuliffe Middle School, has 85% African Americans, 10% Hispanics, 3% Asians, and 2% Others. It is located within the city limits of Houston, Texas and borders the suburb of Missouri City. Thirty-eight percent of the school's population is on free or reduced lunch.

The third school, Missouri City Middle School, has 80% African Americans, 19% Hispanics, and 1% White Americans. Thirty-five percent of the school's population is on free lunch. This school lies within Missouri City's border but is near the Houston city limits. The majority of the African American population that attends this school lives within Houston's city limits. All three schools are serviced by this suburban school district because they are all located in the Fort Bend County area. The variables within each school, SES and student populations, are an enhancement to this study.

METHODOLOGY

This study was originally conducted in 1994 and repeated in 1997. The surveys were administered during the spring of 1994 and spring 1997. In both studies a modified version of the "Middle School Students' Interest Survey" (Su, 1992) was used to measure the students' interest in five areas. This instrument consisted of five sections, but for these studies only two sections, the Science Topics Interest section and the Demographic section, were used. The "Cultural Inclusion" portion of the Science Topics Interest section surveys the science topics from a cultural viewpoint.

The students were given individual instruments with answer sheets and were allowed to answer all open-ended items directly on the instrument. For the 1994 study a sample of 130 African American eighth-grade science students were surveyed. The sample consisted of 64 males and

66 females from three different middle schools in a suburban school district in the southwestern United States. The ethnicity of the school district was 57% White Americans and 43% students of color.

The 1997 study was repeated in the same district at one of the middle schools used in the 1994 study, with a 90% African American student population. The 1997 sample included 51 African American students, 25 males and 26 females.

The investigator and teachers supervised all classes while the survey was being administered. Approximately 45 minutes were required to complete the instrument. The instruments were then collected, separated by ethnicity and schools, then analyzed using an IBM computer with the Statistical Package for the Social Sciences (SPSS) statistical program.

Statistical tests used to analyze the data for this study were the dependent t-test, the two group multivariate analysis of variance (MANOVA), the Hotelling's T^2, Cochran's univariate test of homogeneity, Box's M multivariate test of normality, normal plots, and frequencies.

RESULTS

The focus of the studies was to evaluate the perceived interests of African American eighth-grade science students concerning culturally inclusive science topics in a traditional science curriculum and the nontraditional science curriculum, STS (Science-Technology-Society). Students' interests were evaluated on many topics and issues in STS and traditional science. Specific research questions examined were:

1. Is there a statistically significant difference in the perceived interest of African American eighth-grade science students concerning topics presented in a traditional science curriculum versus topics presented in a nontraditional science curriculum, Science-Technology-Society (STS)?

2. Is there a statistically significant difference by gender in the perceived interest of African American eighth-grade science students concerning topics presented in a traditional science curriculum versus topics presented in a nontraditional science curriculum, Science-Technology-Society (STS)?

3. Is there a statistically significant difference in the perceived interest of African American eighth-grade science students concerning topics presented in a traditional science curriculum versus culturally inclusive topics presented in a traditional science curriculum?

4. Is there a statistically significant difference in the perceived interests of African American eighth-grade science students concerning topics presented in a nontraditional curriculum, Science-Technology-Society (STS), versus culturally inclusive topics presented in a nontraditional curriculum, Science-Technology-Society (STS)?

5. Is there a statistically significant difference in the perceived interest of African American eighth-grade science students concerning culturally inclusive topics presented in a traditional science curriculum versus culturally inclusive topics presented in a nontraditional science curriculum, Science-Technology-Society (STS)?

6. Is there a statistically significant difference by gender in the perceived interest of African American eighth-grade science students concerning culturally inclusive topics presented in a traditional science curriculum versus culturally inclusive topics presented in a nontraditional science curriculum, Science-Technology-Society (STS)?

The results from the research questions that evaluated African American perceptions toward culturally inclusive topics did reveal some significant findings. There was a statistically significant difference in the perceived interests of African American eighth-grade science students concerning topics presented in a traditional science curriculum versus topics presented in a culturally inclusive traditional curriculum. The 1994 results indicated a level of significance at $p=.001$ and in 1997, $p=.000$. The data indicated that the subjects had a greater perceived interest in the culturally inclusive traditional science topics than the traditional topics without the integration of their culture.

Likewise, there was a statistically significant difference in the perceived interest of African American eighth-grade science students concerning topics presented in the nontraditional science curriculum, STS (Science-Technology Society), versus culturally inclusive topics in the nontraditional science curriculum, STS (Science-Technology Society). The 1994 and 1997 data indicated a level of significance at $p=.001$.

There was not a significant difference in the perceived interest of African American eighth-grade science students concerning topics without the cultural inclusive element in the 1994 study. The traditional science curriculum topics and the nontraditional Science-Technology-Society (STS) science curriculum topics were insignificant at $p=.102$ in 1994 but significant in 1997 at $p=.002$. This difference in 1997 was shown to be contributed to by gender preferences. The females preferred the STS topics at a significantly higher rate than the males. Yet neither the STS

means and the traditional curriculum means were as high as the culturally inclusive means.

There was not a statistically significant difference in the traditional
culturally inclusive topics versus the nontraditional STS culturally inclusive topics. The students showed no perceived preference between
culturally inclusive topics in the 1994 and 1997 studies.

Neither was there a statistically significant difference by gender in
the perceived interests of African American eighth-grade science students concerning topics presented in a traditional science curriculum
versus topics presented in the nontraditional Science-Technology-Society
(STS) curriculum in 1994 and 1997. The fact that these students did not
prefer culturally inclusive topics in a traditional science curriculum over
culturally inclusive (CI) topics presented in a Science-
Technology-Society (STS) curriculum confirmed the hypothesis that
cultural inclusion is an important element to them. It can be summarized
that both males and females in this study equally prefer the culturally inclusive topics. In the 1994 study, neither group indicated a greater
interest in traditional curricular topics or nontraditional curricular topics
such as STS, but in the 1997 study, the females showed a preference for
the STS science topics over the traditional science topics.

CONCLUSION

This study concludes that the African American eighth-grade science
students in this study perceive themselves as being interested in studying
science topics that relate to their culture more than topics that do not relate to their culture. It did not matter whether it was traditional or STS.
Female African American students as well as male African American
students were more interested in curricular topics that related to their
culture but there was no significance due to gender. Cultural inclusion
may be a classroom vehicle to enhance African American students' interests and thus their academic achievement in different types of science
curricula. It may be the factor that links the perceived view of success by
African American students with actual success and the involvement of
more females and other students of color in science.

The STS curricular topics showed higher means than the traditional
topics throughout this study. This implies that African American students
perceive themselves as being more interested in STS science topics than
traditional ones. This curriculum through students' interest might en-

hance their achievement in science. The 1997 study showed that the African American females significantly preferred the STS topics in comparison to the males. This data implies that the STS science topics may be used to enhance the interest and achievement of all African American students and especially the females. Since engaging more female students in science is a national problem, using the STS science topics may engage more African American females in science courses and thus science careers.

IMPLICATIONS

Currently no science curriculum has included the culture of African American students as a viable curricular component. Curricula continue to treat cultures, other than the White culture, episodically. Information about scientists of color is usually added to the end of a chapter as an example but not included as an integral part of the curriculum and used as a means to help convey the concepts. This study, as others have done, suggests the importance of the inclusion of the culture into the curriculum. This study indicates that the African American students sampled responded positively to the culturally inclusive science topics and that there is a statistically significant perceived interest in science topics when there is a cultural element involved in the topics. Further, it might benefit this population to allow them to study science in a culturally inclusive curriculum. It may also benefit science education if science educators would research the effect of cultural inclusion on the various curricula and disciplines during the current science reform. Finally as good science pedagogy implies, one can never lose by allowing students to study what interests them.

REFERENCES

Atwater, M. (1994). Research on cultural diversity in the classroom. In D. Gabel (Ed.), *Handbook on research in science teaching and learning* (pp. 558–576). New York: Macmillan.

Banks, J., & Banks, C. (Eds.). (1995). *Handbook of research on multicultural education*. New York: Macmillan.

Banks, J., & Banks, C. (Eds.). (1989). *Multicultural education: Issues and perspectives*. Boston: Allyn & Bacon.

Baptiste, P. (1991). *Developing the multicultural process in classroom instruction: Competencies for teachers. (2nd ed.).* An unpublished manuscript.

Baptiste, P. & Key, S. (1996). Cultural inclusion: Where does your program stand? *Science Teacher, 63*(2), 32–35.

Barba, R. (1995). *Science in the multicultural classroom.* Boston: Allyn & Bacon.

Bennett, C. (1989). *Comprehensive multicultural education: Theory and practice.* Boston: Allyn & Bacon.

Cummins, J. (1986). Empowering minority students: A framework for intervention. *Harvard Educational Review, 56*(1), 18–36.

Daponte, T. (1992). *Investigating students' understanding of Newton's laws of motion through schema theory and sporting activities.* Unpublished doctoral dissertation, University of Houston, Houston, TX.

Dimensions: Attitudes about school subjects. (1993, March). *Education Week*, p. 1.

Forgione, P. (1998). What we've learned from TIMSS about science education in the United States. Address to the 1998 Conference of the National Science Teachers' Association. Las Vegas, NV. http://nces.ed.gov

Graham, S. (1994). Motivation in African Americans. *Review of Educational Research, 64*(1), 55–117.

Hewson, M., & Hewson, P. (1983). Effects of instruction using students' prior knowledge and conceptual change strategies on science learning. *Journal of Research in Science Teaching, 20* (8), 731–743.

Hollins, E. (1990a). Debunking the myth of a monolithic white American culture; or, moving toward cultural inclusion. *American Behavioral Scientist, 34*(2), 201–209.

Hollins, E. (1990b, June). Professional development for teachers of "at-risk" students: A comprehensive plan. Paper presented at the Interstate New Teacher Assessment and Support Consortium Seminar, Kansas City, MO.

Hollins, E., & Spencer, K. (1990). Restructuring schools for cultural inclusion: changing the schooling process for African American youngsters. *Journal of Education, 172*(2), 89–100.

Jegede, O., & Okebukola, P. (1991). The effect of instruction on sociocultural beliefs hindering the learning of science. *Journal of Research in Science Teaching, 28*(3), 275–285.

Johnson, J., Collins, H., Dupuis, V., & Johansen, J. (1988). *Introduction to the foundations of American education.* Boston: Allyn and Bacon.

Johnson, J., Mitchell, C. & Kean, E. (1991). *Improving science teaching in multicultural settings: A qualitative study.* An unpublished paper, University of Oklahoma.

The Joint Center for Political Studies. (1989). *Visions of a better way: A Black appraisal of public schooling.* Washington, DC: Joint Center for Political Studies.

Kahle, J. (1982). Can positive minority attitudes lead to achievement gain in science? Analysis of the 1977 national assessment of educational progress. Attitudes toward science. *Science Education, 66*(4), 539–546.

Key, S. (1998). An elementary preservice class perception of cultural inclusion (work in progress).

Key, S. (1995). African American eighth-grade science students' perceived interest in topics taught in traditional and nontraditional science curricula. *Dissertation Abstract International, 56*(5), 1725.

Key, S. & Kline-Cherry, S. (1998). A partnership enhancing mathematics and science education for students of color (work in progress).

Kunjufu, A. (1988). *To be popular or smart: The Black peer group.* Chicago: African American Images.

Ladson-Billings, G. (1994). *Dreamkeepers: Successful teachers of African-American children.* San Francisco: Jossey-Bass.

Matthews, C., & Smith, W. (1991, April). *Effect of using culturally-relevant science curriculum materials on Native American elementary students.* Paper presented at the National Association for Research in Science Teaching Conference, Lake Geneva, WI.

Ogbu, J. (1990). Minority education in comparative perspective. *Journal of Negro Education, 59*(1), 45–55.

Su, H. (1992). A survey of middle school students' interests in environmental issues as they relate to science instruction. Ed.D. Dissertation, University of Houston, Houston, Texas.

Valverde, G., & Schmidt, W. (1998). Refocusing U.S. math and science education. *Issues in Science and Technology, 14*(2), 60–66.

CHAPTER 6

Native American Science Education
and Its Implications for Multicultural
Science Education

Paul McD. Rowland
and Carol R. Adkins

Imagine three classrooms. The first classroom consists of all White students who speak English as a first language and whose parents were second (or greater) generation Americans; the second classroom consists of students from 15 different ethnic groups and 10 different first language groups and who are first generation Americans; our third classroom consists of a group of students who are all Hopi, who are somewhat bilingual in English and Hopi and who are considered indigenous people. What does multicultural science education mean in each of these classrooms? What is the purpose of multicultural science education in these classrooms?

In this chapter we will examine multicultural science education through a special lens: that of Native American Indian science education (for a discussion of the various labels used to identify the indigenous people of North America see Cornelius, 1999. In this essay Native American, First Nations, American Indian, indigenous people, and Native people will be used interchangeably). Native American Indian science education provides a special vantage point from which the assumptions, goals, processes, and outcomes of multicultural science education can be examined. We begin with a review of the existing literature of Native American Indian science education and some of our work with native educators with the intent of returning to fundamental questions of multicultural science education with this lens.

SCIENCE EDUCATION FOR NATIVE AMERICAN STUDENTS

A review of the literature about science education for Native Americans reveals two themes for the improvement of science education for Native Americans. The first theme is to *increase and improve science instruction*, while the second theme is *to connect science education to Native science*, especially by recognizing the Native American connection to the earth through environmental science themes.

Improvement of Science Instruction

Many authors' suggestions for improving Native American science education are the same as the suggestions being put forth in the national science education reform literature for all students. That is, the strategies are not specific to Native American students, but their repeated occurrence in the Native American science education literature may indicate the acuteness of the need for these strategies with this group of students. According to Garcia and Ahler (1992):

> [T]eaching Indian children is no different from teaching other children. This does not mean that Indian children are exactly the same as non-Indian children. Actually, teaching children as though they were the same robs children of their unique individuality. Good teaching requires that teachers understand and respect the individuality of all children. Neither appreciation nor respect are possible without knowing the children's cultural and environmental backgrounds. (pp. 13–14)

However, the uniqueness of the Native American child's cultural and environmental background radically changes the context for teaching, and these differences need to be recognized.

Cooperative learning or group problem solving has been a common recommendation for teaching Native American students. There is some evidence that Native American students are predisposed to cooperative approaches to learning and do poorly in competitive classroom settings (Swisher & Deyhle, 1992). Gilliland (1992b) claimed that "group problem solving is part of Native American culture" (p. 151). The use of cooperative learning was considered by Garcia and Ahler (1992) to be an effective strategy for teaching Native American students in that it is culturally compatible and may help achieve cultural continuity. Native American students have been found to "respond enthusiastically to problem-solving through small group activities" (Hoffman, 1992, p.

140). In fact, a cultural bias toward cooperative behaviors may result in a reluctance of Indian children to compete with peers (Leacock, 1976 in Swisher & Deyhle, 1992). Hirst and Slavik (1989) suggested that using cooperative learning groups in science can improve not only science learning but also the learning of language. Cohen (1994) has shown that the effectiveness of small group learning is rather complex and various conditions, especially type of task, can influence its effectiveness. This literature review found no research that indicated any consideration of this complexity in the teaching of science to Native American children. However, Gilliland (1992a) noted that the effectiveness of small group work may differ among the various tribes, depending on the local community structure.

Another approach commonly recommended is active/experiential/hands-on learning. Gilliland (1992a) claimed that "most Native American children learn much more readily when instruction is multisensory, relevant and active ...and they have the memory of concrete experience to which they can tie the principle" (p. 59). In a paper entitled *Helping Indian Students Understand Basic Science Concepts* (ORBIS Associates, no date), the list of Guidelines for Implementing Science Activities emphasizes having students "do science" and use materials to learn science.

Another recommendation is to teach science integrated with other subjects. Ovando (1992) pointed out that the multidisciplinary teaching of science concepts is especially compatible with the ways many Native American cultures organize knowledge. He quoted Cajete as saying,

> There is no word in any traditional Native American language which can be translated to mean science as it is viewed in modern Western society. Rather the thought process of "science" which includes rational observation of natural phenomena, classification, problem solving, the use of symbol systems, and applications of technical knowledge, was integrated with all other aspects of Native American cultural organizations. (p. 233)

Some Indian educators have argued that an integrated (non- or inter- or multidisciplinary) approach may be more appropriate than a Western disciplinary approach to the way knowledge is framed by the native culture. Both Ovando (1992) and Gilliland (1992b) argue for the integration of science with other subjects throughout the school day. In particular, these authors suggest that the teaching of language through science activities may be an especially appropriate strategy.

Making connections to the world of the learner is another common recommendation found in the literature. This recommendation not only has the benefit of connecting new learning to prior knowledge but also serves a larger function.

> It is important that Indian students understand what science is and learn to appreciate how science affects their daily lives. By doing so, Indian students can see that science is something that is useful to them and not something which only relates to non-Indian culture. (ORBIS Associates, no date, p. 2)

Ovando (1992) discussed the value of creating a connection between the school culture and the home culture such that school and home learning are not distinct. Gilbert and Carrasco, developers of the Native Science Connections Project at Northern Arizona University, have noted that development of science curriculum for Native American students must be based on their experiences (Williamson, 1994).

A strategy common to work with all types of Limited English Proficient (LEP) students is to specifically teach the language of science when teaching the concepts of science. This approach has been advocated by several Native American educators (Allen & Seumptewa, 1993; Gilliland, 1992b; Ovando, 1992). A variety of content reading and bilingual education strategies have been recommended as ways to assist Native American learners.

Connections to Native Science
The second theme that is found throughout the Native American science education literature is the importance of connecting science education to Native science based on the strong Native American relationship to the land. There are several ways connections can be made to Native science including connections to the scientific knowledge of Native people, connections to native ways of knowing about the world, or connections to the land/earth-based ethic of Native people.

One approach for connecting to Native science is to begin the teaching of science topics by relating the topics to knowledge that Native cultures have developed to help them survive in the world (Carrasco, quoted in Williamson, 1994). Cajete (1994) has advocated the teaching of principles of science through "the use of Indian cultural examples, perspective and field experiences" (p. 47). Gilliland (1992b) also advocated the use of teaching students about the pre-Columbian scientific knowledge of Native Americans. Ovando (1992) gave several references for studying ethnoscience based on local culture and science.

A second approach to connecting to Native science is to come to understand the cultural difference between Western science and Native science. Simonelli (1994) explained the difference as follows:

> Indian science, or "indigenous science" as it's sometimes called, is "full-spectrum science." It draws freely on all four of the gifts that have been given to us as human beings: the spiritual, emotional, mental, and physical. By contrast, Western science dwells mostly on the physical and mental, often rejecting the spiritual and feeling or emotional qualities of life with great arrogance and finality. (p. 37)

According to this view, students should be given opportunities to explore phenomena using both Western science and indigenous science. For example, a study of mining practices could be investigated using Western methods of scientific analyses found in environmental impact studies and then explored using Native knowledge from spiritual and emotional ways of knowing. Each of these ways of knowing can be represented by different questions. For example, a spiritual question might be framed in terms of the appropriateness of taking the minerals from Mother Earth for profit. An emotional approach to mining that we have used is to have learners draw pictures of a personal special place and then to have another person draw on top of the original picture what it would look like with mining taking place.

Kawagley and Barnhardt (1999) have suggested that fundamentally different worldviews are the basis of the differences between indigenous science and Western sciences. However, they argue that the bulk of the literature on Native education focuses on "how to get Native people to understand the Western/scientific view of the world" (p. 126). They argue that Native people need to understand Western science but not at the expense of what they already know. They propose an education for Native people that seeks linkages across the worldviews and is based "in the culture rather than education about the culture" (p. 139). Furthermore, they argue that other people "need to recognize the existence of multiple worldviews and knowledge systems, and find ways to understand and relate to the world in its multiple dimensions and varied perspectives" (p. 139).

A similar bicultural approach is advocated by Garrison, Denetclaw, and Scott (1995), who argue that Navajo cultural knowledge expands the ways of knowing the world and thus serves as a broader background for developing hypotheses and alternative hypotheses about the universe. They suggest that the best possible science education for Navajo students presents "both Navajo cultural knowledge and Western cultural knowledge on an equal basis to Navajo students and helping those students use both of those cultural backgrounds in developing alternative ways of explaining what is happening in the universe" (p. 5).

A cross-cultural approach to science curriculum for First Nations science education is advocated by Aikenhead (1997). His argument is based on a view of science as a subculture of Euro-American culture and the need for Native learners to cross cultural borders when they attempt to learn science. (The cultural perspective argues that the learning of science is essentially cultural acquisition.) Thus, Aikenhead suggests that students learning (Euro-American) science may undergo assimilation (learn the content of science by replacing indigenous views with EuroAmerican views) or enculturation (learn the content of science by incorporating that content into a person's view of the world that includes scientific thinking as an enhancement to everyday thinking). He argues for a science education that is practical and situated. "If science education is going to contribute to First Nations economic development, environmental responsibility and cultural survival, students will need to learn and to eclectically use in practical everyday situations, many ways of knowing: Aboriginal common sense, Aboriginal and Western technology, and Aboriginal and Western knowledge of nature" (p. 228). He proposes a curriculum that recognizes the cultural differences and the necessity for border crossings while "teaching the knowledge and skills of Western science and technology in the context of societal roles (social, political, economic, etc.) including the role of hegemonic icon of cultural imperialism" (p. 229). He specifically argues for "A cross-cultural STS curriculum (that) would emphasize cultural border crossing for the purpose of enhancing students' capabilities and motivations to eclectically draw upon Aboriginal cultures and upon the subculture of science and technology for the purpose of taking practical action toward economic development, environmental responsibility, and cultural survival" (p. 229).

A third approach to integrating Native views of science into the curriculum is to recognize and incorporate the land-based ethic into the curriculum. Historically, Native Americans have developed a special relationship to the land that is based in a unified knowledge of a variety of scientific knowledge, spiritual beliefs, and traditions (Cajete, 1994). This ethical connection to the land provides a basis for connecting Native American students to science through scientific studies of the environment. In addition, Native cultures are rich with legends and stories that provide an entry to science through Native legends (Gilliland, 1992b). For example, the Cherokee story of the "Coming of Corn" (Caduto & Bruchac, 1989) could be used to introduce the study of plant life cycles. Cajete (1994) has challenged students to create new legends and myths to unify new scientific knowledge with traditional knowledge. Like other writers, he has emphasized the importance of a nature-based science education.

A special consideration a few authors highlight in teaching Native American students is understanding local cultural taboos. Allen and Seumptewa (1993) advocate teacher orientations that make new teachers aware of cultural taboos. Gilliland (1992b) stresses the importance of discussing plans for biological experiments with knowledgeable Native students, parents, or friends. Alcoze has pointed out that to keep Native students interested in the sciences, taboo activities such as frog dissections and the inappropriate use of beans in school must be avoided (Greer, 1992).

Summary of Literature Review

The major recommendations for improving science education for Native Americans included the general improvement of science education that has been recommended for all students. Changes in curriculum and teaching strategies such as the use of cooperative learning; active, hands–on learning; integration of science with other subjects; making connections to the world of the learner; and special attention to teaching the language of science have been advocated. A second set of recommendations called for making connections to the students' cultural knowledge of science by: 1) including in science education the contributions made by Native people, 2) viewing science broadly to include Native ways of knowing the world and their cultural basis, and 3) centering Native science education on the study of the environment and relating that study to the Native beliefs that connect them to the earth.

NATIVE AMERICAN SCIENCE EDUCATION: A RATIONALE

Native American education holds a special place both in the United States and in Canada. In the United States, Native American education has legal responsibilities with respect to language and cultural preservation (Native American Languages Act of 1990, 1996). Consequently, we must realize that the education of Native Americans (at least legally) is different from that of other ethnic groups. On the other hand, an understanding of Native American education can help us identify and address issues related to the education of other minority ethnic groups (see Rowland, Prater, & Minner, in press, for a discussion of the use of this term).

If we ask the question, What is the basis for a different kind of education for Native American learners?, we find at least three key responses. First, we argue from a cognitive perspective that culture-based instruction will facilitate learning. Second, we argue from an affective perspective that a culture-based education provides greater motivation to learn. Third, we argue from an ethical perspective that it is right or good to provide an education that facilitates cultural survival.

The cognitive argument serves as the basis for recommendations that students learn about science through lenses that they have already acquired within their traditional culture. This argument assumes that the learner has an existing schema that reflects the knowledge, beliefs, norms, etc., of the Native culture. Ovando (1992) extends this argument from a linguistic perspective and argues that Native students should be able to use a bilingual approach to learning science so they have a fuller social/cultural context for their learning. A teacher in an all-Hopi classroom would need to understand the most common aspects of that culture (and language) to understand fundamental aspects of the Hopi child's schema. This understanding of the culture could then serve as a basis for connecting new knowledge to the prior knowledge of the child. The assumptions behind this rationale are somewhat questionable. The first assumption is that the Native culture is indeed a part of all Native children's schema. Among the Hopi, for example, there is a great deal of diversity of adherence to traditional Hopi practices, use of the Hopi language, and understanding of Hopi cultural stories and beliefs. Despite this warning against overgeneralizing, it does appear to be beneficial for teachers of Hopi children to understand Hopi culture for the cognitive benefits such understanding may bring to planning lessons and for facilitating learners as they attempt to connect new knowledge to their existing schema.

The cognitive argument may be extended to include the idea that a bicultural schema that integrates both indigenous and Western science is a richer schema and provides more alternatives to thought. Several authors have described how Native ways of knowing provide alternative approaches to problem solving that typically Western ways of knowing fail to use (Aikenhead, 1997; Cornelius, 1999; Garrison, Denetclaw, & Scott, 1995; Kawagley & Barnhardt, 1999), thus one might argue that the bicultural approach would result in more divergent approaches to problem solving. Ovando (1992) compares the bicultural approach in science education to that of bilingual education and claims that "just as additive bilingualism enriches the child's first and second language, additive science education can enrich the Indian student's traditional heritage at the same time that it prepares the student for mastery of scholastic science content and processes" (p. 240).

Our second argument is simply that Native American students will be more motivated to learn about those things connected to their own culture than they will be motivated to learn about Euro-American culture. Curricular arguments for the inclusion of stories from and about Native Americans often are based on this premise (Caduto & Bruchac, 1989; Gilliland, 1992a, 1992b). This argument often uses the term "relevance" to describe how such and approach improves student performance. Many curricular materials (see Ovando, 1992, for a list) have been developed on this premise.

The third rationale for Native American science education is based on an ethical argument. Simply put, a humane pluralistic democracy has a responsibility to maintain the diversity of its people, especially those who are involuntary minorities. This argument underlies Aikenhead's (1997) cross-cultural approach, which seeks to prepare learners for "cultural survival." The argument is also found in Kawagley and Barnhardt's (1999) advocacy of a science education contextualized by aboriginal rights to self-determination and self-government. It might be argued that the commitments of the governments of both the United States and Canada to indigenous education are also based on this ethical argument.

NATIVE AMERICAN SCIENCE EDUCATION
AND OTHER LEARNERS

Of what value is Native American science education to other learners? One might argue that it does not have to be of any value; that the value of it to Native people is enough justification for an effort to be made to understand and implement this type of education. However, arguments for the understanding of diverse cultures by all people would suggest that some aspects of Native American science education might be useful for all people to understand Native American culture. Indeed, Aikenhead (1997) suggests that "Non-Aboriginal students, as well as scientists and engineers, have much to learn from First Nations cultures" (p. 233). Specifically, he points out that the relationship to the natural world is one area for learning. He also claims that comparing Western science to Aboriginal knowledge of nature would develop a multiscience perspective and insights into the nature of Western science. Smith (1998) uses Native American science education with other people to develop an alternative (to a Western science) approach to understanding nature that can become part of a "powerful synthesis." More generally, Cornelius (1999) provides a framework for a Native American culture-based curriculum based on the recognition that all cultures have fundamental value and integrity. (The subtitle of her book is "A framework for respectfully teaching about cultures). Her goal is to move the integration of ethnic content (Banks, 1989) from the additive approach to a transformational approach wherein students come to respect the worldview of Native people while at the same time, addressing and eliminating the stereotypes of Native people that are prevalent in many educational materials. It is not unreasonable to argue that respectful encounters with Native American science education by other students might be a powerful tool for both increasing understanding of other cultures and developing a better understanding of ways of knowing.

ISSUES IN MULTICULTURAL SCIENCE EDUCATION

More than one-fourth of the students in American schools are identified as members of minority ethnic groups. The ethnic identification of a student, whether a self-identification or identification by another, is a critical part of how a student interacts with others. If we assume that most learning takes place as a result of interactions between a learner and others (including authors and media producers), then it seems clear that ethnic identity is a critical part of a student's learning.

Our first argument and challenge focuses on science education that meets the needs of this growing body of minority ethnic students, who are, as a group, less successful in science classes and underrepresented in the science professions (Atwater, 1994). It is clear that currently, science education fails to meet the needs of ethnic minority populations in U.S. schools.

Baptiste and Key (1996) have described the need for multicultural education as follows:

> Science should be presented in a non-elitist, culturally diverse context that includes all students. Presenting science as a hands-on, activity-based, problem solving instructional program couched in constructivist theory, enables all students, including students of color, to excel in science. (p. 32)

A fundamental challenge for science educators is providing successful science learning experiences to all students. The problem with meeting this goal is that students do not start at the same point and these differences vary across a variety of factors including ethnicity. Furthermore, it is well accepted that providing the same experiences does not provide all students with equal learning opportunities. "Children of different cultures have constructed culture-based information in different ways, and thus bring different perceptions and understandings to the classroom" (Martin, 1997, p. 243). Constructivist educators like Martin and Atwater (1996) argue for the use of a constructivist approach to science education that recognizes the role of ethnicity and culture in developing the learner's schema or prior knowledge. Multicultural science education is viewed as "a special case of individual learning needs" to be addressed by appropriate methodologies (described for various ethnic groups), multicultural curriculum (content areas representative of various ethnic groups), and a general cultural sensitivity (Martin, 1997).

A second argument for multicultural education comes from both majority and minority perspectives. Baptiste and Key (1996) frame this argument as follows: "Cultural inclusion is needed to develop competent science students who are socially responsible participants of a culturally diverse society where group identity is valued and preserved" (p. 34). This argument is similar to that made by Cornelius (1999) who bases her curriculum on a model put forth by Banks (1989). The typology for cultural inclusion put forth by Baptiste and Key appears to be a variation of Banks's model which moves from exposing students to the contributions of the target group (what Baptiste and Key call the Product Level) to a level of social action where students take action on important social issues (Baptiste and Key's Process/philosophical orientation level). Cornelius's cross-cultural approach and Baptiste and Key's cultural inclusion approach both argue for a multicultural education for all students so that they are better able to be successful participants in a diverse democracy. In addition, both arguments make a case for a multicultural approach that serves to maintain different cultures.

Thus, the rationale for multicultural science education follows from three arguments:

Minority ethnic students are not provided an equal opportunity without it.

Majority students need it to develop appropriate skills to succeed in a diverse world.

Valuing and preserving group identity (essential to a culturally diverse society) is promoted by it.

MULTICULTURAL SCIENCE EDUCATION (MSE)
AND NATIVE AMERICAN SCIENCE EDUCATION (NASE)

It is informative to look at MSE and NASE through the following questions: Of what does it consist? What is its purpose and rationale? In doing so we can probe some issues about these two approaches to science education and provide some basis for answering the questions raised at the beginning of this chapter about our three classrooms.

First, of what do MSE and NASE consist? In some science methods textbooks, MSE appears to consist of following various "how to" lists. For example, Esler and Esler (1989) describe how to make a classroom more multicultural through bulletin boards, seating arrangements, audiovisual aids, resource people, and field trips. Suggestions for multicultural effectiveness by Raizen and Michelsohn (1994) refer to teacher characteristics in terms of ensuring fairness, spotting bias in materials, and establishing learning environments where all students learn science. Martin (1997) suggests that students from different ethnic groups need different methodologies. In addition, he suggests that the curriculum be altered to fit the ethnic makeup of the classroom. However, Martin's main suggestions are based on his claim that "general characteristics of effective multicultural teaching are essentially the same as the general characteristics of constructivist inquiry teaching" (p. 245). NASE has been characterized by Rowland and Adkins (1995) as consisting of improved science instruction using a variety of techniques such as cooperative learning groups, experiential learning, integration with other subjects, and connections to the world of the learner, as well as making connections to Native science through relating science education to topics or themes important to Native people, exploring the differences between Native science and Western science, and integrating a land-based ethic into the curriculum. These same ideas are found in Cornelius's (1999) Iroquois corn culture–based curriculum, which is aimed at both Native students and other students. Fundamentally, it appears that MSE and NASE consist of the same kinds of practices.

Second, what are their purpose and rationale? Multicultural education appears to have two audiences: minority ethnic students and majority students. For minority students, the promise of MSE is greater success in science classes and greater potential for membership in science-related professions as well as cultural maintenance. For majority students, the promise is a better understanding of how students of other cultures view the world and an improvement in working with populations of diverse people. NASE is primarily focused on Native learners. Its purpose is both improvement in academic performance in the science classroom and cultural preservation. Once again it appears that MSE and NASE are fundamentally the same.

The differences between MSE and NASE in terms of theoretical purposes and practice are not that great; however, the differences in context make NASE and MSE different enterprises. If we return to our second and third classrooms, we can see that the all-Hopi classroom can easily be accommodated by the notions of NASE developed above. Compared to many classrooms, the Hopi class is not a very diverse classroom. The basic language and cultural norms are fairly similar for all students. Thus, it is relatively easy for a teacher to try to understand the culture of the students, to provide students with appropriate instructional strategies, and to use a curriculum based in Native culture in the context of whole class instruction. The classroom teacher who faces 15 ethnicities and 10 language groups has a very different problem. Although at first glance the problem is one of logistics (how can one teacher provide appropriate methods and curriculum to a group of students this diverse) the problem is also one of purpose and rationale.

To clarify this problem it is useful to separate the achievement rationale (cognitive and affective) for NASE and MSE from the ethical rationale. The achievement rationale involves making connections to the learner's culture to improve both motivation and schema building. This problem is one of logistics. Although it may be desirable to connect to a student's culture, it is clear that in a very diverse classroom such connections will be rare and dependent on a teacher who can engage in conversations with students to surface relevant connections (Rowland, Prater & Minner, in press).

The ethical rationale is equally complex. Both NASE and MSE argue that cultural preservation is a good and necessary responsibility of the schools. For Native American education this is not only a moral right but a legal right under federal law (Native American Languages Act of 1990, 1996). The question that emerges for MSE is whether or not there is an ethical obligation to provide science education that promotes the cultural preservation for all cultures found in a classroom. Many new immigrants to the United States are less concerned about schools providing cultural maintenance than they are about schools providing academic success for their children and improving the economic opportunities for their children. In these cases of voluntary immigrants, MSE might be useful for its cognitive functions but considered a waste of time that detracts from assimilation. An extreme example illustrates this point: Consider a graduate student in electrical engineering from Pakistan. It is unlikely that this student would find a curriculum adjusted to his culture very useful. It may be helpful to use Ogbu's (1978) categories of voluntary and involuntary immigrants to help sort out the ethical rationale. Involuntary immigrants (he includes American Indians, African Americans, and Hispanos) may be "owed" a cultural maintenance because they were deprived of their culture through force. On the other hand, immigrants who came to the United States voluntarily to join the pluralistic American society have a right to continue their cultural practices but the society and its institutions are not obligated to provide mechanisms for cultural maintenance. We put forth this modification of the ethical rationale as a basis for further discussion of what kind of science education is appropriate when the goal is equity and a sound science education for all students.

CRITIQUE OF MSE AND NASE

MSE and NASE share a common problem. They describe students of a particular group through the use of stereotypes based on limited research findings or limited experiences (Rowland, Prater, & Minner, in press). A very real issue is the within-group variance on any parameter, whether it be an assumption about cultural knowledge and practice or cognitive style. The category of ethnicity may be less important than other categories such as ruralness or economic status. For Native American students, life on the reservation is very different from life in large cities. For Native students who live in cities the main purpose of NASE may be cultural preservation, while on the reservation the purpose may focus on student achievement. These differences in purpose need to be clear. Likewise, MSE must be clear about what its purpose is.

Another problem in both approaches is that of language. Little research has been conducted on the effects of first or native language on learning science. The findings thus far are inconclusive in this essential area (Atwater, 1994). Eleanor Wilson Orr's (1997) findings that Black English Vernacular interferes with learning mathematics and science raises serious issues about the importance of language learning to conceptual understanding of science. Clearly we need more research on the relationship between language learning and science understanding if we are to help students of limited English proficiency, a factor affecting many minority ethnic students. The extent to which bilingualism enhances or constrains science learning needs to be more clearly established.

The future of MSE and NASE may hinge on providing both clear rationales for their use and evidence for their effectiveness at meeting their stated goals. For Native Americans, NASE has both practical and legal support based on assertions of self-determination and claims in the economic future of the Indian nations. NASE can be easily justified through ethical arguments that appeal to cultural preservation as well as to students' academic success. On the other hand, MSE, especially for voluntary minorities, cannot be justified on this basis. MSE for minority ethnic students needs to be justified and supported by research demonstrating its effectiveness at meeting academic goals. Likewise, MSE needs to be shown effective at meeting goals for majority students in terms of improving their understanding of science and their ability to work with diverse populations. From an individual empowerment perspective we can argue for MSE as a way to provide a sound science program for all. We now need to determine whether or not it delivers.

REFERENCES

Aikenhead, G. S. (1997). Toward a First Nations cross-cultural science and technology curriculum. *Science Education, 81*(2), 217–238.

Allen, G. C. & Seumptewa, O. (1993). The need for strengthening Native American science and mathematics education. In S. J. Carey (Ed.), *Science for all cultures* (pp. 38–43). Washington, DC: National Science Teachers Association.

Atwater, M. M. (1996). Social constructivism: Infusion into the multicultural science education research agenda. *Journal of Research in Science Teaching, 33*(8), 821–837.

Atwater, M. M. (1994). Research on cultural diversity in the classroom. In D. L. Gabel (Ed.), *Handbook of research on science teaching and learning* (pp. 558–576). New York: Macmillan.

Banks, J. (1989). *Multicultural education: Issues and perspectives.* Needham Height, MA: Allyn and Bacon.

Baptiste, H. P. & Key, S. G. (1996). Cultural inclusion. *Science Teacher, 63*(2), 32–35.

Caduto, M. J., & Bruchac, J. (1989). *Keepers of the earth.* Golden, CO: Fulcrum.

Cajete, G. A. (1994). Land and education. *Winds of Change, 8*(1), 42–47.

Cohen, E. G. (1994). Restructuring the classroom: Conditions for productive small groups. *Review of Educational Research, 64*(1), 1–35.

Cornelius, C. (1999). Iroquois corn in a culture-based curriculum: A framework for respectfully teaching about cultures. Albany: State University of New York Press.

Esler, W. K. & Esler, M. K. (1989). *Teaching elementary science* (5th ed.). Belmont, CA: Wadsworth.

Garcia, R. L. & Ahler, J. G. (1992). Indian education: Assumptions, ideologies, strategies. In J. Reyhner (Ed.), *Teaching American Indian students* (pp. 13–32). Norman: University of Oklahoma Press.

Garrison, E. R., Denetclaw, W. F. & Scott, O. T. (1995). Navajo scientists of the next century—Laanaa hasin. *Journal of Navajo Education, 12*(3), 3–7.

Gilliland, H. (1992a). Growth through Native American learning styles. In H. Gilliland (Ed.), *Teaching the Native American* (pp. 51–62). Dubuque, IA: Kendall Hunt.

Gilliland, H. (1992b). Science for Native Americans. In H. Gilliland (Ed.), *Teaching the Native American* (pp. 149–153). Dubuque, IA: Kendall Hunt.

Greer, A. (1992). Science: It's not just a white man's thing. *Winds of Change, 7*(2), 12–18.

Hirst, L. A., & Slavik, C. (1989). *Cooperative approaches to language learning.* (ERIC Document Reproduction Service No. ED 354 775).

Hoffman, E. (1992). Oral language development. In J. Reyhner (Ed.), *Teaching American Indian Students* (pp. 132–142). Norman: University of Oklahoma Press.

Kawagley, A. O., & Barnhardt, R. (1999). Education indigenous to place: Western science meets Native reality. In G. Smith and D. R. Williams (Eds.), *Ecological education in action: On weaving education, culture, and the environment* (pp. 117–140). Albany: State University of New York Press.

Martin, D. J. (1997). *Elementary science methods: A constructivist approach.* Albany, NY: Delmar.

Native American Languages Act of 1990. (1996). In G. Cantoni (Ed.), *Stabilizing indigenous languages.* Flagstaff, AZ: Northern Arizona University Press

Ogbu, J. (1978). *Minority education and caste: The American system in cross-cultural perspective.* New York: Academic Press.

ORBIS Associates (n. d.). *Helping Indian students understand basic science concepts.* Washington, DC: Author.

Orr, E. W. (1997). *Twice as less: Black English and the performance of Black students in mathematics and science.* New York: W. W. Norton.

Ovando, C. J. (1992). Science. In J. Reyhner (Ed.), *Teaching American Indian students* (pp. 223–240). Norman: University of Oklahoma Press.

Raizen, S. A. & Michelsohn, A. M. (Eds.). (1994). *The future of science in elementary schools: Educating prospective teachers.* San Francisco: Jossey-Bass.

Rowland, P. McD. & Adkins, C. (1995). Teacher education for teaching science to American Indian students. *Journal of Navajo Education, 12*(3), 35–41.

Rowland, P., Prater, G., & Minner, S. (in press). Teaching science to diverse learners: A professional development perspective. In J. Rhoton and P. Bowers (Eds.), *Professional development in science teaching and learning*. Washington, DC: National Science Teachers Association.

Simonelli, R. (1994). Toward a sustainable science. *Winds of Change,* *8*(2), 36–37.

Smith, W. S. (1998). Native American perspectives. *Science Teacher,* *65*(3), 32–36.

Swisher, K. & Deyhle, D. (1992). Adapting instruction to culture. In J. Reyhner (Ed.), *Teaching American Indian students* (pp. 81–95). Norman: University of Oklahoma Press.

Williamson, B. (1994, July 4). Native American science project launched. *Mountain Campus News*, pps. 1, 4.

CHAPTER 7

Multicultural Science Education
Program Demonstrates
Equity and Excellence

Charles E. Simmons

From former President Bill Clinton, Congress, and corporate executives, the call for high-tech literacy is being heard throughout the nation to prepare American youth for the demand for the information society. That society is already making its presence felt to such an extent that Congress and state governments are seeking to increase by hundreds of thousands the numbers of high-tech trained immigrants. As Clinton told an audience at the Massachusetts Institute of Technology in Cambridge in June 1998, "We shouldn't let a child graduate from middle school anymore without knowing how to use new technologies to learn" (Bennet, 1998). It is certainly true that the majority of students in urban and rural public schools lack sufficient technological training. However, among those programs that focus on math/science education in an urban setting is the Detroit Area Pre-College Engineering Program (DAPCEP), an academic enrichment organization, which services some 73 middle and high school campuses. For 23 years, DAPCEP has been on the track toward preparing inner city pre-college students for careers in engineering (Hill, 1990).

Chances are that if you drive a car anywhere in the nation that was manufactured in the last 15 years, an alumnus of DAPCEP or another enrichment program for minorities may have contributed to the design. Or if you are a consumer of a Michigan electrical or gas utility, a DAPCEP alumnus may have been involved in the preparation or delivery of that product. DAPCEP alumni engineers are now represented throughout the Detroit high-tech sector, contributing to automobile design and manufacturing, chemical processing, computer hardware and software, and public utilities. Some are providing medical care, and others are involved in research. Some are employed and others are entrepreneurs. One alumnus is an executive at a major Wall Street corporation (DAPCEP Tracking Report, 1996).

"My first job out of high school was with a company that does engineering work, and I got it through the DAPCEP Summer Bridge Program," says Yvette Cloyd, now a project manager at Ford Motor Company's Plastic and Trim Products Division (Simmons, 1994). Cloyd says that DAPCEP has opened many doors for her since her summer experience years ago. The program has placed hundreds of college-bound students since 1983. A 1988 graduate of the University of Detroit–Mercy with a bachelor of science degree in math, Cloyd also has a master's degree in computer science and has been a mentor in the program for 11 years. Among DAPCEP alumni and students, Cloyd is not unique, for most of the DAPCEP students are girls, and half of the program's founders were women of high achievement in math/science education (Y. Cloyd, personal interview, 1994).

For instance, the late Esther Caddell, a veteran science teacher and medical researcher, was known as the First Lady of DAPCEP. Caddell, an alumnus of Kentucky State and West Virginia State colleges, was denied admission to medical school because of a policy against the enrollment of women. Some 35 years ago, Mrs. Caddell developed a project-oriented teaching and study method called SUAM DWYPES, which made the scientific method user-friendly to urban boys and girls and was applicable to any area of learning for all ages of students. Caddell's methods involved helping students channel their own resources by tailoring each project individually, expanding the student's preexisting interest. The project also involved the parents as judges, so they would become aware of the student's academic activities. The method provided support and included skill building not only in math/science curriculum, but also an overall development of language skills. According to longtime friend and mentee Kenneth Hill, Mrs. Caddell, who died in 1995, "took the complex scientific method and broke it down into finite steps so that anyone could follow it." She turned her home into a science learning camp for youth whose enthusiasm for their projects was so high that alumni from her tutelage are now long advanced into their own successful professional practices as engineers, surgeons, or top administrators (K. Hill, personal interview, Feb. 10, 1994).

Another alumnus reflects on his DAPCEP experience. "I've always been curious about how things are made," says Wayne Askew (Simmons, 1994). "When I got involved in the after-school program in the tenth grade, I didn't really understand what engineering was all about. But through DAPCEP, I met Black engineers who described the projects they were working on. We took field trips to the MichCon Gas Company, General Motors, and other manufacturers in the Detroit area. I was only in the program for a little while before I knew that I didn't want to work on an assembly line. I wanted to help decide what was made on the line."

Currently an engineer at TRW, Askew has worked as a product design engineer at the Ford Motor Company's Plastic and Trim Products Division. The DAPCEP alumnus holds degrees in mechanical engineering and engineering management from the University of Detroit–Mercy. Askew also mentors middle and high school students in the same program that sparked his interest in engineering. "While in college, I worked as a counselor to kids in the DAPCEP Summer Program, and I've worked with Ford Motor Company's Teacher Partners program, spending several hours each month with an adopted classroom, which gives students a chance to see a real, live engineer and ask questions," he says. "It's exciting now to be able to give something back" (Simmons, 1994).

But these views and developments are not consistent with much of the thinking about urban education. Since scholarly studies and the mass media so often emphasize the high dropout rates and low achievement of minorities at middle and secondary school levels, many lay people and scholars conclude that youth of color are too genetically or culturally inferior to succeed in careers requiring advanced education in the humanities, the social sciences, or math and science. It is true that a declining but unacceptable gap still exists between achievement of Whites and minorities (defined for this study as African American, Hispanics, and Native Americans), yet the facts are that over the past 15 years the high dropout rates have been declining. In addition, more students of color are graduating from high school and going on to college, and low test scores are also improving at some grade levels (Jones-Wilson, 1990; Malcolm, 1990). But it is also true, and this is often dismissed as inaccurate or inappropriate testing, that the average test scores of American students of all races and classes are lower than those of students in other industrialized and some developing nations (Steinberg, 1996). This is especially true in the math and science areas.

Although minorities comprise 20% of the labor force, they are only 8% of the math/science/engineering profession (National Science Foundation, 1994). Minorities will compose one third of the nation's workforce in the 2000s. The goal set by the United States for the year 2000 is to increase underrepresented minorities and women to the level of numerical equity.

BARRIERS TO ACHIEVEMENT BY MINORITIES AND WOMEN

For centuries, those who argue that people of color, minorities, and females have lower abilities to learn math, science, and other academic disciplines have given numerous reasons for that perceived inferior condition (Takaki, 1993). There are the biological determinism arguments that gained international popularity in the 19th century but that stubbornly persist today in some circles (Gould, 1981). These views hold that shared behavioral norms, and the social and economic differences between racial, gender, and class groups, are based on inherited traits of inferiority. Therefore, they reason, any resulting social or economic hierarchy is simply a precise reflection of those genetic differences, and it would be foolish to try to change them. The major scientific basis underlying these views have been the measurement of the skull or brain and psychological testing. Tracing the history of these ideas in the 1970s with thorough research published in *The Mismeasurement of Man*, the author, Stephen Jay Gould, quotes the century-old ideas of E. Huschke, a German anthropologist, who wrote in 1854: "The Negro brain possesses a spinal cord of the type found in children and women, and beyond this, approaches the type of brain found in higher apes" (Mall, 1909, pp. 1–2, cited in Gould, 1981).

Gould also cites another German scholar of anatomy, Dr. Carl Vogt, who wrote during the same era in 1864 in the name of science:

> By its round apex and less developed posterior lobe, the Negro brain resembles that of our children, and by the protuberance of the parietal lobe, that of our females.... the grown-up Negro partakes, as regards his intellectual faculties, of the nature of the child, the female, and the senile white.... Some tribes have founded states, possessing a peculiar organization; but as to the rest, we may boldly assert that the whole race has, neither in the past nor in the present, performed anything

tending to the progress of humanity or worthy of preservation. (1864, pp. 183–192)

Gould also notes that as recently as the 1960s, the *Encyclopedia Britannica* in its 18th edition of 1964 still listed "a small brain in relation to their size," along with woolly hair as characteristic of Black people (Gould, 1981).

Fast forward to even more modern ideas about inferior abilities of women and minorities, and the student will find them expressed in sociocultural and often overlapping themes that prevailed during the time that DAPCEP began (Crow, 1966). Those arguments suggest that inner city urban children and children born to single parents or other alternative family configurations are also doomed to failure. This cultural inferiority is the result of a combination of external forces such as high crime, low school budgets, lack of social exposure to the mainstream, no books in the home, no role models, poor reading skills, and the catch-all attitude similar to the genetic model that minorities and females have a long history of poor achievement. That just about completes the circle of doom.

On the other side of the argument have been numerous scholars who have refuted their opponents' rationale. Earlier in this century, African American scholars, including Dr. Carter G. Woodson and Dr. W. E. B. DuBois, tackled the issue head-on in their classic works, *Miseducation of the Negro* and *Black Reconstruction in America,* respectively (Woodson, 1933; Dubois, 1935). These views were amplified during the DAPCEP era by scholars such as Asa G. Hilliard, III (Hilliard, 1990). That group asserted the view that brain size and skull shape have no relationship whatsoever to intelligence. In addition, these scholars have explained that intelligence testing merely measures experience rather than ability, and that the author of the original intelligence test admitted that it was not intended to determine one's intellectual ability. Unfortunately, that is exactly how the test ended up being used. Also unfortunate is that too many educators, administrators, policy makers and parents did not hear or believe this side of the story.

The scholars who refuted the idea of innate inferiority have also championed civil rights and have fought for the need to eliminate the various detrimental social forces identified above. They all agree that those factors negatively impact the learning process. However, as Dr. Kenneth B. Clark points out, there is no reason that the social ills cannot be resolved simultaneously while serious teaching and learning is going on (Clark, 1967). As Clark explains:

> The educators who argue that the schools cannot do any better job than they are now doing in educating minority group youngsters at the same time tend to argue that the society should turn itself around and become more just. The society should clean up its slums; the society should rid itself of racism; the society should cure all the ills and pathologies which afflict ghetto areas before the schools will be able to reach children in the second, third, or fourth grade how to read or how to do arithmetic.... It is extremely hard for me to say, yes, all these things should be done, but we should not wait until they are done before the schools teach these children how to read and how to do arithmetic. I do not see that there is any real conflict between the society's taking care of its unfinished racial business and the schools doing what schools are supposed to do: namely, teach children. (p. 96)

Without hesitation, DAPCEP pioneers adopted the attitude that teaching and learning must be done right now and for all children within their reach. For the past 23 years their collective energy has been directed toward that philosophy, that all youth can learn under the right conditions. They set out to create those conditions in spite of any negative external factors.

There is much literature about the fact that academic enrichment programs have been shown to be successful in increasing minority and female participation and achievement in math/science/engineering courses (Oden, 1992). In addition, ample studies have demonstrated that multicultural education is one of the major factors that accounts for that success (Ladson-Billings, 1995). Ladson-Billings argues that academic enrichment programs and multicultural education have been a part of African American scholarly thought for a long time prior to the current debate. Building on those ideas and standing on the shoulders of giants, the Detroit Area Pre-College Engineering Program is one of the most highly successful intervention programs in the nation and has consistently equated excellence with equity (Oden, 1992; Clewell, Anderson, & Thorpe, 1992; DAPCEP Tracking Report, 1996). This chapter will discuss the DAPCEP program's administrators, teachers, and parents, and their implementation of multicultural education as a component for the achievement of excellence.

Started with a grant from the Sloan Foundation and 245 students, the Detroit Area Pre-College Engineering Program was founded in 1976 as an academic math and science enrichment program for public school students in Detroit's inner city. Its first location was in one of the poorest areas of the city. According to James Foster, a retired principal and one of the programs' founders, "I was told by my associates that I was out of my mind for going to that school in the first place. There were so many broken windows when I arrived. But afterwards, that area of the city actually became the home of the best kept school in the city because I opened the school to the community and the parents felt that it belonged to them" (J. Foster, personal interview, June 5, 1996). Because of the program's success, every year some 2,000 of the city's public school students and some private school students, are very competitive with their suburban counterparts in math and science. The racial composition of the students reflects the demographics of the city, which is over 80% African American but includes White, Latino and Arab American youth.

"Be part of the solution," is the motto of Kenneth Hill, the DAPCEP executive director and one of the founders, who holds a degree in civil engineering from Howard University and a master's degree in education from Wayne State University (K. Hill, personal interview, Feb 10, 1994). Hill believes that the high rate of achievement among DAPCEP students stems from many factors. "Public school educators, volunteer mentors, and parents are driven by the old-fashioned belief that everyone can learn and a pit bull determination to inspire youth," he says. The program's enhanced curriculum is taught during weekdays, weekends, and in summer sessions at local universities, through field trips and college lectures, as well as internships at local corporations, including the auto manufacturers and parts suppliers.

A key to DAPCEP's success is its operation as a partnership that includes, on its board of directors, representatives of the public school system, corporations, foundations, seven universities, and very active parents. Corporate involvement offers a unique advantage, with many Detroit-based companies providing field experiences that supplement classroom learning. In addition to their financial support, corporations have provided essential hands-on training experiences by opening their plants to field trips, encouraging staff engineers to act as mentors and role models, and hiring DAPCEP participants for summer jobs. For example, in the Ford Partnership Program, 47 volunteer engineer mentors have developed a close relationship with public school teachers, with whom they conduct field trips, assist with science fair projects, teach classes, and mentor students (Gargaro, 1995).

General Motors sponsors an annual Paper Vehicle Project, now in its ninth year, that allows teams of high school students working closely with GM engineers, mentors, and teachers, to design and build life-size model cars using only paper products. The concept of building paper vehicles originated with three young African American engineers at General Motors. Mark Thomas, Vincent Lyons, and Elliot Lyons developed the idea at Stanford University while they were graduate students. For 12 weeks, student team members learn principles of automotive engineering through classes and lectures. The project culminates in a period of "build days," during which the teams of engineers and students assemble the cars. Each school works with a different team of engineers, and each project group arrives at a different design solution (Donley, 1994).

In another example of how the big three U.S. automakers are involved in DAPCEP, the Daimer-Chrysler Corporation teamed up with Michigan State University to provide six engineering seminars to 1,800 DAPCEP students from 35 middle schools and 14 high schools. Other corporations and institutions that have offered seminars are Dow Chemical, Michigan Bell, Detroit Edison, and five Detroit-area universities (Toporek, 1996).

PROGRAM ADMINISTRATORS

James Buri

DAPCEP program administrators have all served as classroom teachers who enjoyed and excelled in their student contact. In addition, they have all worked either as school administrators or instructional specialists. One among the four has served as an assistant principal. In its infancy, DAPCEP won a grant to write a curriculum guide and thereby formalize its middle school program. Kenneth Hill needed two visionary but disciplined educators to direct the writing of that curriculum, a huge job that took five years and became a 500-page document with a six-part training video. The $600,000 grant process also involved writers and work and review committees. An assistant principal, James Buri, who is White, was selected as one director, and the other was instructional specialist Laverne Ethridge, an African American. When the two began working together on the project, they kept their day jobs and worked frantically in the evenings and weekends at Buri's house, where the massive paperwork and documents were "spread out all over the place for five years"

(J. Buri, Personal interview, Sept. 10, 1997; L. Estridge, Personal interview, June 25, 1997).

Buri and Ethridge hired the writers and reviewed the materials prior to sending them to the various DAPCEP committees. The project also included working with technical writers and illustrators, monitoring the printing, and in between there was the videotape preparation. All the time Ethridge and Buri were becoming experts in the new curriculum. A rich diversity of classroom and administrative experience, and advanced training in the National Teacher's Corps combined with a philosophy that everyone can learn, made Program Director James Buri a major force in the DAPCEP leadership team.

Buri graduated from Albion College with a degree in economics, then went on to earn a master's degree from Oakland University. After two years in the National Teacher Corps, he returned to his native Detroit inner city community and began a love affair with elementary school science. He started on the lower West Side at Franklin Elementary by Tiger Stadium and after a year transferred to the East Side and taught third-through sixth-grade science. "Then I taught kids like boxer Tommy Hearns and that group until the school closed. Then for a year I taught at Balch Elementary School, which is now the Golightly Educational Center near the Detroit Institute of Arts. I had a good relationship with the students, especially the older ones," says Buri, now a veteran with 33 years of service in the Detroit public schools (J. Buri, personal interview, Sept. 10, 1997).

Buri's reputation traveled throughout the system, and when he was invited to teach at Pelham Middle School in his former neighborhood, he "did a lot with their science fair and curriculum and was good at it." So when DAPCEP had its first major expansion from its infant organization, Executive Director Kenneth Hill approached Buri and his principal, requesting that the dynamic young educator teach a class.

But let us return to the National Teacher Corps (NTC). During the 1960s and early 1970s of the Vietnam War era, there had been a need for male teachers in urban and rural schools but the country wasn't attracting them. With the youthful spirit of a domestic Peace Corps originated by President John F. Kennedy, the NTC was a two-year program that took applicants with a bachelor's degree in any subject and awarded a master's degree along with a teaching certificate. In Buri's program there were about 120 mostly male students who held sessions at a house on East Jefferson guided by master classroom teachers. Rather than empha-

size the traditional methods courses, the NTC focus was hands-on classroom applications for the urban teacher of the 1960s, when young people
acted and dressed with a free spirit. As Buri puts it, "We were kind of a
rebel group. When I first began teaching I had jeans and a ponytail and
hip boots." In his NTC program there were six student teachers in a room
for half a year until they had their own classroom. "We had to sink or
swim and I guess I learned to swim real quick, and I liked it!" (J. Buri,
personal interview, Sept. 10, 1997).

When Buri looks back over his two decades of teaching and admini-
stration to compare the teachers with traditional education with that of
the NTC alumni, he firmly chooses the latter. In his view, the traditional
method is probably a thing of the past. "It's not functional anymore, and
the old song and dance is keeping many young applicants out of the field.
It's really a roadblock. I'm sure it helps some people, but this career is
really about relating to kids. You have to have the content knowledge,
but at the lower grades if you can't relate to the kids it doesn't matter
how much you know, because it's also about wanting to be there for
them, about having that kind of direction in your life, about that kind of
giving."

In addition, Buri, who was on his way to becoming an accountant
when the NTC came along and placed him in a science classroom, is
equally convinced that the nontraditional approach prepared him better
for the actual classroom experience. "After two years I was ready because I had done it. It was obvious by the end of the two years who could
and who couldn't do it where in a traditional program you don't know
until you go out and get that probationary contract. But at the end of our
program everyone knew who could handle it and who couldn't. Our
classmates would self-select out if they couldn't make it, because you
can't exist in those classrooms unless you really feel like you're making
progress" (J. Buri, personal interview, Sept. 10, 1997).

Laverne A. Ethridge

A product of a Detroit East Side neighborhood of homeowners where the
men worked in the auto factories and the women worked at home,
Laverne Ethridge attended Williams Elementary, Greusel Junior High,
then Cass Technical High School. Ethridge's playmates, who were
among the many first generation Detroiters, had their bicycles, roller
skates, and piano and dance lessons, and they never wanted for anything.
"The way we see Blacks portrayed on television a lot of times is not nec-

essarily the way that all Black folk were brought up," says Ethridge, fondly recalling the family garden and trips to the Eastern Farmers Market with her grandmother and mother, both of whom were and still are (L. Ethridge, personal interview, June 25, 1997).

In high school, Ethridge majored in home economics because she had enjoyed sewing since the seventh grade. However, she didn't like and never took cooking, and because Cass was a college prep school, everyone was required to take the core courses in math and science, including biology, chemistry, algebra, and geometry. "I was always basically a smart kid, and although my mother didn't press for excellence, she told me to do a good job. Since I'm the type of person who did whatever my mother wanted me to do, and could have gotten all As. But she was happy that I got Bs and Cs and so was I. Yet when I went to college, I felt it was a more serious matter" (L. Ethridge, personal interview, June 25, 1997).

Ethridge enrolled at Highland Park Junior College (HPJC) on graduation from high School because her grade point average was not high enough to enter Wayne State University. Many students at HPJC were preparing to transfer to the University of Michigan in Ann Arbor, which everyone said was a good school, and she really wanted to go there. However, her father couldn't afford it, so she attended Wayne State University. "When I got there I met Claude, fell in love, and we got married." Shortly afterward, Claude was drafted into the Army, and the couple moved to Massachusetts. On their return to Detroit, Ethridge enrolled at Eastern Michigan University, in Ypsilanti, decided that a science concentration was more marketable than her major in social studies/home economics, and changed her major. It was a thoughtful change. Ethridge still wanted to teach home economics, however, but discovered that Black students were not encouraged to take that major, which required living in a house on campus. That was during the time just before the end of official segregation, when Black students were not allowed to live in those houses. Instead they would have to live with a woman in Ypsilanti. "The same environment existed at WSU," says Ethridge. "If you talk to anyone who taught home economics and who is over 50, their degree probably came from the southern Black colleges," she said. "When I realized that I wasn't going to teach home economics, that was another reason why I got into science although I always liked it" (L. Ethridge, personal interview, June 25, 1997).

Following her student teaching in science at an elementary school in Ypsilanti and graduation with a B.S. in Science, when Ethridge applied for a job as a science teacher she was hired immediately and found that she loved the work. "As a brand-new teacher, I became an elementary science teacher at the brand new Jamison Elementary School on Philadelphia. I was the first person who taught in that classroom and I had a ball. I had chicks and ducks and even a garden. We did everything that you could think of. We planted our seeds in the spring and the custodian would water the plants in the summer. In the fall we would harvest the crops and cook all the greens. I was just nutty, that was almost home economics again but it was a science course" (L. Ethridge, personal interview, June 25, 1997).

> Jamison was a small school with about 600 students and staff and an intercom system. But after I returned from my pregnancy leave with my first child, I was assigned to a huge school with over 1,000 students in the middle of the Herman Gardens project. The project was converting from White to African American and the teachers had all been there for 30 years and had never taught African American kids. When the African American children arrived, the administration lost control and the building was on the wild. There was no intercom system, and you would look out your door and the kids would be running up and down the halls, while at Jamison if you saw a student in the hall alone you would push a button and an adult would come right away" (L. Ethridge, personal interview, June 25, 1997).

In 1971 Ethridge began teaching science in Detroit's Region Five. "When I arrived there the class had no chairs, books, nor supplies. It took us a couple of years to get all the books and to get things organized into the middle school atmosphere. But this became my niche. Middle school students were much more challenging. I was the 'senior' science teacher who taught the Science Fair project while my partner, Izola Norrell, was the seventh-grade science teacher as well as the DAPCEP teacher" (L. Ethridge, personal interview, June 25, 1997). During that time Ethridge also earned a master of science degree at the University of Detroit with a major in Reading and Learning Disabilities. Subsequently Ms. Norrell left and was replaced by a new teacher, Suzanne Wasson.

As Ethridge explained, "Suzanne Wasson was not originally a science teacher but it shows you that if a person is a good teacher they will do well in whatever they teach, and she did" (L. Ethridge, personal interview, June 25, 1997). Ethridge and Wasson also worked together as a team. But then Ethridge was promoted and left the classroom for the Regional Area Office as an Instructional Specialist. Ethridge was subsequently promoted to positions as Math Improvement Teacher and Staff Coordinator. During that time she was also a coordinator for development and writing of the DAPCEP Middle School Curriculum Guide and companion videotapes which received national recognition. In 1990 she became a DAPCEP program manager. She retired in 1998 and continues to serve as a consultant.

MULTICULTURAL CONTRIBUTORS TO SCIENCE

Laverne Ethridge, one of the originators of the Multicultural Contributors Program as well as an author of the DAPCEP Curriculum Guide, talks about the DAPCEP experience in her own words.

> We've always had a unit on the contributions of minorities to science in the DAPCEP curriculum, but we found that some of the teachers taught the unit and some did not because it was an elective class. Some teachers did a real good job, some didn't teach anything at all, some people kind of tacked it on at the end. But one of the things that happens when you have a "Show and Tell" unit is that it forces teachers to have something to show and tell. The first year it was an idea that James Buri and me came up with to have everybody bring their notebooks to the DAPCEP office. Initially all you had to do was make some notes on about 15 minority inventors or contributors, including independent research for one person, and a written report on all 15.

> We did a lot with presentation skills and required all the students in the class to research and present on one contributor while the class would take notes. For example, when I gave my report, you take notes. When you gave your report, I would take notes. Then when I wrote my report, I would base my notes on what you told me. So I would write a one-page synopsis on 14 contributors, and then write what we call a major report on my own contributor. And that would be the minority contributor notebook. Then we thought, if we're going to have a notebook, they ought to also have an exhibit to go with it. That's really the kind of setup we're talking about, a notebook and an exhibit, two finalists from each school. The first time we did it we had it in a little room upstairs, and we had about 20 notebooks and exhibits. Of course, at that time, we were in the process of building the program so I don't know how many schools we had, probably 15 to 17 schools because all of them didn't participate.

The Minority Contributors Contest began in 1990. The next year we did it we felt the room was too small because we had judges, so we moved it to the Detroit Public Library. By then everybody saw what the other teachers had done, then we put a little pressure on the schools by telling the school representatives about the contest and showing them the list of teachers and student participants. So if you're the principal and you're reading this and you don't see your school's name there you want to know why, similarly to people making contributions at a Baptist church, they want to see their name on the list. So the following year the other teachers wanted to make sure they had something. That's right, Call the roll! That year the library was filled with lots of nice exhibits for viewing by teachers and administrators, and some teachers asked, "Why can't the students attend?" So we moved the event downstairs to the ballroom and began bringing students there to see it. We held it there for the next two years until the building was sold and we had to find another site, which is how we moved to the State Fairgrounds and have held it there for the past three years. In 1996 we had some 112 projects, which represents about 54 schools because some schools only have one representative, some don't participate, and some have two teachers.

Only two projects may be entered per school. If we did three per school, then we'd take up more space. We brought in 40 schools, 40 groups of children to see the exhibits, and then we had the program at night from 6:00 to 8:00 P.M. and we usually have the school band. Since they play, we try to get the people to come at 5:30 or 5:45 so the band plays their last song at 6 P.M. We call all the children's names who have an exhibit, and they receive a medallion and a neck ring. Each student who has an exhibit is already a winner at their own school; then we choose the best of those and everything works out very nicely. It's a nice program; the parents come and they are able to go into the exhibit hall and view their children's projects, and then they take them home" (L. Ethridge, personal interview, June 25, 1997).

DAPCEP TEACHERS

Teachers are the hub of the DAPCEP partnership. Many participate as mentors and hold special classes during and after school for participating students. Most teachers consult with parents regularly on the students' progress and work with engineers to assist their pupils with science fair projects. They also attend monthly DAPCEP In Service Training classes, in which senior DAPCEP teachers teach the junior faculty about their teaching methods and the specially prepared DAPCEP curriculum guide (J. Buri, personal interview, Sept. 10, 1997). A more intensive workshop is held during the summer. The new teachers are recruited by senior DAPCEP teachers and program administrators based on their enthusiasm for working with students and their high standards of teaching, and because they believe that all students can learn math and science regardless of their race, class, gender, or family configuration. The teachers are given an additional stipend by DAPCEP and required to spend extra time with the students. They also receive additional funds to pay for science fair supplies for the students.

Sharon Lee is one example. Lee, an African American teacher who received an "Outstanding Teacher Award" from the Detroit Science Teachers Association, has been teaching science at Detroit's Grant Middle School for eight years, and her students have won more gold ribbons at the science fairs than participants in other DAPCEP classes. DAPCEP's in-school administrator, James Buri, says that Lee has been inventive at using feedback from the science fair judges to help her students improve the quality of their projects. Lee believes that anything worth doing takes time and commitment.

> These youngsters are used to fast food, but the process of developing a science fair project helps them become self-directed. My students understand that if they are in DAPCEP, they are expected to behave and perform in a certain way. I don't accept excuses. I expect the very best from my students. Anything less is unacceptable.

> The conventional wisdom is that these students are overcome by a sense of helplessness, but I discourage that attitude and build into them the idea that they can take control. If they can afford expensive gym shoes and candy, they can be committed to their education. There is no question that they have my commitment: I will stay with them day and night to help them finish their projects (Simmons, 1994).

A New Teacher's Impressions

A new teacher's impression of DAPCEP can be found by listening to the experiences of Ingrid Heckman (I. Heckman, personal interview, June 13, 1995). "If I had to define DAPCEP in a phrase, I'd have to say, 'Well Organized!'" That's Heckman's opinion after completing her first full year in the math-science enrichment program. Prior to joining the faculty at Hally Middle School, Heckman worked and interned at the White

House, and then taught K–7 science for two years in Dominique as a Peace Corps volunteer. "I really enjoyed the wonderful Dominique program. There were helpful teachers and a principal who put up with my learning their culture and learning to teach simultaneously," said Heckman, who used the school garden as a laboratory for classes that integrated science, math, and social studies (I. Heckman, personal interview, June 13, 1995).

The West Indian classes were a great introduction because the method was completely hands-on and called a "Life Lab," says Heckman. She finds the experiences in the Peace Corps and the DAPCEP method quite similar, for both have "clear goals and a lot of hands-on activities where the students are completely involved and have an end product to show. In Dominique, it was the garden project, and with DAPCEP it's the minority contributor and science fair projects," she added. In both situations the teacher spends more time helping students with their projects while they're doing research and footwork, a method she well identifies with because that has been her own ideal learning model, says Heckman.

Born in Port Huron, Michigan, Heckman attended High School in Redding Pennsylvania, and moved to Virginia to study at James Madison ,where she majored in telecommunications and public relations. Following her Peace Corps service, Heckman attended the University of Michigan, where she received her master's degree in education.

INSERVICE TRAINING

The DAPCEP program administrators organize a monthly inservice training workshop that is taught by master classroom teachers based on their use of the DAPCEP curriculum guide. The teachers learn about classroom practices, field trip preparation and implementation, the Multicultural Contributors project (formerly called "Minority Contributors"), and the annual Metropolitan Detroit Science and Engineering Fair.

According to Ingrid Heckman, "DAPCEP is so much a part of Hally Middle School that it's hard not to be a part of the program, but I was confused as to why I needed to attend an inservice workshop when I had been teaching for two years and had already been entering students in the Science Fair. But when I attended all the questions were answered because I thought I was teaching right but found out that I have a lot to learn," says Heckman. "I began to understand the Minority Contributors and what the notebook meant. The workshops were helpful even during the school year, but the Summer Institute builds the camaraderie which teachers usually don't have," she says (I. Heckman, personal interview, June 13, 1995).

Listening to other teacher-mentors, and seeing other teachers who work very hard, have great ideas, and who have been in the system long enough to know which ideas will work, are important parts of the Institute, Heckman explains. In addition, she is impressed by the fact that the classes are taught by real classroom teachers rather than administrators or consultants who were in the classroom long ago. "I really learned what's expected of the teacher, and what my course outline should look like. That helped me to set up my outlines before I returned to school in the fall, and I really worked toward that goal throughout the school year," she added (I. Heckman, personal interview, June 13, 1995).

The only way to get kids computer literate is to have them actually work on computers, says Heckman, who was trained by DAPCEP to use the Internet during her first semester as a result of a grant from the Ameritech Company. She is now helping to teach her students on the computer. "At Halley, I can require all students to type because we have the computer for them if they don't have access at home. We have Saturday classes and after-school tutoring. You should see all the student files on the computer in my classroom," she says (I. Heckman, personal interview, June 13, 1995).

DAPCEP Resources Versus Spending Your Own Money

As Heckman puts it, "I can't tell you how good it feels as a teacher to walk into the school and have an expense account for supplies there for you; I felt like the biggest wheel!" Last year Heckman had spent a lot of her own money to buy student supplies, and although other teachers had helped her with funds the first year, "I felt like a peon whispering that it was under another teacher's account."

> DAPCEP pays for the science fair project supplies for the students enrolled in their classes, but once when I called a mother of a non-DAPCEP student to report that he hadn't turned in his science fair project, she told me that she wasn't speaking to her son at the time and that we were asking too much from the parents. He was a bright student and ended up out of sheer guts completing the project and bringing it in on a cardboard box. I knew he did the project but it's pretty difficult to grade based on the requirement that they have a special board, and I

would have purchased it for him if I had known. He presented his project on that box and I had so much respect for him because I saw in a real sense what economics can do to a child (I. Heckman, personal interview, June 13, 1995).

DAPCEP CORPORATE PARTNERS AND MENTORS

In October 1995, Heckman's DAPCEP classes were assigned a young engineer from General Motors, Peter Bejin, who visits the class alternate months with demonstrations of engineering activities and information about career preparation. The students enjoyed the air bag demonstration using an actual product. Another favorite was the viscosity lesson, in which the students had an assortment of liquids in test tubes. "They would drop their little lead ball and time it to see how long it would take to drop to the bottom in water compared with Karo syrup, for example. He tied it all into the subject of automobile lubricants and their importance to engineers," Heckman says.

Subsequently, according to Heckman, one of the students also did a science fair project comparing viscosity of oils. "The engineer-mentor was especially helpful because he's a real person who's out in the profession every day, and it's a refreshing break for the students rather than to have to listen to the same teacher every day. He was even brave enough to come during the last week of school. On their evaluation the students gave him the highest mark," Heckman added (I. Heckman, personal interview, June 13, 1995).

Other highlights observed by the new teacher included her first time on the DAPCEP-organized field trip to the Cranbrook Science Museum in metropolitan Detroit, which requires students to answer specific questions about the exhibits. That was her third Science Fair, which gave students the opportunity to take their projects to Cobo Hall one day and return to view all the exhibits the next day. And she recalled her second journey on the all-expense paid Toronto, Ontario, trip for the Science Fair Grand Award and Gold Award winners. On such trips, about 200 students and their teachers travel via Amtrak and spend the night at a hotel in Toronto. Says an enthusiastic Heckman, "DAPCEP is so well organized! Either you know what you're doing or you don't. It doesn't leave much room for ambiguity" (I. Heckman, personal interview, June 13, 1995).

THE METROPOLITAN DETROIT SCIENCE
AND ENGINEERING FAIR

A consistent measure of DAPCEP's success has been the student participants' increasingly high achievement record in the annual regional Metropolitan Detroit Science and Engineering Fair, in which both urban and suburban students compete. Although when Detroit students first competed in 1976, they received less than 6% of the awards at the fair, they now take more than half the Grand Awards in the first place category, and nearly two-thirds of the second-place Gold Ribbons. More importantly, 70% of the DAPCEP secondary school graduates are pursuing engineering, math, or science majors in college, and 74% of DAPCEP college graduates have majored in science, math, or engineering (DAPCEP Tracking Report, 1996).

PARENTAL INVOLVEMENT IN DAPCEP

The Parent Advisory Committee (PAC) is an integral component of the DAPCEP program, and the chairperson of the PAC sits on the Board of Directors of DAPCEP. PAC members assist in writing proposals and fund-raising they help to organize the program's twice-a-year recruitment efforts; they organize forums to help parents better assist their students, and they hold other forums to educate parents and students about scholarship opportunities, college selection, and preparation of applications. The parents also raise money for scholarships for DAPCEP students. One former PAC chairperson, Denise Reid, a dressmaker, found that the exposure to higher education she received while assisting her children with DAPCEP not only helped her children, but also encouraged her to return to school for a college degree (D. Reid, personal interview, Feb. 12, 1998).

PAC member Denise Reid, who served her second year as chairperson of the DAPCEP support group in 1998, grew up in Detroit's historic Black Bottom. She lived with her father, who had abandoned cotton farming in Mississippi for greener pastures in the Motor City, and her mother, a nurse raised in Detroit. Her father had a third-grade education and could neither read nor write when he moved to Michigan, but the children and mother taught their dad how to read and write, beginning with the Bible, and he became quite good at it. That really instilled the importance of education in the youngest daughter of eight children. Reid's father was employed at the Local 338 Building Trade Union and worked his way up to a contract negotiator. In her words, "Since nursing was an easier occupation for Black women to get into, my mother became a registered nurse. They both had good jobs and we didn't suffer" (D. Reid, personal interview, Feb. 12, 1998). Reid's husband, Moses, is an independent plumbing and carpenter contractor and the couple has three children: Chloe, 16; Christian, 14; and Joshua, 12. She is a dressmaker and works at her home office.

All three of Reid's children have been involved in the DAPCEP program.

> My neighbor who had two children in DAPCEP suggested that I should enroll my children in the program. Since my children all did well in school and had lots of activities, I didn't get involved at first. But she bugged me for a couple of years until I attended an open house and enrolled my daughter, Chloe, when she was in 6th grade (D. Reid, personal interview, Feb. 12, 1998).

Reid liked the idea of Saturday and summer classes. They would keep Chloe away from the TV, which Reid dislikes intensely. Although Chloe didn't like the first three Saturdays, it soon became fun and she got hooked on the hands-on experiments. The DAPCEP activities branched over into her other studies, and she learned how to organize her time. After that, it was no problem getting her up in the morning. She started talking about the program to her siblings and showed them some of her experiments. She also liked the snacks. It was Chloe who got her two younger siblings into the program, says Reid.

Reid says she signed up to start attending the parent meetings because she wanted to know when the next open house would be, so all of her children would all get into the program. " I kept involved and started taking notes at the meetings. DAPCEP really helps the kids broaden their horizons and teaches them to work at things" (D. Reid, personal interview, Feb. 12, 1998).

Reid enrolled her daughter Chrissy in sixth grade and she wanted to go. Chrissy participated in the summer program every day from 8:00 A.M. to 3:30 P.M., and she liked it. She got some nice T-shirts, and her mother made matching shorts.

> There was a lot of homework and she said it was like school, but it hit her in a different way. As a talkative child, it gave her the opportunity to talk to people beyond her instructors at school. She likes to find out

about things and relate that information to other things (D. Reid, personal interview, Feb. 12, 1998).

Reid's son, Josh, "was already so involved in experiments that I thought he'd love it," says Reid.

> He wanted to build an airplane and rocket like his sisters. I signed him up in fifth grade because it started by then at that level. His classes were mostly paperwork and they didn't do as many projects, so it wasn't as exciting as he thought. He was bored and didn't want to go back, and I didn't see any impact on him. But in the sixth grade, when they did rockets, motors, and engines, that got him. By the seventh grade, he was very good in math. He's also a little more neat and organized at home too, and I credit that to DAPCEP (D. Reid, personal interview, Feb. 12, 1998).

Regarding the children's career plans, Reid says that DAPCEP has had some impact on their motivation, although only one of the three youngsters is considering engineering.

> Chloe, who is out of DAPCEP now and into another enrichment program, wants to be an interior decorator. She's planning to go to Lawrence Tech. I attribute much of what she's done to DAPCEP. Chrissy wants to be a lawyer or work in the political arena. She's still in DAPCEP, but I think she'll phase herself out in the next year. None really want to get into engineering, but I'm pushing Josh toward civil engineering. He likes art and is an artistic person, but I think he needs this to fall back on. I'm going to keep him in the program (D. Reid, personal interview, Feb. 12, 1998).

What Reid Got Out of DAPCEP

> What I got out of DAPCEP was two and a half years ago the PAC was taking work site tours to engineering sites. We took four busloads of kids to a sunroof manufacturer, window manufacturer, and Focus Hope and watched what the engineers do. They showed us the Fast Track program, and I signed up. I passed and moved on to the next phase to train in engineering. I found out that I didn't want to go into engineering, but I wanted to get an education. I enrolled in the Detroit College of Business to get a two-year degree in business administration. I'm still working on that degree right now. Without DAPCEP, it wouldn't have crossed my mind that I could be somebody, and it made the world seem bigger. I'd like to open a light manufacturing business like special

wear—bridal gowns. The degree will help me learn, and I've gained
daily confidence in math and time management. It gives me a focus (D.
Reid, personal interview, Feb. 12, 1998).

What Reid Expects of her Children

My kids were always in school and not out playing in the streets. I
liked the programs because it gave them the opportunity to have it better than I had. That's what all parents want. The children are all
entrepreneurs in some way. They all have their own chores and responsibilities with my business and my husband's business at home. One
gets on the computer and works with her dad's business, another will
answer the phones, and Chloe is a dressmaker, too (D. Reid, personal
interview, Feb. 12, 1998).

Reid's Role in the PAC

I wanted to show my support for DAPCEP, so I became a member and
somehow am now the president [of the PAC]. I conduct regular meetings and outreach programs. Our purpose is to raise money for
DAPCEP, so we run one major event at Cobo Hall for the Scholarship
Dinner, which includes an auction, and we give out scholarships. Any
money we get above costs goes to the students. The scholarships are for
$1000 to $1500 and are based on financial need. We have one scholarship named after a student who was in a severe auto accident and
persevered. That is given to a student who overcomes some obstacles to
reach success. I support an agenda where minorities help each other to
go on and reach their potential. We meet once a month except in the
summer. I really enjoy my involvement as well as delegating to the
other members (D. Reid, personal interview, Feb. 12, 1998).

The Metropolitan Detroit Science and Engineering Fair

Two of my children have participated in the fair and I've chaperoned it.
One project was based on growing beans and the other tested the fire
safety of various fabrics. My kids aren't really so interested in science,
so it wasn't that important to them. The youngest one is the only one
who may still be interested in participating, but I'm not going to push
him (D. Reid, personal interview, Feb. 12, 1998).

Significance of DAPCEP

It's a good program to take advantage of and it offers opportunity. DAPCEP may educate 100 children and some percentage of those will go into science and math, but all 100 are far better for doing it than without it. It's not just geared toward engineering. It allows students to find out what they can be the best in (D. Reid, personal interview, Feb. 12, 1998).

SUMMARY

With a national shortage of math, science, and engineering professionals, measured in the hundreds of thousands, predicted for the new millennium, many corporations are scrambling to find ways to fill the projected gap. To the extent that American youth will be the ones to fill the gap, the nation must find ways to interest, educate, and retain an increasingly diverse group of students, some of whom have been considered either culturally or genetically inferior in advanced math and science. The DAPCEP program has demonstrated that it is possible to combine equity and excellence in the process of motivating and educating women and minorities at the pre-college level, who will then go on to achieve in the universities and in the professions.

The elements of the successful program include the following: Program founders who refused to accept the view that minority and female youth could not learn and be high achievers in math, science, and engineering careers. On the contrary, they strongly believed that all students can learn given the appropriate conditions. Those conditions include administrators who believe in the DAPCEP mission of preparing minority students for engineering careers. They established their own curriculum to address the fact that there are numerous fields in engineering that students need to be aware of, that hands-on instruction methods can work along with textbook instruction. In addition, the administrators provide a broad array of practical support to the classroom teacher, such as funding for science fair projects, planning and transportation for field trips, and inservice training that utilizes classroom teachers for workshop instructors. This combination of support and interaction results in a strong feeling of camaraderie among the teachers. Another element of the program is the classroom teacher, who provides traditional and hands-on instruction to implement the DAPCEP curriculum. The teacher works closely with parents on the Metropolitan Detroit Science and Engineering Fair and the Multicultural Contributor projects, and works closely with engineer mentors who visit the classes armed with their actual work assignments on which DAPCEP students can participate. Teachers receive funding for their extra work but are selected because they have already demonstrated special concern for students.

The major projects of the DAPCEP program in which all students are required to participate annually are the Metropolitan Detroit Science and Engineering Program and the Multicultural Contributors. Both programs require extensive research preparation in and out of the classroom, and both programs give highly visible rewards for student achievement. While the science fair develops math and science skills, the Multicultural Contributors component heightens the students' awareness of a history of high achievement by minority and female scientists and engineers, resulting in a higher level of confidence among the student participants.

The Student Tracking Report Summary of Findings based on a survey of 2,500 alumni, reveals the following: Based on grade point average (GPA), California Achievement Test (CAT), and High School Proficiency Test results, DAPCEP students are better prepared to attend college and are more likely to stay in school than non-DAPCEP students (according to a Detroit Public Schools special report of 1993 and 1994 high school graduates). According to the same study:

> More than 75% of DAPCEP students enroll in four or five year colleges and universities, compared with 51% of non-DAPCEP graduates of the Detroit Public Schools system.
> Eighty-three percent of the DAPCEP students are either college graduates or are currently enrolled in college.
> Nearly 50% of DAPCEP students currently enrolled in college are majoring in engineering, science, or mathematics-related fields.
> Seventy-two percent of DAPCEP college graduates have earned degrees in engineering, science or mathematics-related fields.
> Sixty percent of college graduates attended one of DAPCEP's partner universities.

DAPCEP Executive Director Kenneth Hill says with confidence that some of the people who will fill the ranks of the nation's scientists and engineers in the near future are now in the various DAPCEP programs. "Through our mentors, supportive teachers, weekend classes, and summer programs, we are working to ensure that our students have the best possible chance to succeed in university environments and go on to take their places in the professional world as engineers, physicians, and scientific researchers" (K. Hill, personal interview, Feb. 10, 1994).

REFERENCES

Bennet, J. (1998, June 6). Clinton calls for techno-literacy in schools, New York Times, p. 1.

Callas, K. (Ed.), (1998, Summer). Science fair investment pays off. *Moving Up, DAPCEP Newsletter Science Fair Edition*, 1.

Clark, J. H. (1995). The African in the new world: Their contribution to science and technology. In H. Boyd & R. Allen (Eds.), *Brotherman: The odyssey of Black men in America—An anthology*, (pp. 691–697). New York: Ballantine.

Clark, K. (1967). *Dark ghetto: Dilemmas of social power*. New York: Harper Torchbooks.

Clewell, C., Anderson, B., & Thorpe, M. (1992). *Breaking the barriers: Helping female and minority students succeed in mathematics and science*. San Francisco: Jossey-Bass.

Crow, L. (1966). *Educating the culturally disadvantaged child: Principles and programs*. New York: David McKay.

The Detroit Area Pre-College Engineering Program. (1996). *The tracking report*. Detroit, MI: Institutional.

Donley, R. (1994, June 20). Service leads to honors for young GM engineers. *Tech Center News*, pps. 1, 24.

DuBois, W. E. B. (1983). Black reconstruction in America. In A. Meier (Ed.), *Studies in American Negro life, report of 1935 edition*. New York: Atheneum.

Gargaro, P. (1995, December 20). Best-managed non profit: DAPCEP takes a big step. *Crain's' Detroit Business*, p. 1.

Gould, S. (1981). *The mismeasurement of man*. New York: Norton.

Hill, K. (1990). The Detroit Area Pre-College Engineering Program, Inc. *Journal of Negro Education, 59*(3), 439–448.

Hilliard, A. (1990). Limitations of current academic achievement measures. In K. Lomotey (Ed.), *Going to school* (pp. 135–142). Albany: State University of New York Press.

Jones-Wilson, F. (1990). The state of African American education. In K. Lomotey (Ed.), *Going to school* (pp. 31–51). Albany: State University of New York Press.

Ladson-Billings, G. (1995). Making mathematics meaningful in multicultural contexts. In W. Secada, E. Fennema, & L. B. Adajian (Eds.), *New directions for equity in mathematics education* (pp. 126–145).

Malcolm, S. (1990). Reclaiming our past. *Journal of Negro Education, 59*(3), 246–259.

National Science Foundation (1994). Second national conference on diversity in the scientific and technological workforce, October 28–30. Washington, DC: Conference Proceedings.

Oden, S. (1992). *Challenging the potential: Programs for talented disadvantaged youth.* Ypsilanti, MI: High Scope.

Simmons, C. (1994, Nov.–Dec.). It starts with paper cars. *FOCUS Magazine of the Joint Center for Political and Economic Studies, 22,* 11–12.

Sizemore, B. (1985). The Madison elementary school: A turnaround case. *Journal of Negro Education, 57*(3), 243–266.

Steinberg, L. (1996). *Beyond the classroom* New York: Simon & Schuster.

Takaki, R. (1993). *A different mirror: A history of multicultural America.* New York: Little, Brown.

Toporek, T. (1996, August 5). UDM hosts car program for students. *Tech Center News, 20*(49), p.11.

Woodson, C. G. (1933). *The miseducation of the Negro.* Washington, DC: Associated.

CHAPTER 8

Good Versus Bad Culturally Relevant Science: Avoiding the Pitfalls

Cathleen C. Loving
and Bernard R. Ortiz de Montellano

INTRODUCTION

In 1991 the Detroit Board of Education adopted its "Suggested Criteria for Reviewing Educational Textbooks and Materials" (Detroit Public Schools, 1991). Included in these criteria are explicit references to multicultural/multiethnic content in textbooks and other learning materials. Items are required to be screened for truth, balance, order, harmony, and the degree to which they are bias-free and multicultural. What do these components entail? What led to this explicit reference to multicultural content? What is the state of existing materials hoping to be considered for such adoptions?

The authors explore these questions from two perspectives—that of a practicing anthropologist who specializes in Mesoamerican studies (Ortiz de Montellano, 1990) and that of a science educator particularly interested in the relationship between student and teacher views of the nature of science and scientific literacy (Loving, 1997). Both researchers have written about the status, evolution, and quality of multicultural or culturally relevant science materials available for U.S. classrooms (Haslip-Viera, Ortiz de Montellano, & Barbour, 1997; Loving, 1998; Ortiz de Montellano, 1996; Ortiz de Montellano, Haslip-Viera, & Barbour, 1997). Both are concerned that many materials currently in wide distribution across the country do, in fact, represent bad science. We use the Detroit Board's criteria combined with our assessment of a number of examples to provide the reader with our set of criteria for selecting good culturally relevant science materials.

What philosophical perspective do we assume in this study of culturally relevant science materials? First, we acknowledge that science is not culturally neutral and that culture is an important component in much science. Naturally, culture will play a larger and more direct role in anthropology, as humans study humans, than, say, in theoretical physics. Research suggests, however, that worldview—"the culturally dependent, implicit, fundamental organization of the mind... composed of presuppositions or assumptions which predispose one to feel, think, and act in predictable patterns" (Cobern, 1991, p. 19)—varies among different ethnic groups. The extent to which science teachers use culturally relevant materials and pedagogical techniques can often determine the extent of successful learning in many sciences.

We wish to avoid labeling ourselves as objectivists or subjectivists, realists or nonrealists, or any of an array of constructivists. We take a centrist position, agreeing with fundamental notions of good science by well-known science educators such as Matthews (1994) and Driver, Leach, Millar, and Scott (1996). This stance allows us to highlight the central tenets of good science—the quality of the evidence and the explanation, and the relationship between the two.

Our challenge in science education is to do what Cortés (1994) calls the "Great American Balancing Act" (p. 6). He is referring to the notion of providing an education that will enrich and acculturate all students, yet not require assimilation. His brand of culturally relevant science would acknowledge and make best use of student backgrounds, while at the same time moving them toward important mainstream understanding. He uses the expression "E Pluribus Unum"—out of many, one—to remind us what our goal should be in all classrooms. Students should feel part of a culture that goes beyond what they individually bring to class. Culturally relevant teaching results in "adducation," not "subtractucation," according to Cortés.

STATUS OF CURRENT CULTURALLY RELEVANT MATERIALS

There is a glaring underrepresentation of minorities in science professions (National Science Foundation, 1996) and significantly lower achievement in secondary school science and mathematics among ethnic minorities (National Center for Educational Statistics, 1995). While attempts to increase minority role models in science and science teaching are a start, this is not enough. There is a great demand for approaches that tie culture with science, and the refusal of scientists and science educators to develop accurate and valid materials of this type has fostered the development of alternative science materials of dubious quality and their adoption by school districts with large minority enrollments. In 1987, the Portland Oregon School District published the *African American Baseline Essays*, a set of six essays providing resource materials and references for teachers on the knowledge and contributions of Africans and African Americans.

Our discussion will focus on the Science Baseline Essay written by Hunter Havelin Adams (1990) and a few other works. There are serious problems with this baseline essay, but because of the current pressure on school districts to incorporate multicultural material into the classroom and because of the dearth of this kind of material, it has been widely distributed. Hundreds of copies of the Baseline Essays have been sent to school districts across the country. They have been adopted or are being seriously considered by school districts as diverse as Fort Lauderdale, Detroit, Milwaukee, Atlanta, Chicago, Prince George County (MD) and Washington, DC. Even more widely distributed is its predecessor, *Blacks in Science: Ancient and Modern*, edited by Ivan Van Sertima (1984). Vine DeLoria, who is involved with Indian science education through the American Indian Science and Engineering Society (AISES) has recently published a book entitled *Red Earth, White Lies: Native Americans and the Myth of Scientific Facts* (DeLoria, 1995).

These supplements on multicultural science (Adams, 1990; DeLoria, 1995; Van Sertima, 1984), expressly intended to "raise the self-esteem" of students, adopt a triumphalist approach to the scientific knowledge covered. That is, they present the achievements and the beliefs of the group described as superior and anticipatory to the achievements and beliefs of modern "Western" science. Thus, the Dogon of Mali studied Sirius B, which is invisible to the naked eye, hundreds of years ago. The Egyptians foreshadowed the theory of evolution thousands of years ago; the Egyptians also anticipated many of the philosophical aspects of quantum theory (Adams, 1990, p. 20), and they knew the particle/wave nature of light (p. 26).

Similarly, the need to defend Native myths and religion as scientific and factual inevitably leads to antiscience and pseudoscience. Native

American religions involve the creation of man in the New World. DeLoria (1995) defends this view by denying that modern humans evolved in Africa and that subsequently Paleoindians migrated across the Bering Strait to people the New World. Instead, DeLoria presents a scenario in which in the distant past four groups—the Salish, the Sioux, the Algonquians, and "mean-spirited, white-skinned, bearded people" (p. 77)—lived in North America. The first three groups remained in North America and the fourth migrated eastward to enter Europe as the Cro-Magnons (pp. 77–78). This contradicts all the paleontological evidence that humans evolved in Africa and that no skeleton of a hominid prior to "truly modern humans" has ever been found in the New World.

The defense of Indian myths as factual leads DeLoria (1995) to deny the validity of basic tenets of geology, physics, and biology—essentially aping the stance of defendants of another religious myth—Scientific Creationists, who claim the earth to be 6,000 years old. Myths of the Warm Springs Reservation, Oregon, describe an eyewitness view of the creation of Mt. Multnomah, but potassium/argon dating shows that this range was formed between 25 and 27 million years ago. DeLoria, denying the validity of radioactive dating as he earlier denied the validity of the standard geological sequence, argues that this mountain is very recent and that the Indian forefathers actually saw the formation of the mountain (pp. 200–204). A further example of the "young earth" approach is DeLoria's claim that petroglyphs prove that Indians in Missouri actually saw a stegosaurus, perhaps as late as the 19th century, and that Indians in Arizona saw a diplodocus (pp. 240–244).

Other examples of triumphalist or pseudoscientific approaches to multicultural science that are not based on any reliable scientific evidence come from Jose C. Argüelles (1987) and Richard King (1990). Argüelles (1987) claims that Maya calendrical myths are factual and that there will be a great crisis in A.D. 2012 because the Maya predict it. King (1990) writes that melanin has extraordinary properties, and that these properties confer great powers on people with a large amount of it. Some of the properties attributed to melanin are that it is a superconductor, that it absorbs all frequencies of electromagnetic radiation, that it can detect and be influenced by weak magnetic fields, and that granules of melanin can function as microcomputers and process information. Melanin is supposed to regulate all physiological and psychological processes in humans. Melanin is responsible for the superior intelligence, the potential extrasensory ability, and the greater degree of spirituality of Black people, according to King.

AVOIDING THE PITFALLS OF BAD CULTURALLY RELEVANT SCIENCE

The brief examples from Adams, Van Sertima, DeLoria, King, and Argüelles set the stage for our suggested criteria to be used by teachers as they choose culturally relevant science materials. The six criteria below, with additional examples, should aid teachers in avoiding the pitfalls of blatantly bad science and, we hope, encourage selection of materials that represent bona fide science from various cultures. The criteria ask teachers to check for: (a) author's credentials, (b) sufficient documentation, (c) political agenda, (d) "newspeak," (e) sufficient depth and evidence, and (f) pseudoscience, myth, religion, or postmodern New Age beliefs.

Author's Credentials

The credentials an author possesses to write about science should not be the only factor in credibility because ultimately that should depend on the reasoning and the evidence presented. However, credentials are an important factor to consider. Credentials should be written in such a way that it is clear that the person has some sustained or formal education in an area related to the topic being discussed, or has significant experience in that area as reflected by peer-reviewed publications and/or reputation among qualified peers. Typical credentials would be a Ph.D. in a field related to the science in question—indicating some formal background in the discipline—or some track record of doing sustained work in a new field as an extension of one's original specialty.

Teachers and science educators selecting curricula should be alert for descriptions that imply but do not clearly state an author's qualifications. For example, the description "a professor at Wayne State University" does not mean that the person is qualified to write about chemistry. He/she may be a professor in literature, political science, or drama. Some physicians (M.D.) and lawyers feel that they are qualified to write on any topic. Most are clinical practitioners without advanced research degrees, and they are not trained as researchers.

We do not wish to discourage the growing trend of viewing disciplines like science in a more integrative fashion. We also encourage continued learning beyond one's formal education that tends to broaden our scope of understanding. This extension into other areas, however, often has its limitations—and the writer or speaker needs to acknowledge the areas in which he/she is "dabbling."

Examples of writers who blur the line between expert and novice:

1. Hunter Havelin Adams is described in the introduction to the Portland Baseline Essay (1990) as a "research scientist at Argonne National Laboratory." Actually, Mr. Adams is an industrial-hygiene technician who "does no research on any topic at Argonne," and whose highest degree is a high school diploma (Baurac, 1991; Marriot, 1991).

2. Vine DeLoria (1995) is a political scientist with a law degree who writes of Native Americans evolving in the New World based on the concept that their origin myths are veridical.

3. Richard King (1990) is a psychiatrist with a M.D. but does no laboratory research on melanin. In his book he fails to make the crucial point that there is no relationship between melanin in the skin and melanin in the nervous system.

4. José C. Argüelles has a degree in art and writes about how human history has been shaped during the time of the great Maya Calendar Cycle, 3113 B.C. to A.D. 2012, by a galactic beam through which the earth and sun have been passing. He claims his insight into the Maya came in a vision (1987, p. 21).

Documentation

A very important thing to do before using any material is to check the documentation provided to determine how trustworthy and reliable is the material.

1. There is an order of credibility of sources of scientific information. In order of decreasing credibility they are: peer-reviewed scientific journals; texts from publishers such as Academic Press or Wiley Interscience; journals such as *Scientific American, Bio-Science,* or *Natural History.* Books from university presses and commercial publishers can be good or bad, as some presses are quite selective, with excellent editorial staffs, and others are not. One should be suspicious of an over-reliance on newspapers, popular magazines, and vanity press books. Currently, there is much information obtainable from the Internet that goes through no peer review whatsoever. (However, there are a growing number of relatively young, but peer-reviewed, electronic journals). Peer review gives some assurance that knowledgeable people have checked the work to see

if sources are adequate and are cited correctly, whether claims are supported by evidence, and whether scientific claims are credible.

2. Information should come from primary sources. Authors should ordinarily provide you with citations to the original source of the information. Consistent reliance on paraphrases from second- or third-hand sources, or summaries in newspapers or magazines, should make you suspicious about the accuracy and worth of the information.

3. One should be suspicious of a great reliance on old and obsolete sources. Acceptable scientific explanations and any given body of knowledge change over time. Science books and journal articles can become obsolete, or at least their explanations can become incomplete, in a few years. Sometimes this aspect is hard to verify with books because reprint editions may be cited without giving the original dates of publication.

Example: King (1990, pp. 53–55) uses Churchward (1913, 1921) to claim that the Twa pygmies of Africa are *Homo erectus* and the ancestors of the rest of humanity. Pygmies are modern humans, *Homo sapiens sapiens*. King ignores 80 years of research to cite a work that was erroneous even in 1913.

4. Check for complete citations (i.e., author, title, place of publication, publisher, year and page number). If these data are consistently missing, there is cause not to trust the material. Authors who are citing works carefully and accurately want their readers to be able to check their citations; those who may be misrepresenting their sources do not want readers to check their citations.

Example: Adams (1990) fails this test. He does not distinguish between what would be considered serious academic sources (i.e., refereed journals, academic press books), intermediate sources (popular science journals), very old sources that might be obsolete, and unreliable or very questionable sources (newspapers, magazines, vanity press books, and "New Age" publications). Adams's citation style is not helpful either to teachers who want to get more information or to readers who want to verify quotations. For example, often quotations in the text are cited by author and title but the book is not included in the bibliography, and even when books are included, page numbers are not given in the footnote.

5. Watch out for lots of typographical or spelling errors. Authors who are careless on the little details tend to be careless with the larger facts.

Example: King (1990) argues that Black people are superior to Whites because they have a lot of melanin. Much of the book, however, has passages such as the following: "Elevated levels of pineal MSH are strongly implicated in extrasensory perception and emotionality. The amino acid tyrosine, which is produced in the process of producing melanin, is also the precursor of coedine [sic], murphine [sic], mescaline, LSD, thyroxin, and norepinephrine (Riley 1972). These are chemicals that range from the psychedelic drugs mescaline, L.S.D. [sic], D.M.T. [sic], through the euphoric addictive drugs morphine and coedine [sic]" (King, 1990, p. 120). Or, for example, "Calcium in the form of hydroxy appetite [sic apatite] or bone formation is found in the structure of the pineal gland" (pp. 58–59).

Example: Amen (1993) argues that Egyptians had advanced knowledge of electronics, but there is not a single citation or footnote in the book. The bibliography at the end is quite incomplete. The book is full of spelling and grammatical errors.

A Political Agenda Can Distort Even Simple Facts

One aim of Afrocentrism is to show that Egyptians and their culture actually had their roots in Sub-Saharan Africa (Asante, 1993–94; Bernal, 1987, 1991; Diop, 1991). In support of this claim, Adams (1990, p. 14) quotes the following:

> "They come, the waters of life which are in the sky,
> They come, the waters of life which are in the earth...
> The sky is aflame for you, the earth trembles for you,
> before the divine birth of Osiris-Nile." (Third Dynasty Pyramid Texts
>   of Unas [2063]).

On this basis, Adams claims that:

> "This profound statement symbolically speaks to the ancient Egyptian people's recognition that the river Nile was the umbilical cord that annually deposited the nutrient-laden, life-regenerating alluvial earth from the womb of the world, the Great Lakes/Mountains of the Moon region near the equator, all throughout the valley. Moreover, it indicates that the ancient Egyptians' belief of a celestial source of the Nile River. Supporting their extra-terrestrial origin of the Nile theory, evidence has been recently found showing that the earth today and for hundreds of millions of years, has been inundated by water-laden, micro-comets, which not only over time were the source of the ocean's water, but of river's water like the Nile." [Adams does not cite any source for this evidence] (p.)

The problem with this explanation is that the silt that is brought to Egypt comes from monsoon rains in Ethiopia carried by the Blue Nile—called that precisely because of its load of silt (Baines & Marek, 1980; Shaw & Nicholson, 1995). The Great Lakes/Mountains of the Moon area is the source of the headwaters of the White Nile. The White Nile doesn't figure at all in the silt deposition. Any Egyptologist would know this, and these sources can be verified in any map.

Melanists like Adams (1987, 1988) and King (1990) make a number of claims about the superiority of Blacks based on the properties of neuromelanin (melanin in the human brain), β-MSH (beta-melanin stimulating hormone), and melatonin and their higher concentration in Black people compared to Whites. However, there is no β-MSH in adult humans (Robins, 1991, pp. 33–34), and melatonin has little if any role in human physiology. There is no relationship between skin melanin and neuromelanin (Robins, 1991, p. 81). Melatonin got its name because it causes blanching of frog skin. It has no relationship or similarity to melanin. Melatonin has no impact on puberty or skin color (Ebling & Foster, 1989; Hastings, Vance, & Maywood, 1989; Robins, 1991, pp. 34–37; Sizonenko, Lang, & Aubert, 1982).

"Newspeak"

Watch out for the use of scientific-sounding terminology or the inappropriate use of scientific terms. This is a tip-off either to sloppy thinking or to a fast one being pulled on you. Clear writing means clear thinking. If you cannot understand what a paragraph says, be suspicious of the author's intent. You should be able to tell someone else what a paragraph means. Try to render the following examples into simple declarative sentences and explain what the author really means.

1. Adams (1990) argues that mainstream scholars have failed to get the REAL meaning of Egyptian hieroglyphs.

> [T]housands of hieroglyphic inscriptions, and yet over a hundred years and hundreds of scholars devoting their lives to translation, the essence of their meaning eludes us. This is primarily because the ancient Egyptians' polyocular epistemology renders their written style of communication, multicontextural. That is to say, there is a high degree of simultaneity and spontaneity, and also rhythm and symbolic logic in their thought; for example, superimposed upon a single image are many points of view and moments of time. For an "expert" unfamiliar with

Egyptian lifeways, translation could give the antithesis of the author's original intent. (p. 30)

2. "The reason for the intense subjective effects experienced by the human psyche lies in the overall impact of radioactivity and electromagnetic pollution on the infrastructure of the DNA, causing increased randomness and entropy of behavior. But this response of DNA experienced as socially disruptive behavior in the human realm, inclusive of rises in the incidence of cancer and new diseases like AIDS, is actually only a complement of what is occurring in the larger host organism, Earth" (Argüelles, 1987, p. 146).

3. "As resonant structures, symbols literally create, work with, and inform the light body. The light body is the electro-resonant galactic code bank that informs the genetic code bank. It is the stuff of imagination, insight, all true understanding—and more! While the foundation of our light body corresponds to the vibratory infrastructure of the DNA, it can only be activated through a knowing use of symbols. Nor should this symbol-thriving light body be seen as separate from what we call our physical body. Rather, the resonant light body underlies and interpenetrates all of our functions" (Argüelles, 1987, p. 89).

4. "The resonant body of the Earth, the vibratory infrastructure that literally holds together the sense-perceptible body of the Earth, is in a condition of intense 'fever' called resonant dissonance. Remembering the planets as gyroscopes holding the frequency pattern of their particular orbits, we see that environmentally impactful effects since 1945 have actually set in motion a dissonant vibratory wave affecting the overall spin of the planet. If the dissonance is not checked, then, similar to an uncontrolled nuclear reaction, the end-result would be the development of a wobble in the spin and a consequent shattering of the planetary form. The Earth could be broken up into smaller bodies not unlike the Asteroid belt" (Argüelles, 1987, p.146).

5. "As ideographic symbols, there are many different ways in which these Signs can be read. Dense with meanings, the Signs demand an analogical understanding. Analogical thinking randomly floats and leaps to a conclusion by a like association linking dissimilar things. Analogical thinking is also that which creates form on the basis of like proportions. As we have already seen, the Mayan number symbolism is completely based on fractal harmonics which are based on like proportions" (Argüelles, 1987, p. 97).

6. "Using the Harmonic Module as the template of the circuitry of the light body, and understanding the light body to be the true skeleton of the physical body, we can assert that the diseases and plagues which ails us—cancer and AIDS—are not cellular in cause but instead are the direct result of immersion in and addiction to various feedback effects of our deleterious technological environment. The cure to these Late Industrial Age diseases, therefore, is not to be found in chemicals or radioactive treatment, but in a radical shift in disposition accompanied by the development of genuine bioelectromagnetic medicine that accounts for the natural, organic restoration of intrinsic resonance as key factors in healing" (Argüelles, 1987, p. 182).

7. "Melanin granules act like tiny primitive eyes, forming a large neural network structure, whose function is to absorb and decode electromagnetic waves. Neural-network computers are learning machines which are made with a number of receptors that can adjust their weights (quantitative properties) to produce a specific output. The body of Africans contain massive amounts of melanocytes that encode all life experiences in their melanin production, with the aim of creating an actual-reality state after death" (Amen, 1993, p. 29).

8. "At low frequencies the conductivity of melanin is small, but at ultra high frequencies (UHF), melanin is a superconductor. Maximum current flows only in the skin, due to the skin-effect, at melanin's UHF resonant frequency. Melanin is the most important substance in the human body. It is an oxidized form of RNA, which enables the body to coordinate the production of proteins needed in cellular repair. Wherever there is cell damage melanin is seen surrounding the site, functioning as a neuro-transmitter in coordination with melanocyte protein production for the repair of damaged DNA. Knowledge of the medical value of melanin is suppressed by the Medical Establishment, in order to deny its supremacy" (Amen, 1993, p. 29).

9. "This myth handed down from Ancient Times, relate the events occurring in the eye of a radio galaxy. Where stars and planets are swallowed by the central black hole and resurrected as fourth-dimensional matter (plasma) [sic]. A plasma is characterized by its high electron content. About 95% of the matter of the universe is in this state. A low pressure gas plasma need not be strongly ionized to or [sic] produce electromagnetic effects. Black skin, which is composed of a layer of organic semiconductors can be considered a plasma or fourth-dimensional matter. And since neuro-melanin and melanocytes are the basis of higher

mental activity, it stands to reason that our moral nature is an expression of more direct contact with God through the spirit" (Amen, 1993, p. 61).

Sufficient Depth

Topics should be presented in enough detail that teachers can go beyond the topic facts and deal with the evidence, which should be included to support any claims made.

1. Culturally relevant science materials must avoid a long laundry list of the achievements of a particular culture without sufficient detail to understanding the concepts being listed (the "mentioning problem"), or lists of achievements that do not pertain to the grade levels being taught.

Example: Adams, (1990) work, which is aimed at the elementary school level, claims that Egyptians were the first to discover Darwin's theory of evolution, quantum mechanics, the wave/particle of nature of light, electroplating of gold, glider flight, etc. with no explanation of what these theories entail.

2. Conclusions should be stated with sufficient evidence. This is particularly important when extraordinary or very unorthodox claims are made; "extraordinary claims require extraordinary proof."

Example: To state that Brazil is hot does not require much evidence besides pointing to the fact that it is near the equator. On the other hand, to say that the Maya people were transmitted through space in the form of DNA code (claimed by Argüelles, 1987, p. 59) requires an enormous amount of proof (none was given).

Example Claim: "[The ancient Egyptians]...anticipate many of the philosophical aspects of the quantum theory in contemporary physics" (Adams, 1990, p. 20).

Evidence Presented:

> Chicago computer scientist, Levia Hoppzallern, offers more valuable insights. To the Egyptians, he points out, time as a unit of energy expressed in the form of an entity or process that can be measured by its duration. Prior to an entity's or processes' manifestation, its 'time' does not exist. As such, they recognized that an entity or process exists in two states: Potential—a functional or trans-material existence before its 'first time', and actual—its period of manifestation or duration from its 'first time' until completion of its life cycle, its eternity. Thus each thing represents a unique dimension of time. Time was therefore multidimensional. In the 'Book of Caverns' (Quererets), a phrase illustrates this:

'Unin-nefer of the living who passes through millions of time dimensions," (Adams, 1990, p. 20).

Pseudoscience, Myth, Religion, Postmodern/New Age Beliefs

Some explanations presented as science are in fact pseudoscience, myth, religion, supernatural beliefs, magic or postmodern/New Age beliefs masquerading as science. Be suspect if you see highly unusual methods, aims, theories, vocabularies, or conclusions.

Examples:

1. "Psychoenergetics (also known in the scientific community as parapsychology and psychotronics) is the multidisciplinary study of the interface and interaction of human consciousness with energy and matter. Magic is the conscious attempt of an individual to 'imitate' through ordinary sensorimotor means the operation of psychoenergetic (psi) phenomena. Thus, genuine psi phenomena such as precognition, psychokinesis, and remote viewing in the distant past as well as the present has always been closely associated with "magic", and the attempt to separate the two has only been a fairly recent activity. Psi, as a true scientific discipline, is being seriously investigated at prestigious universities all over the world" (Adams, 1987, p. 41).

2. Quoting Lucy Lamy—"Maat is Cosmic Consciousness, the ultimate goal of creation and of every creature, the immortal fruit of a constant acquisition. Maat is the greatest treasure that a being might wish for." Adams (1987, pp. 11–14) concludes that "This concept called Maat represents the first set of scientific paradigms: A set of general principles which serve as the basis from which the ancient Egyptians did all types of scientific investigations."

3. "If the Indian legend demonstrates the presence of people in North America, or even the Western Hemisphere, tens of thousands of years ago—or in the case of Mount Multnomah 25 million years ago—then that discrepancy should alert scientists and they should reexamine their doctrines in the light of the conflicting interpretations. The idea that people have only been in the Western Hemisphere for 12,000 years is simply an agreement among scholars who neither think nor read and who have been stuck on a few Clovis and Folsom sites for a generation. I personally cannot believe that any people could remember these geological events for tens of thousands of years. My conclusion is that these are eyewitness accounts [formation of Mt. Mazama, Crater Lake, Mount

Multnomah, the Puget Sound] but that the events they describe are well within the past 3,000 years. It is past time that this resistance be ended and a new scenario for the Western Hemisphere be constructed" (DeLoria, 1995, p. 206).

4. "A number of tribal traditions describe creatures that may have been dinosaurs. Again, the Pacific Northwest peoples have a number of stories concerning oversized animals in their lakes and rivers. Since the current trend in dinosaur research suggests that these creatures, for the most part, were warm-blooded and had social and instinctual characteristics reminiscent of mammals of today, there is no reason to hesitate suggesting that some of these creatures, described as animals or large fish by observers, were surviving individuals of some presently classified dinosaur species. That is to say, humans and some creatures we have classified as dinosaurs were contemporaries (DeLoria, 1995, pp. 240–241); the Sioux have a tale about such a monster in the Missouri river...I suspect that the dinosaur in question here must be a stegosaurus" (p. 243).

GOOD CULTURALLY RELEVANT SCIENCE

In addition to the six criteria for selecting curricula mentioned in the previous section, there are other classroom decisions to help assure teachers that they are providing a culturally relevant science experience for students. We agree with Oakes & Lipton (1999) that teachers must do more than value cultural relevancy; they must act on that value (p. 261). This requires both general and specific strategies as well as content decisions.

A philosophical framework that should be present in all classrooms, but is particularly critical in culturally diverse classrooms, has to do with the belief that children need to be "mined" for their knowledge and that teachers are the miner-artists (Ladson-Billings, 1994). This helps provide an environment for democratic, culturally relevant classrooms—where ethnic, racial, or cultural differences are not ignored or hidden but are openly discussed as worthy and interesting (Paley, 1995). In our view, involvement of parents and other cultural role models not ad hoc, but as an integral part of the science subject matter, is also critical and is supported by the work of others (Paley, 1995; Cortés, 1994).

As suggested previously (the "mentioning problem"), science concepts need to be emphasized that are age-appropriate, in a context deep enough for meaningful learning, and aligned with state standards for scientific literacy. With 49 states officially claiming standards documents, curriculum writers should pay attention to these learning priorities. It is, therefore, crucial that scientific, historical, and anthropological examples used in culturally relevant science classes be as accurate as possible. There is little room for "centric" teaching—claims of first discoveries to raise self-esteem of children, with little or no supporting scientific evidence. Instead of claims of a particular culture being first or best, students can, for example, spend time learning how both African and Aztec cultures had a process and an explanation for the evaporation of seawater, resulting in the removal of salt. While the best explanation today may differ from either culture's, students still are able to get a sense that mathematics, science, and general problem-solving are not alien to their culture.

In fact, our notion of improving self-esteem involves students succeeding at increasingly complex tasks in a rigorous, but highly supportive, environment. Teaching should be done constructively so that students can develop their own explanations and test their hypotheses—requiring fewer topics in more depth. Written curricular materials for teachers must contain enough detail so they get the necessary background to provide activities and resources for students to understand the scientific explanations—without having to do a lot of research on their own. One of the authors recently worked with teachers in the Detroit area. If teachers learn a little anthropology and history associated with a particular scientific phenomena, followed by developing culturally relevant curricula and then returning home to try activities with students, initial results appear promising.

Some important science concepts follow that might be found in standards documents for which there are culturally relevant examples. Both Egyptian and Aztecs used honey to treat wounds. Why? Bacteria die by having osmotic pressure dry them up. Experiments using typical osmosis-diffusion set-ups can be enhanced with these story-examples, while also serving to show the important role of models in science. Numerous foods and food groups can be studied to teach the nature or methods of science, as well as important concepts related to nutrition and human health. George Washington Carver's work with peanuts is well known, but the emphasis on his contribution to the understanding of the role of niacin in preventing pellagra needs to be emphasized. Another effective cultural-scientific story is of New World natives discovering that by adding beans to their niacin-poor corn diet they could prevent pellagra. The knowledge of how vitamin-deficiency diseases work in the system is, of course, the ultimate goal for students, but getting there can be a more meaningful trip through such culturally rich examples.

Use of food examples provides a natural bridge to many other disciplines—geography, history, literature, art—and helps link to knowledge of parents and other family members. How universal can we claim the four food groups are—including meats and dairy products—to good nutrition, when many cultures eat healthy diets without much of either? We are not attacking the Western food pyramid (which has changed recently to reflect healthier eating), but rather we are promoting alternative examples which have evidentiary support. Suppose students learned of the nutritional value of corn or beans and then were asked to each contribute a favorite recipe from home that used one as the primary ingredient. Better yet, family contributions of a dish identified by its ingredients could result in quite a nice "smorgasbord," where different cultures display—and everyone gets to try—their representative dishes.

Just as culturally relevant science teaching using examples for biological concepts integrates disciplines, the same is true with numerous concepts in the physical sciences. In addition to the obvious integration of mathematics, there are anthropological and other social science connections to make. Dyes and pigments are interesting. Fundamental chemical principles can be taught using the same chemical molecule that seems to be used by many different cultures—indigo. Consisting of a configuration of carbon, nitrogen, hydrogen, and oxygen, indigo is found in many different plants but seems almost universally used as a dye. With the addition of two bromine atoms, the molecule becomes Tyrian purple. Even the Anglo-Saxons painted their faces blue (remember the movie *Braveheart*)!

The connection between scientific breakthroughs, technological innovations that follow, and the resulting impact on society is an interesting socio-political-cultural study. All of this can be part of a culturally relevant science lesson. Concepts related to chelation of metal ions in chemistry can be made relevant by using the example of lead-based paints. An anthropological behavior term ,"pica," describes certain animals' indiscriminate, omnivorous eating habits—from magpies to small children in a ghetto apartment chewing the peeling paint from windowsills. The knowledge that kids chew on windowsills and that lead is poisonous to humans led to the technological breakthrough of lead-free paints as well as the scientific knowledge related to medical treatment for lead poisoning using EDTA (Edathamil tetrasodium). There are, however, sociopolitical dimensions to all of this. The neighborhoods most affected are often more disenfranchised and take longer to have the results of the science and technology available to them. The physical sciences also include concepts that can be illustrated by discussing nuclear power plants, waste dumps, or high voltage apparatus. All of these have traditionally been found closer to certain ethnic minority neighborhoods.

Students might be surprised to learn that just as the Mayan religious fascination with time compelled them to study the sky, Isaac Newton studied the skies to demonstrate the perfection of God's creation. The fact that Newton came up with some of the best mathematical explanations for his observations is only part of his story. Culturally relevant science examples should help students see that all cultures are capable of doing science. At-home projects like reading electric meters or keeping a list of the foods a family eats in 24 hours can enhance the degree to which students feel part of a scientifically literate community.

CONCLUSION

We admit there is a paucity of good culturally relevant curricula ready for teacher use. Our examples are an attempt to begin correcting this. Plans are underway to work with other colleagues (e.g., Diana Marinez, Texas A&M, Corpus Christi) on developing a series on culturally relevant science materials that will provide teachers with background, activities, and resources. In the meantime, we ask the teachers in Detroit and other districts to abide by their written criteria (truth, balance, harmony, order, with bias-free multicultural materials) and to avoid substituting "centric" materials that do an injustice to students, their culture, and to science.

Science teachers need to be alert when selecting all texts and curriculum materials. In the current milieu, with emphasis on diversity, equity, and multicultural education, they need to be particularly alert to the above six criteria as they seek to be more inclusive of all students in their teaching. While appealing to unique cultures and issues of equity and justice, culturally relevant science materials must be judged by a standard that gives both teacher and student some assurance that what is being presented is supported by evidence and is an accurate version of science, history, and anthropology.

REFERENCES

Adams, H. H. 1987/1990. *African and African American contributions to science [Baseline Essay]*. Portland, OR: Multnomah School District.

Adams, H. H. (1988). Lecture Second melanin conference: New York. Broadcast on *African American World View*, WDTR 90.9 FM, Detroit Public School's Radio, October 2.

Adams, H. H. (1987, Sept. 16–18). Lecture: First melanin conference: San Francisco. Broadcast on *African American World View*, WDTR 90.9 FM, Detroit Public School's Radio, September 25, 1990.

Amen, N. A. (1993). *African origin of electromagnetism*. Jamaica, NY: Nur Ankh Amen Co.

Argüelles, J. C. (1987). *The Mayan factor: Path beyond technology*. Santa Fe, NM: Bear & Co.

Asante, M. K. (1993–94). On the wings of nonsense. *Black Books Bulletin: WordsWork 16*(1–2), 38.

Baines, J. & Marek, J. (1980). *Atlas of ancient Egypt*. New York: Facts on File.

Baurac, D. (1991). Director of Public Information, Argonne National Laboratory. Letter to Christopher Trey, May 22.

Bernal, M. (1991). *The Afroasiatic roots of civilization*, Vol. 2, New Brunswick, NJ: Rutgers University Press.

Bernal, M. (1987). *The Afroasiatic roots of civilization*, Vol. 1, New Brunswick, NJ: Rutgers University Press.

Churchward, A. (1921). *The origin and evolution of the human race*. London: G. Allen & Unwin.

Churchward, A. (1913). *The signs and symbols of primordial man*. London: G. Allen & Unwin.

Cobern, W. W. (1991). *World view theory and science education research*, NARST Monograph No. 3. Cincinnati, OH: National Association for Research in Science Teaching.

Cortés, C. E. (1994). Limits to "Pluribus," limits to "Unum": Unity, diversity and the great American balancing act. *National Forum: Phi Kappa Phi, 74*(1), 6–8.

DeLoria, V. (1995). *Red earth, white lies: Native Americans and the myth of scientific facts*. New York: Scribners.

Detroit Public Schools (1991). *Suggested criteria for reviewing educational textbooks and materials, March 1992*. Detroit, MI: Detroit Board of Education.

Diop, C. A. (1991). *Civilization or barbarism: An authentic anthropology.* (Yaa-Lengi Meema Ngemi, Trans.). Brooklyn, NY: Lawrence Hill.

Driver, R., Leach, J., Millar, R., & Scott, P. (1996). *Young people's images of science.* Buckingham, UK: Open University Press.

Ebling, F. J. P., & Foster, D. L. (1989). Pineal melatonin rhythms and their timing of puberty in mammals. *Experientia, 45,* 946–952.

Haslip-Viera, G., Ortiz de Montellano, B. R., & Barbour, W. (1997). Robbing Native American cultures: Van Sertima and the Omecs. *Current Anthropology, 38*(3), 419–441.

Hastings, M. H., Vance, G. & Maywood, E. (1989). Phylogeny and function of the pineal. *Experientia, 45,* 903–906.

King, R. (1990). *African origin of biological psychiatry.* Germantown, TN: Seymour Smith.

Ladson-Billings, G. (1994). *The dreamkeepers: Successful teachers of African-American children.* San Francisco: Jossey-Bass.

Loving, C. C. (1997). From the summit of truth to its slippery slopes: Science education's journey through positivist-postmodern territory. *American Educational Research Journal, 34*(3), 421–452.

Loving, C. C. (1998). Cortés' multicultural empowerment model and generative teaching and learning in science. *Science and Education, 7*(5), 533–552.

Marriot, M. (1991, August 11). *New York Times,* pp. K 1,12.

Matthews, M. R. (1994). *Science teaching: The role of history and philosophy of science.* London: Routledge.

National Center for Educational Statistics. (1995). *Understanding racial-ethnic differences in secondary school science and mathematics achievement.* Washington, DC: U.S. Department of Education Office of Research and Improvement (OERI).

National Science Foundation. (1996). *Indicators of science and mathematics success, 1995.* (L. Suter, Ed.). Arlington, VA: National Science Foundation.

Oakes, J., & Lipton, M. (1999). *Teaching to change the world.* Boston: McGraw-Hill College.

Ortiz de Montellano, B. R. (1990). *Aztec medicine, health and nutrition.* New Brunswick, NJ: Rutgers University Press.

Ortiz de Montellano, B. R. (1996). Afrocentric pseudoscience: The miseducation of African Americans. *Annals of the New York Academy of Science, 775,* 561–572.

Ortiz de Montellano, B. R., Haslip-Viera, G., & Barbour, W. (1997). They were NOT here before Columbus: Afrocentric hyperdiffusionism in the 1990s. *Ethnohistory, 44*(2), 200–233.

Paley, V. G. (1995). *Kwanzaa and me*. Cambridge: Harvard University Press.

Robins, A. H. (1991). *Biological perspectives on human pigmentation*. Cambridge: Cambridge University Press.

Shaw, I., & Nicholson, P. (1995). *The dictionary of ancient Egypt*. London: The British Museum.

Sizonenko, P. C., Lang, U. & Aubert, M. L. (1982). Neuroendocrinology of puberty: The role of melatonin in man. *Annals of the York Academy of Science, 43*(6), 453–464.

Van Sertima, I. (1984). *Blacks in science: Ancient and modern*. New Brunswick, NJ: Transaction Books.

CHAPTER 9

Rethinking Multicultural Science Education: Representations, Identities, and Texts

Peter Ninnes

INTRODUCTION

The last 15 years have seen a substantial increase in the interest in the relationship between science and culture, particularly the possibilities and problems associated with science teaching in culturally diverse contexts. One central element in the debates arising in this area concerns the way school curricula in general and science curricula in particular should respond to cultural diversity, especially the presence in science classes of non-Western, Indigenous, and minority group learners. Within this "crisis of narratives" (Lyotard, 1984, xxiii) some authors such as Good (1995) and Loving (1995) have argued that since science is universal, the concept of multicultural science education is highly problematic. In contrast, many authors believe that Indigenous and minority groups have their own knowledges that can contribute to scientific understandings, their own unique ways of knowing the world, or indeed their own kind of science (e.g. Aikenhead, 1997a, 1997b; Christie, 1991; Gordon, 1990; McKinley, 1996; Ninnes, 1994, 1995, 1996; Roberts, 1998; Snively & Corsiglia, 1998).

As a number of authors have pointed out, much of this debate in science education has drawn on theoretical frameworks developed in anthropology, especially educational anthropology (see, for example, Aikenhead, 1996; Krugly-Smolska, 1999). As a result, a range of general and specific anthropological concepts and constructs have been appropriated into the discourse of multicultural education and in particular science education. These concepts and constructs include, among others, worldview (Cobern, 1996; Fleer, 1997; George, 1999), cultural border-crossing (Aikenhead, 1996), culturally derived (or even determined) science content and learning styles (Bisbee, 1996; Ninnes, 1994, 1995, 1996), First Nations science (Aikenhead, 1997a), Aboriginal science (Christie, 1991), Indigenous science (Snively & Corsiglia, 1998), different cultural understandings (Fleer, 1996), African American epistemology (Gordon, 1990), traditional cosmology (Ogawa, 1997), Indigenous curricula (McKinley, 1996), Indigenous knowledge (Roberts, 1998; Swift, 1992), cultural knowledge (Keating, 1997), Native American perspectives (Smith, 1998), cross-cultural science (Taylor, 1999) and traditional beliefs (Taylor & McPherson, 1997).

Krugly-Smolska (1999) notes the time lag of about 10 years between the development of multicultural education and the development of multicultural science education. It is useful, therefore, to ask whether recent developments in and thinking about multicultural education, particularly the use of the concept of culture, can inform an understanding of and assist in rethinking multicultural science education. In particular, postcolonial theory has begun to be used to examine issues of culture, identity, and diversity in educational contexts. Crowley and McConaghy (1998) argue that

> Postcolonialism can point to the fissures and gaps in extant theorising and practice and especially perhaps in the tensions surrounding subjectivity, identity and difference. Postcolonialism...is critical to deconstructing binaries that reify and normalise, fix and stabilise, erase and efface. (p. 270)

This emphasis on examining issues related to difference, subjectivity and identity is particularly useful in the realm of ethnicity and culture, because in multicultural science education the approach has often focused on cultural differences, as noted above, which in turn suggests the creation of identities and subjectivities through particular multicultural pedagogies and practices.

A number of other issues are raised by Hickling-Hudson (1998), who contends that postcolonial approaches explore issues of interconnectedness, discontinuity, hybridity, ambiguity, power, and knowledge, which tend to be glossed over in modernist, postmodernist, and Marxist accounts. Furthermore, a postcolonial approach is not only about looking back at the past, as some authors have argued (e.g. Gandhi, 1998; McClintock, 1995). "Poco" approaches also examine how colonial experiences are manifest in post colonial presents (Hickling-Hudson, 1998) and the way colonising discourses and practices reproduce themselves in apparently postcolonial states and their institutions such as education (McConaghy, 1997, 1998a).

A specific example from within multicultural education discourses in Australia illustrates the need to continue to develop our thinking in this area. McConaghy (1997, 1998a, 1998b) has pointed out that the recognition of cultural differences in learning among Australia's Indigenous people, epitomised by the groundbreaking work of Harris (1984) and Christie (1984, 1985), occurred in a specific historical context, namely of a principally assimilationist approach to Indigenous education. As such, their ideas were quite radical, and led to a wide range of developments in Indigenous education, including attempts to include Indigenous cultural content and learning styles into schooling, and the development of bilingual education and two-way education (see, for example, Harris, 1990, 1988; Wunungmurra, 1988). Yet recently these kinds of approaches, particularly the use of the concept of culture and the construction of oppositional binaries of cultural difference, have been reexamined and problematized from a number of perspectives. In particular, writers such as McConaghy (1998b) have critiqued the notions of cultural difference that these programs promoted and have explored their unintended consequences. McConaghy argues that specific sets of ideas about Indigenous education may either reproduce colonial oppressions or disrupt them. Those narratives that reproduce colonial oppressions may unwittingly be "a continuation of resilient discourses of white supremacy" (McConaghy 1998b, 124). In particular, McConaghy draws on Bain Attwood's (1992) work to identify three aspects of educational discourses of Aboriginality that may equally apply to multicultural science education.

Paraphrasing McConaghy's (1998b, 125–127) account of these three aspects of educational discourses, a rethinking of multicultural science education could address issues of ownership and representation of Indigenous and minority knolwedges and identities in school science curricula and classrooms. Who speaks for Indigenous and minority groups in the development of science curricula? Who controls the process of curriculum development? What are the unintended consequences of making Indigenous and minority groups and their knowledges and ways of knowing the objects of study in science curricula and class-rooms? To what extent does teaching about Indigenous and minority ways of knowing and knowledges become in fact a process of speaking for Indigenous and minority groups? Second, we could ask about the nature of the representations of Indigenous and minority groups' ways of knowing and knowledges found in science teaching materials and sci-ence classrooms. How does the use of the notion of culture and particularly of cultural differences help or hinder this process? To what extent does a focus on cultural differences result in the construction of cultural and epistemological binaries, which in turn (mis)represent groups as widely different from each other? To what extent do cultural difference approaches lead to the construction of notions of the "essen-tial" or "authentic" ethnic or Indigenous subject? Do these essentialist notions mask diversity within groups and allow those in positions of power to create identities for marginalised groups to their detriment? Third, and still loosely following McConaghy (1998b) and Attwood (1992), to what extent do the use of culture and concepts of cultural dif-ference enhance educational and administrative control over Indigenous and minority group members in science classrooms? To what extent do practices and discourses of cultural difference in the multicultural school and (science) classroom include, exclude, or disenfranchise Indigenous or minority group members?

It is the aim of this chapter to explore this reconceptualization of multicultural science education through the examination of the use of cultural difference approaches in the incorporation of multicultural, and especially Indigenous, perspectives into school science textbooks. The research on science textbooks that is used to inform the discussion here is part of an ongoing project concerning the representation of diverse knowledges and identities in texts (Ninnes, 1998, 1999, forthcoming a, forthcoming b). This chapter particularly draws on textual analysis, and as such focuses on the representations of Indigenous knowledges and identities that are found in the textbooks. That is, its main focus is on the second set of questions that Attwood (1992) and McConaghy (1998b) raise. The wider project also involves an examination of the first and third set of questions above, particularly the ways in which the texts have been developed and the relations of power involved in textbook produc-tion. However, this aspect of the research is ongoing and is not presented here.

The four texts used in the analysis come from two plural societies, Australia and Canada. The *Science Probe* series (Baumann, et al., 1995; Beckett et al., 1995; Bullard et al., 1996) is used in years 7–9 in British Columbia, Canada. This is the sole text recommended by the British Columbia ministry of education, and as such is used extensively throughout the province. The current edition, published by Nelson, was developed from a previous edition published by Wiley. All of the listed authors are Canadian, and most are from British Columbia. A small number are from Ontario. The *Science Directions* (Roberts, et al., 1989, 1991a, 1991b) series was developed specifically for junior science classes in Alberta, in close consultation with the provincial ministry of education, Alberta Education. It is the largest selling junior secondary science text in that province (G. S. Aikenhead, personal communication). Several of the authors who worked on the *Science Directions* series also contributed to *Science Probe*. The *Dynamic Science* (Wilson & Bauer, 1991, 1992, 1994, 1995) series of texts is used extensively in New South Wales, Australia, and is based on the syllabus prescribed by the ministry of education in that state. The *Australian Secondary Science* series (Dangerfield, et al., 1995, 1996, 1998) was designed and structured to match the National Science Profiles and the Victorian Curriculum Standards Framework. Unlike their Canadian counterparts, ministries of education in Australian states do not usually work closely with textbook authors. Rather, the ministries tend to produce syllabi and curricula, and then authors and publishers respond to these in a relatively *ad hoc* way.

The examples from the texts provided in the following narrative were identified through a process of textual analysis based on the methods espoused by Foucault (1972) and Luke (1989), which focused on identifying not only the ideology presented in the text (what was said) but also the linguistic elements of the text, especially syntax and lexicon, used to convey particular ideologies. Text here refers to not just the words, but also the graphical components of the textbooks, and the spatial arrangement of words and graphics. As well as the explicit references to particular knowledges and identities, the texts were also analysed regarding the nature of the implied or explicit comparisons made between knowledge types, that is, the way the texts constructed relations of power among knowledge types.

REPRESENTATIONS OF INDIGENOUS IDENTITIES
AND KNOWLEDGES

A series of textual effects are examined in addressing the second set of questions paraphrased from McConaghy (1998b) related to the representation of Indigenous identities and knowledges. For the sake of brevity, the focus here is on Indigeneity, rather than other minority groups, although many of the same effects are seen with regard to non-Indigenous minorities. In particular, I look at the extent to which Indigenous knowledges and identities are represented in each set of texts, essentialism and the use of discourses of traditionality, the use of binaries or other more complex conceptualizations of Indigenous diversity, the temporal location of Indigeneity, the representation of contemporary identities, and discourses that privilege scientific knowledges over Indigenous knowledges.

Extent of Representations of Indigenous
Knowledges and Identities

Before examining the nature of the representations of Indigenous knowledges, ways of knowing, and identities that are presented in the texts, it is useful to compare the texts in terms of the extent of coverage that they give to these issues. The analysis involved the identification of discrete sections of text concerning Indigeneity. The discrete sections of text were defined as part of a sentence, a whole sentence, a paragraph, a box of text, a graphic or a page or more of text discussing an aspect of Indigenous knowledges, separated from other representations of Indigenous knowledge by text related to non-Indigenous topics. The *Dynamic Science* series gives the most comprehensive coverage to Indigenous issues. In the four books in this series there are a total of 55 discrete references to Indigenous issues and these occur in all but six of the 27 chapters (that is, 78%). In the *Australian Secondary Science* series, 17 discrete references are made to Indigenous issues in 11 of the 36 chapters (31%) in the three books in this series. The *Science Probe* series presents 27 discrete references to Indigenous issues in 13 of the 64 chapters (20%) in the three books of the series. The three books in the *Science Directions* series provide only nine references to Indigenous issues in three of the 18 units (17%).

Essentialism and Discourses of Traditionality

As can be seen from the previous section, each set of textbooks does identify and discuss to some extent a set of knowledges and ways of knowing that are represented as belonging to Indigenous people. Each set of texts thus purports to know Indigenous people. It is difficult to evaluate the merits of including Indigenous knowledges in this way. A later stage of this research project aims to determine the processes by which particular knowledges were categorised as Indigenous, and the means by which they were collected and incorporated in the texts. It may be that representing Indigenous knowledges, even in essentialist ways, may be necessary in certain historical circumstance such as an assimilationist climate. In Spivak's terms, at times it may be strategically useful for educators to temporarily adopt essentialist positions while at the same time "remaining vigilant about our own practice" (Spivak, 1990, p. 11), in order to achieve a wider goal, such as an explication of practices that ignore the possibility of alternative ways of knowing and knowledges and thus disadvantage particular groups in society. While it may be appropriate for Indigenous people to adopt essentialist positions about themselves in order to achieve a political purpose, I am more concerned here with the ways in which the textbooks construct essentialist identities of Indigenous people, that is, the ways they speak both about and for Indigenous people.

One of the major ways identified here in which the textbooks construct essentialist identities is through what I call a discourse of traditionality. The *Dynamic Science* series adopts this approach much more frequently than the other textbooks. The *Dynamic Science* series develops an extensive discourse around the notion of tradition through the use of phrases such as "traditional Aboriginal people" or "traditional Australian Aboriginal" or Aboriginal people living a "traditional lifestyle" or in a "traditional setting." These phrases occur a total of 26 times in the archive of verbatim statements collected from the texts, while very little is said about either the difficulties of defining "traditional" or the nature of "nontraditional" Aboriginal lives. It appears that for some reason, the authors considered maintenance of a traditional lifestyle a marker of authenticity. Or they simply may have wished, for other unknown reasons, to distinguish between what they perceived to be differing life situations of various Indigenous peoples. In contrast to *Dynamic Science*, the *Australian Secondary Science* series uses the terms tradition or traditional in relation to Indigenous people on only five occasions, *Science Probe* on two occasions, and *Science Directions* not at all.

Binaries or Other Conceptualizations of Indigenous Diversity

Another way in which essentialist notions of Indigenous identity are established in the texts is through the generalisation of Indigenous knowledges and practices to all Indigenous groups. In effect, this type of practice sets up binaries between Indigenous and non-Indigenous knowledges which homogenise Indigenous identities, mask diversity within Indigenous populations, and possibly exaggerate differences between knowledge types. Alternatively, the texts at times disrupt this essentialising tendency by referring to the knowledges of specific groups, thus acknowledging diversity and breaking down simple Indigenous–non-Indigenous binaries. None of the textbooks are particularly consistent in the approach they take to this issue. *Dynamic Science* refers to only one particular group of Australian Indigenous people, the Pitjantjatjara people, while the *Australian Secondary Science* series refers only to the Anangu people. The *Science Probe* books mention the Haida, Bella Coola, Tlingit, Tsimshianor, Cree, Saanich, Objiway, Kwakiutl, Nuxalk, Shuswap, Loucheux, and Inuit, whereas the *Science Directions* series refers only to the Iroquois and Inuit. In *Science Directions* (Book 7, p. 101) there is also a photograph of the Interpretive Centre at the Head-Smashed-In Buffalo Jump, which, according to Corbett (1997), is a site formerly used for buffalo hunting by Blackfoot-speaking people from the Peigan and Blood bands.

At times some of the textbooks refer to Indigenous groups from particular geographic areas. The *Dynamic Science* series mentions people from the mouth of the Murray River and from the Flinders Ranges, while the *Australian Secondary Science* series mentions groups living along the Hawkesbury River. The *Science Probe* series refers to West Coast native peoples, of which there are a substantial number of different groups or bands, but the *Science Directions* series makes no mention of groups from particular areas. The use of generic terms such as Aboriginal people, Aboriginal peoples, Aboriginal and Torres Strait Island people(s), is quite common in a number of the textbooks. As noted above, these kinds of homogenising terms are used quite extensively in the *Dynamic Science* series, particularly in conjunction with modifiers indicating traditionality, although at times modifiers such as "some" are used which indicate that certain practices were restricted to particular Indigenous groups. The *Australian Secondary Science* series uses generic terms of this kind on 16 occasions, although on three occasions the modifiers "some," "most," and "often" are used, which to some extent indicate diversity within Indigenous identities and practices. Furthermore, these texts often use plural forms such as "Aboriginal and Torres Strait Islander peoples" which also indicate a diversity of group identities. Although the *Science Probe* series most commonly mentions specific groups, on three occasions it uses homogenising forms, while the *Science Directions* series makes two references of this kind.

The Temporal Location of Indigeneity

McClintock (1995) argues that imperial and colonial ideologies represented the culture of the colonised as anachronistic: "The stubborn and threatening heterogeneity of the colonies was contained and disciplined not as socially or geographically different from Europe and thus equally valid, but as temporally different and thus as irrevocably superannuated by history" (p. 40). Furthermore, drawing on the work of Fabian (1983, cited in McClintock, 1995, p. 37), McClintock (1995) argues that through the rise of social evolutionary thinking, "time became a geography of social power, a map from which to read a global allegory of 'natural' social difference" (p. 37). In other words, non-European cultures and peoples were represented as relics from the past, located in antiquity, socially inferior, and superseded by European progress. European cultures were represented as existing in the present, as being modern, and hence socially superior. These arguments have important implications for the ways in which Indigenous knowledges and ways of knowing are represented in science textbooks in particular, but in other curriculum materials and curriculum areas in general. If Indigeneity is represented as belonging principally to the past, it could be argued that this is a practice that far from contributing to the inclusion of Indigenous knowledges in curricula on equal terms with other forms of knowledge, in fact is a means for (intentionally or unintentionally) subjugating, colonising or, in Foucauldian terms, disciplining, these knowledges and bringing them under the control of dominant knowledge forms (Foucault, 1977).

The discourse of traditionality referred to above can be thought of as part of this process of locating indigenous knowledges in antiquity or representing them as atavistic. Another mechanism by which this representation is achieved is through grammatical devices such as the use of tense. If textbooks and other curriculum materials use past tense to describe practices and beliefs that could be reasonably expected to be extant, then it could be argued that the textbooks are representing these knowledges and beliefs as superseded, or in McClintock's terms, superannuated by history. In passages concerning Indigenous knowledges and identities in the *Dynamic Science* series in which the tense is clearly identifiable and the belief, technology, or practice described could reasonably be expected to be extant, present tense is used approximately four times as often as past tense when describing these kinds of Indigenous beliefs and technologies. In the *Australian Secondary Science* series, present tense is used nearly three times as often as past tense. However, in the *Science Probe* series, past and present tense are used in approximately equal proportions in these situations. It is difficult to perform this kind of analysis on the *Science Directions* texts because they contain so few representations of Indigenous knowledges. The historical representations in the *Science Directions* texts are described in more detail below. Thus it would appear that two sets of textbooks (*Dynamic Science* and *Australian Secondary Science*) rarely represent extant knowledges as located in the past, whereas the *Science Probe* series is much less successful in avoiding this problem.

Representations of Contemporary Identities

In addition to the discourses of traditionality and the use of tense identified above, the texts can be analysed in terms of the extent to which they present contemporary Indigenous knowledges, lifestyles, and identities. If a text emphasises practices and beliefs from the past with no coverage of contemporary identities, then it could also be argued that the textbook is misrepresenting Indigenous identities by locating them in antiquity. The *Dynamic Science* series makes little mention of contemporary Indigenous identities. As noted above, it constructs a discourse around supposedly traditional Indigenous practices. Similarly, the scant attention paid to Indigenous issues in the *Science Directions* series is almost entirely limited to historical representations. These include a picture of people wearing loincloths and hollowing out a log (*Science Directions* 7, pp. 86–7); reference to the Head-Smashed-In Buffalo Jump museum, mentioned above (*Science Directions* 7, p. 101); the saving of a 16th-century French exploration party by Iroquois knowledge of treatments for scurvy (*Science Directions* 8, pp. 252–3); and the picture of "Native Canadians farming in the eighteenth century" (*Science Directions* 9, p.

238), also mentioned above. The *Australian Secondary Science* series fares slightly better in terms of representing contemporary Indigenous identities. This series does present some historical material, such as the warnings provided by Indigenous peoples to Europeans of the tendency of the Hawkesbury river to flood, a warning that was ignored with devastating results (*Australian Secondary Science* 1, p. 179). However, it also mentions current efforts to record Indigenous knowledge of herbal medicines (*Australian Secondary Science* 1, p. 3), the role of Indigenous people in seed collection and revegetation at Weipa (*Australian Secondary Science* 2, p. 208), and the Anangu people's role in managing Uluru-Kata Juta National Park (*Australian Secondary Science* 3, p. 3). Compared with the other texts, the *Science Probe* series provides the most diverse range of contemporary Indigenous identities and knowledges. These include the use of precious metals in art (*Science Probe* 9, p. 48), contemporary fishing techniques such as seine netting (*Science Probe* 9, p. 505), struggles and disputes over land ownership and land use (*Science Probe* 8, p. 498, 499, *Science Probe* 8, p. 521), and contemporary Indigenous peoples' careers as foresters (*Science Probe* 8, p. 512), fish and wildlife habitat officers (*Science Probe* 9, p. 515), and antipollution campaigners and educational innovators (*Science Probe* 10, p. 469).

Privileging Scientific Knowledges

One of the probably unintended consequences of making Indigenous and minority groups and their knowledges and ways of knowing the objects of study in science curricula and classrooms can be the status elevation or privileging of scientific knowledges at the expense of Indigenous and minority knowledges. Although these "other" knowledges are included in the curriculum, the result may be their diminution and the promulgation of the myth of positivism. These ideas can best be illustrated by examples from the four sets of texts.

In the *Dynamic Science* texts, the spatial organization of the texts suggests that Indigenous knowledges are peripheral to mainstream scientific knowledge. While examples of Indigenous knowledges are incorporated into the main narrative in these texts, many of the examples of Indigenous knowledges occur within shaded boxes separated from the main narrative and labeled "Did you know?" Thus these kinds of knowledge may appear as curiosities, as side issues, or as peripheral to the main thrust of the text.

A second spatial technique for privileging scientific knowledge involves discussing various Indigenous, minority group, or ancient explanations of natural phenomena and then rounding off the discussion with the "scientific" explanation. For example, in the *Science Probe* series, the perspectives of "ancient peoples" concerning solar eclipses are discussed, including the suggestion that they were "frightening" (*Science Probe* 8, p. 331) and that people "screamed and yelled" (p. 331) at them. This discussion then concludes with a scientific explanation of how eclipses occur. A similar pattern is followed in the discussion of lunar eclipses, with an example provided of "the Kwakiutl people of the West Coast [who] believed that a lunar eclipse was caused by a sky monster who tried to swallow the moon" (*Science Probe* 8, p. 333). Again a 'scientific' explanation follows this discussion. A further example is provided in discussion of the motion of the sun and the planets. In *Science Probe* 8 (p. 315) the beliefs of ancient Egyptians and the Nuxalk people of British Columbia are canvassed, after which the text provides a scientific explanation, including: "Many things about the sun have been discovered since the times of these explanations. The sun does not travel across the sky. It only appears to travel..." (p. 315). As well as privileging scientific knowledge, these explanations also disregard the complex purposes of Indigenous knowledges. That is, they provide no sense that these stories and explanations had important social and cultural purposes; they did not exist simply to explain physical phenomena.

While the texts rarely explicitly compare and judge the various explanations, the fact that they are science textbooks and the "scientific" explanation is provided last implies the superiority of the scientific explanation; such an arrangement is perhaps a textual and epistemological equivalent of the "family of man" diagrams that first appeared in the late 19th century in evolutionary and anthropological writings and that McClintock (1995, pp. 38–9) argues were a visible representation of the superiority of Europeans. These family of man diagrams illustrate a linearly arranged series of human and other primate phenotypes, with the European type at the apex. In fairness, it must be said that the *Science Probe* series at times appears to acknowledge the differing purposes of scientific and Indigenous explanations of physical phenomena. For example, in *Science Probe* 9 (p. 270) students are encouraged to research Indigenous myths concerning the universe. The textbook points out that such knowledge was "kept by special people in their communities. These special people were able to remember all this information; it was not written down." The readers are then asked, "Why do you think they did not write this information down?" While an obvious answer might be a lack of written language, the question may also imply an understanding by the author of the diverse social and cultural purposes of knowledge.

Another technique used by the texts to privilege scientific knowledge is simply to dismiss or ignore other forms of knowledge, or to argue that scientific knowledge is superior or that other beliefs are mistaken. In the *Australian Secondary Science* series, for example, firewalking is treated as follows:

> Firewalking has an almost magical image and is often used as an example of how the mind can influence the body, but really it is just another example of energy transfer—or to be correct the lack of energy transfer. (Book 1, p. 139)

In the same series the following exercise subtly advances the merits of scientific knowledge and its benefits for apparently ignorant local villagers in need of patronage, who presumably have no local knowledge of relevance to the issues at hand:

> In less developed countries of the world there is often a shortage of technology due to lack of money.
>
> 1. Imagine you are an Australian aid worker who has been sent to a village to help the local people water their crops. You have instructed them to dig ditches to carry the water but now you need to build a device for getting the water from the river into the ditches to irrigate their land. All you have been given is 30 m of plastic hosing.
> 2. Form a group and devise a simple machine that will help the villagers get the water our of the river and into their irrigation ditches.
> 3. When you have a plan, check it with your teacher and build a model to test that it works. (Book 2, p. 130)

The *Science Probe* series dismisses understandings about nature derived from nonscientific means when it proclaims science as the source of all understanding about nature:

> Science has limits. Scientific knowledge is not absolute truth. Rather it is the *total* of our present understanding about nature. This understanding is subject to constant revision and updating. (*Science Probe* 10, p, 10, emphasis added)

In the *Science Directions* series, as noted above, there are very few representations of Indigenous knowledges. In conjunction with this ignoring of Indigenous perspectives, the texts privilege scientific knowledge by frequently discussing the process of accumulation of scientific evidence to justify their truth claims about scientific knowledge. The word "evidence" is used in this regard on 15 different occasions in the three books in this series when discussing a range of scientific ideas, including Newton's ideas about gravity, particle theory, ice ages, the origins of potash, methods for testing manufacturers' claims, the ages of rocks, predicting earthquakes and the theory of continental drift.

As well as the use of past tense described above, each set of texts at times uses universalizing language to promote the myth of positivism. That is, they suggest that while people had particular perceptions of the world in the past, scientific progress has led to the abandonment of these ideas in favour of "scientific" ideas. The texts imply a universal adoption of scientific ideas and global abandonment of alternative worldviews. In the *Science Probe* series, for example, the following passage uses first person plural pronouns to obtain this effect.

> Knowing about stars and the universe will help *us* understand more about ourselves. Humans have always wondered who *we* are, where *we* came from, and what will eventually happen to *us* and our Earth. *We* can come closer to answering these questions by studying the many changes that are occurring in the solar system and in the universe beyond the solar system. (*Science Probe 9*, p. 343, emphasis added)

Alternatively, universal language is used to prescribe boundaries between Indigenous knowledges and the knowledge of some undescribed group including the reader. For example, in the *Dynamic Science* series contrasts are made between scientific knowledge and Indigenous knowledge. Again, the first person plural pronoun is used, and this gives the impression that the text is not addressing Indigenous people, which is a curious approach given the significant numbers of Indigenous people in some schools in New South Wales and their low retention rates:

> The heavens have always provided people with inspiration for stories. Traditional Aboriginal people have many stories relating to groups of stars that *we* now call constellations. For example, to some groups the Southern Cross is a man called Mululu together with his daughters. The daughters are the four bright stars, while the nearby star Centaurus is their father caring for them. (Book 4, p. 240, emphasis added)

The *Science Probe* series at times takes a similar approach:

> Early native people in Canada also used plants to produce medicines. For example, they boiled willow bark to obtain a substance that relieved pain. *We* now call this substance salicyclic acid. (*Science Probe* 8, p. 85, emphasis added)

RETHINKING MULTICULTURAL SCIENCE EDUCATION: LESSONS FROM THE TEXTS

I began this chapter with an exploration of ways of thinking about multicultural science education on the basis of developments that are occurring in the field of postcolonial theory as applied to issues of cultural diversity in education. The cultural difference approach to science education has been a welcome development because it has been a way for science educators to reflect on the extent to that science curricula and science teaching relate to the diversity found in the wider society in which that education is situated. However, there are some problems with this approach that need to be addressed. The analysis presented here, using examples from four sets of science textbooks used in two plural societies, indicates that a number of these problems relate to discourses and representations of culture and cultural difference, of diverse knowledges and ways of knowing, and of Indigenous identities. The major problems relate to the lack of representations of Indigenous knowledges and identities in some texts; the use of narrowly conceived notions of Indigeneity, such as the discourses around traditionality; the construction of binaries that disguise diversity within Indigenous populations and result in essentialist notions of Indigeneity; and the various means by which science knowledge is privileged to the detriment of other knowledge forms. These are all problems that potentially can be addressed by a reexamination of the way science educators talk and write about diversity. Each of the texts, with the exception of the *Science Directions* series, illustrates a number of practices that curriculum developers, textbook authors, and teachers can employ to more positively represent Indigenous knowledges and identities. These practices include the recognition of diversity within Indigenous populations through the use of particular groups' names, rather than generic terms; the use of modifying language to avoid overgeneralising; the representation of a range of contemporary and historical Indigenous identities and knowledges; and the incorporation of Indigenous knowledges into the main textual narratives alongside but not subordinate to the ideas that are represented as Western scientific ideas.

A number of problems remain unresolved, however. These problems relate to the wider issues concerning the process of the development of multicultural science materials. The ideas presented in this chapter have principally been concerned with the nature of the representations found in the texts and have implications for the actual writing of science curriculum materials. But the first and third sets of questions raised by McConaghy (1998b) and Attwood (1992) inform the wider process of textbook and other curriculum material development. In particular, there are social and political questions concerning who controls the process and to what extent the process of multicultural science curriculum development acts as a means of controlling and disciplining Indigenous and other minority groups. Specifically, further work needs to be undertaken regarding the sources of knowledge pertaining to Indigenous peoples, the extent of involvement of Indigenous people in the production of texts that purport to represent their knowledges and that construct identities for them, and the effects of including material of this kind in science curricula on Indigenous and other students' approaches to learning science.

REFERENCES

Aikenhead, G. S. (1997a). Towards a First Nations cross-cultural science and technology curriculum. *Science Education, 81*(2), 217–238.

Aikenhead, G. S. (1997b). Canada's Indigenous Peoples and Western science education. In M. Ogawa (Ed.), *Effects of Traditional Cosmology on Science Education* (pp. 15–21). Faculty of Education, Ibaraki University, Japan.

Aikenhead, G. S. (1996). Science education: Border crossing into the subculture of science. *Studies in Science Education, 27*, 1–52.

Attwood, B. (1992). Introduction. *Journal of Australian Studies, 35*, i–xvi.

Baumann, F., Bullard, J., Deschner, D., Flood, N., Gore, G., Grace, E., Hirsch, A., McGammon, B., Sieben, G., Vliegenthard, W., & Winter, M. (1995). *Science probe 8* (Student Edition). Toronto, Canada: Nelson.

Beckett, P., Bullard, J., Czernada, J., Flood, N., Freeman, P., Grace, E., Hirsch, A., McGammon, B., Sieben, G., Stokes, T, Winter, M., &

Wootton, A. (1995). *Science Probe 9* (Student Edition). Toronto, Canada: Nelson.

Bisbee, G. (1996). Building a Native American drill. *Science Teacher, 63*(2), 40–41.

Bullard, J., Cloutier, F., Flood, N., Gore, G., Grace, E., Gurney, B., Hirsch, A., Hugh, D., Madhosingh, C., Millett, G., & Wooton, A. (1996). *Science probe 10* (Student Edition). Toronto, Canada: Nelson.

Christie, M. (1991). Aboriginal science for the ecologically sustainable future. *Australian Science Teachers' Journal, 37*, 26–31.

Christie, M. (1985). *Aboriginal perspectives on experience and learning.* Deaking University, Geelong.

Christie, M. (1984). *The classroom world of the Aboriginal child.* Ph.D. thesis, University of Queensland.

Cobern, W. W. (1996). Worldview theory and conceptual change in science education. *Science Education 80*(5), 579–610.

Corbett, B. (1997). Head-Smashed-In Buffalo Jump. [Online] http://www.calexplorer.com/backcountry/head_smashed/index.html. [accessed 24 February 1999]

Crowley, V. & McConaghy, C. (1998). Introduction: Postcolonialism, feminism, pedagogies. *Discourse: Studies in the Cultural Politics of Education 19*(3), 269–273.

Dangerfield, E., Pike, T., Feutrill, H., & Holper, P. (1996). *Australian secondary science 2.* Melbourne: Cambridge.

Dangerfield, E., Pike, T., Feutrill, H., Holper, P., & Lloyd, D. (1998). *Australian secondary science 3.* Melbourne: Cambridge University Press.

Dangerfield, E., Pike, T., Feutrill, H., Holper, P., & Lloyd, D. (1995). *Australian secondary science 1.* Melbourne: Cambridge University Press.

Fleer, M. (1997). Science, technology and culture: Supporting multiple world views in curriculum design. *Australian Science Teachers' Journal, 43*(3), 13–18.

Fleer, M. (1996). Early childhood science education: Acknowledging and valuing differing cultural understandings. *Australian Journal of Early Childhood 21*(3), 11–15.

Foucault, M. (1977). *Discipline and punish.* London: Penguin.

Foucault, M. (1972). *The archeology of knowledge.* London: Travistock.

Gandhi, L. (1998). *Postcolonial theory: A critical introduction.* St Leonards, NSW, Australia: Allen & Unwin.

George, J. (1999). World view analysis of knowledge in a rural village: Implications for science education. *Science Education, 83*, 77–95.

Good, R. (1995). Comments on multicultural science education. *Science Education, 79*(3), 335–336.

Gordon, B. M. (1990). The necessity of African-American epistemology for educational theory. *Journal of Education, 172*(3): 88–106.

Harris, S. (1990). *Two-way Aboriginal schooling: Education and cultural survival.* Canberra, Australia: Aboriginal Studies Press.

Harris, S. (1988). Culture boundaries, culture maintenance-in-change and two-way Aboriginal schools. *Curriculum Perspectives, 8*, 76–83.

Harris, S. (1984). *Culture and learning: Tradition and education in North-East Arnhem Land.* Canberra: Australian Institute of Aboriginal Studies.

Hickling-Hudson, A. (1998). When Marxist and postmodern theories won't do: The potential of postcolonial theory for educational analysis. *Discourse: Studies in the Cultural Politics of Education, 19*(3), 327–339.

Keating, J. F. (1997). Harvesting cultural knowledge. *Science Teacher, 64*(2), 22–25.

Krugly-Smolska, E. (1999). Research on multiculturalism applied to students' learning school science: Some theoretical issues. NARST 99 Workshop Paper. [On-line] http://www.ouhk.edu.hk/cridal/misc/krugly.htm

Loving, C. (1995). Comment on "multiculturalism, universalism, and science education." *Science Education, 79*(3), 341–348.

Luke, A. (1989). Open and closed texts: the ideological/semantic analysis of textbook narratives. *Journal of Pragmatics, 13*, 53–80.

Lyotard, J.-F. (1984). *The postmodern condition: A report on knowledge.* Minneapolis: University of Minnesota Press.

McClintock, A. (1995). *Imperial leather.* New York: Routledge.

McConaghy, C. (1998a). Disrupting reproductive and erasive pedagogies: Educational policy process in postcolonial Australia. *Discourse: Studies in the Cultural Politics of Education, 19*(3), 341–354.

McConaghy, C. (1998b). Constructing Aboriginality, determining significant difference. In T. Maxwell (Ed.), *The context of teaching* (pp. 121–139). Armidale, Australia: Kardoorair Press.

McConaghy, C. (1997). *Rethinking indigenous adult education.* Ph.D. thesis, University of Queensland.

McKinley, E. (1996). Towards an Indigenous science curriculum. *Research in Science Education, 26*(2), 155–167.

Ninnes, P. (Forthcoming a). Representations of diverse knowledges and ways of knowing in junior secondary science texts in Australia. Manuscript submitted to *Science Education.*

Ninnes, P. (Forthcoming b). Representations of indigenous knowledges in secondary school science textbooks in Australia and Canada. Manuscript submitted to *International Journal of Science Education.*

Ninnes, P. (1999, April). Representations of ways of knowing in junior high school science texts in plural societies. Poster presentation at the annual meeting of the American Educational Research Association, Montreal, Canada.

Ninnes, P. (1998, December). Overcoming racist approaches: Innovations in secondary school science textbooks in Australia and Canada. Paper presented at the 26th annual conference of the Australian and New Zealand Comparative and International Education Society, Auckland, New Zealand.

Ninnes, P. (1996). Informal learning strategies in Solomon Islands. *Journal of World Anthropology, 1*(3) [Online]. http://wings.buffalo.edu/academic/department/anthropology/jwa/V1N3/ninnes.art

Ninnes, P. (1995). Informal learning contexts in Solomon Islands and their implications for the cross-cultural classroom. *International Journal of Educational Development, 14*(1), 15–26.

Ninnes, P. (1994). Toward a functional learning system for Solomon Island secondary science classrooms. *International Journal of Science Education, 16*(6), 677–688.

Ogawa, M. (Ed.). (1997). *Effects of traditional cosmology on science education,* Faculty of Education, Japan: Ibaraki University.

Roberts, D. A., Durward, W. C., Grace, E., Krupa, G., Krupa, M., Hirsch, A., Spalding, D. A. E., Baker, B. J., & Wohl, S. M. (1989). *Science Directions 7.* Toronto, Canada: John Wiley & Sons.

Roberts, D. A., Winter, M. K., Gore, G., Grace, E., Lang, H. M., & MacLean, W. (1991a). *Science directions 8.* Toronto, Canada: John Wiley & Sons.

Roberts, D. A., Winter, M. K., Bullard, D., Hirsch, A., Gore, G., Grace, E., Emerson, B., & McLelland, L. W. (1991b). *Science directions 9.* Toronto: John Wiley & Sons.

Roberts, M. (1998). Indigenous knowledge and Western science: Perspectives from the Pacific. In D. Hodson (Ed.), *Science and technology education and ethnicity: An Aotearoa New Zealand per-*

spective (pp. 59–75). Wellington: The Royal Society of New Zealand.

Smith, W. (1998). Native American perspectives. *Science Teacher, 65* (3), 33–36.

Snively, G. & Corsiglia, J. (1998, April). Discovering indigenous science: Implications for science education. Paper presented at the National Association for Research in Science Teaching conference, San Diego, CA.

Spivak, G. (1990). *The post-colonial critic: Interviews, strategies, dialogues.* New York: Routledge.

Swift, D. (1992). Indigenous knowledge in the service of science and technology in developing countries. *Studies in Science Education, 20,* 1–28.

Taylor, N. & McPherson, C. (1997). Traditional and religious beliefs and the teaching of science in Fiji. *New Zealand Journal of Educational Studies, 32*(2), 191–205.

Taylor, P. (1999). Whose interests are being served in cross-cultural science teaching? NARST 99 workshop paper. [On-line] http://www.ouhk.edu.hk/cridal/misc/taylor.htm

Wilson, D., & Bauer, M. (1995). *Dynamic science 4.* Sydney, Australia: McGraw-Hill.

Wilson, D., & Bauer, M. (1994). *Dynamic science 3.* Sydney, Australia: McGraw-Hill.

Wilson, D., & Bauer, M. (1992). *Dynamic science 2.* Sydney, Australia: McGraw-Hill.

Wilson, D., & Bauer, M. (1991). *Dynamic science 1.* Sydney, Australia: McGraw-Hill.

Wunungmurra, W. (1988). Dharwurrpunaramurra: Finding common ground for a new Aboriginal curriculum. *Curriculum Perspectives, 8*(2), 69–71.

CHAPTER 10

Defining a Theoretical Framework for Multicultural Science

Samina Hadi-Tabassum

In the science and engineering fields, the enrollment of African American and Hispanic students is lower than other racial or ethnic groups, and thus, the representation of each group in the scientific workforce is only 2% (Sutman & Guzman, 1993). Since there is a severe underrepresentation of minorities in the science field, it is imperative for schools to increase the scientific literacy of minority students and for universities to recruit minority students into scientific careers. Current reform efforts in science education are addressing the need for promoting scientific literacy for all students by providing inclusive science curricula and training teachers in antidiscriminatory practices that can increase minority student participation in the sciences (Raizen, 1998). In order to create inclusive science classrooms that are democratic learning communities, many educators feel that there is also a need for "multicultural science education," which is defined largely in contrast to the standardized Western science practiced in most schools today: the testing of hypotheses until one arrives at a certain and definitive conclusion; the empirical, objective, formal, and controlled features of scientific explanation; the accuracy of prediction, data consistency, and causal thinking; an objective control over nature; a rational perspective of reality; and the logical measuring and counting of time and space. In contrast to the mainstream positions toward science, multicultural science promotes alternative ways of knowing or epistemologies that approach scientific knowledge from a first world and postcolonial framework that critically questions the empirical characteristics and ontological premise of Western science in order to emphasize the concept of "epistemological pluralism" (Cobern & Loving, 1998; Sleeter, 1996). By reclaiming the indigenous epistemologies of marginalized people, multicultural science encourages a heterogeneous view of the world where science is not culturally defined from a mono-empirical framework. Instead, multiculturalists work toward broadening the philosophy of scientific knowledge to encompass the many distinct cultures and their scientific facts, logic, histories, and achievements. For example, ecologists and biologists are now embracing the "traditional ecological knowledge" of indigenous populations and are advocating the teaching of such knowledge in school-based science education programs (Snively & Corsiglia, 1998). This chapter examines multicultural science programs such as the one described above; however, before examining multicultural practices, it is important to understand the theoretical framework behind such practices and develop connections between theory and practice.

Multicultural science has not been easily and widely accepted by the scientific community, mostly because it challenges the theoretical foundations of science itself by working from a critical paradigm. The idea of multiple views of science and multiple ways of knowing science is a concept that describes the complexities of identity and discourse in our postmodern world. The examination of alternative models, such as traditional ecological knowledge (TEK), is an important dimension to the multicultural science debate that is currently being discussed in the discourses. The Cartesian dualism and strict empiricism of Western science is being challenged through a relational concept of scientific identity that is not entirely synonymous with the Western identity and is open to Other identities such as an indigenous identity of science. With its anti-foundationalism, postmodern theory invokes a criticism of Western science through the refutation of its epistemological grounds. Instead of acknowledging only a single voice in the discourse, multicultural science endorses a postmodern theory that challenges authority and hegemony and accepts a variety of points of views without suppressing them.

In *The Order of Things*, Michel Foucault (1970), who has greatly influenced postmodern theory, traces the evolution of the human sciences and argues that institutions such as schools have perpetuated a structuralist epistemology that inhibits alternative ways of thinking by adhering to conformist forces that strain the sciences with prescriptive rules of formation or epistemes. These conformist forces support a strictly Western epistemology that has controlled scientific institutions from the classical age onward with its rule-based claim of infallible and absolute truths. It was within the classical epistemological age in the European 17th century when "the connections between the various branches of empirical knowledge" developed and are still strongly upheld today (Sheridan, 1980, p. 54). However, Foucault's *Order of Things* ends with him envisioning a new era in which positive self-conscious discourse has the potential to change the discourse of knowledge itself (Gane, 1986). Self-conscious discourse is comprised of what Foucault calls *genealogy* or a historical rendering of the sciences, in which the genealogical researcher "studies conjectures of discourses, searches for ruptures and breaks in social practices, and identifies the formation of new historical conjectures" (Johannesson, 1998, p. 304). By studying how science has been structured and legitimized, opposed and fragmented, both historically and socially, the struggle over the value of ideas and practices in science becomes more apparent once it has been researched from a genealogical perspective that challenges us to reconsider the processes of rational thought that originally create coherent structures. Thus, by questioning the foundational premise of such thinking, reflective talk in the science discourse must now turn to genealogical research that can account for a plurality of epistemologies by first decentering the position of Western science, which has usurped a historically situated utopia in the sciences, and then meditating on multiple sciences. When one does construct and write a noncausal and nonchronological genealogy of the sciences, it is apparent that the historical roots of science form a web of signifying epistemologies that stretches beyond the spatial and temporal configurations of a Western taxonomy and nomenclature, especially in the classification and ordering of nature, where there is a strong presence of first world epistemologies.

Such a plurality of signification can be further defined as a "heterotopia," which Foucault envisions as a new transgressive space of incommensurable identities, differences, and representations that are characterized by both continuous formations and the inconsistencies and incoherences needed to break down structuralist rules of continuous formations. Now, diverse epistemologies and scientific practices can be regrouped to create a multicultural science, which then forms a new episteme that has shifted away from the universalist and homogenous confines of Western science. By transforming the episteme, which is a collective yet difficult process, we can alter the conditions of what is possible within the science classroom by changing the object of what is studied in science and the science in which the object is known. However, critics of multicultural science claim that there is a great deal of discontinuity between the epistemologies of first world cultures and Western cultures, which leads to a paradoxical stance on science. In addition, science practitioners claim that Western science is so powerful that all attempts to reform it will fail in the classroom. Foucault would contest that such discontinuities are bound to surface. This is because when he describes the historical trajectories of the sciences in terms of the formation and production of knowledge, what may have looked as continuous from the perspective of Western science now may seem radically discontinuous to those who still adhere to that perspective. Thus, if the underlying rules of what constitutes scientific knowledge are changed, one will find that the production of scientific discourse will change as well, and we must come to accept this change. Western science has been the foundation of all scientific knowledge for a great stretch of time for of many reasons, but mostly because it imposed linguistic and social conventions in the struggle for agentive control. Today, most science is conducted in the English language because it has been successfully formalized in many countries across the world. However, the rediscovery of first world epistemologies, which were once overlooked because they might have appeared to be discontinuous with Western science, especially in terms of linguistic pragmatism, should now be reinstated into the postmodern science classroom to create an ensemble of multivariated discourses and practices.

How will this postmodern change occur in the science classroom? By making a radical break from previous Western modes of knowledge and representation, postmodernism no longer accepts the "master narrative" of Western science. Instead, science becomes a plurality of scientific discourses from the various world cultures. Postmodern science is no longer the "normal science" defined by Thomas Kuhn as "a practice in which scientists argue by reference to shared exemplars" (Dreyfus & Rabinow, 1986, p. 120). In addition, the concept of multicultural science rejects many modernist assumptions about how science should be defined. For example, the following concepts have often been associated with modernist views of Western science: instrumentalism, hierarchy, autonomy, and universality (Rhoads & Valadez, 1996). Consequently, science classrooms in the modern era became instrumental in that they were thought of as machines designed to serve only specific centralized functions. Even the subcomponents of a science classroom, such as lab experiments, were seen as precision instruments for the performance of specific tasks. Using a machine metaphor (Kliebard, 1995), science classrooms of the modern era carried out precise functions and were organized in a hierarchical fashion so that clear rules and regulations guided the actions of the students. In *Discipline and Punish* (1977), Foucault also talks about how school classrooms can use social mechanisms to turn the teaching of students into a science:

> [S]mall techniques of notation, of registration, of constituting files, of arranging facts in columns and tables that are so familiar to us now, were of decisive importance in the epistemological "thaw" of the sciences of the individual. One is no doubt right to pose the Aristotelian problem: Is science of the individual possible and legitimate? (pp. 202–3)

In this manner, science teachers functioned as classroom managers in order to control and regulate the students' scientific work. From a modernist perspective, science classrooms were seen to exist outside of the natural environment and the school surroundings. Science classrooms were seen as autonomous organisms that took in material resources from the environment and reshaped them to produce a product. Modernist views of science classrooms also stressed universality—a sense of sameness must exist in order for the classroom to be held together with similar values and beliefs. There was no discussion of alternative ways of thinking and knowing. The modern era did not mediate a sense of multiplicity, fragmentation, instability of meaning, dissent and dissolution of grand narratives, and emancipatory practice. Difference and diversity thus posed a threat to the machinelike functioning of the modern science classroom.

On the other hand, the concept of multicultural science is informed by postmodern views of classrooms that do mediate a sense of multiplicity, fragmentation, instability of meaning, dissent and dissolution of grand narratives, and emancipatory practice. Postmodernists, for example, challenge scientific theories that stress prediction and control. They reject the idea that science classrooms are social machines with clearly defined identities in which all students guide their actions as a means to achieve predetermined ends. Instead, many postmodernists see science classrooms as socially constructed, which means that the reality portrayed by Western science is arbitrary and relative. By defining knowledge as socially constructed, postmodernists are emphasizing the social roles both the teacher and the students play in defining and redefining their science classroom. In turn, science classrooms are cultural artifacts in themselves, and in order to understand them, one must go beyond the objectives completed by the students and what goals are met. From a postmodern perspective, the identity of the science classroom is the meaning-making process enacted by all the classroom members to create its own unique web of signification that stretches beyond the walls of the classroom.

Another critique of postmodernism is the social hierarchy established in science classrooms, where there is domination and centralized power instead of a consensual and democratic model of student learning. By focusing on cooperative grouping instead of direct instruction, process-driven instruction instead of product-driven instruction, the science teacher is making vital decisions toward opposing institutional domination and subordination practices that marginalize students. A commitment to equality and active student participation enables the science teacher to create a collaborative environment. Postmodernists also challenge the idea that science classrooms are autonomous. Instead, postmodern science classrooms are seen as intimately interwoven with the external environments so that students are mutually empowered by connecting with their surroundings. And finally, postmodernists critique the essentialist nature of Western science, which eliminates differences. A critical postmodern perspective argues that modernist conceptions of science classrooms based on similarity and harmony deter the possibility of building multicultural classrooms. Science classrooms should be viewed as communities of difference, in which alternative ways of knowing science are not concealed or silenced, but instead form the basis for students coming together to interact and learn from one another and from other cultures. In order for such situations to occur, Burbules & Rice (1991) argue that there needs to, "dialogue across differences" or self-reflective discourse so that we discuss differences instead of eliminating them. Thus, from a postmodern perspective, multicultural science challenges us to create what critical theorist bell hooks (1994) describes as "engaged pedagogy," which brings teachers and students together to talk about how different cultures perceive science differently, even if those differences are conflict-ridden and contradictory, so that there is a democratic vision of science.

DEVELOPING MULTICULTURAL SCIENCE CURRICULA

Since the multicultural perspective toward science is a fairly new phenomenon, there are many diverse definitions as to what constitutes multicultural science and how it can be applied in the science classroom. In response to the struggle over defining multicultural science and its pedagogy, Pomeroy (1994) listed nine significant and overarching research agendas that define and propel multicultural science in today's classrooms and universities: (a) science and engineering career support services for minority students; (b) an indigenous social issues context for science content; (c) culturally sensitive instructional practices; (d) historical non-Western role models; (e) demystification of stereotyped images of science; (f) science communication for language minorities; (g) indigenous content for science to explain; (h) comparison and bridging of students' worldviews and the worldview of science; and (i) exploration of the content and epistemology of Western and first world knowledge of the physical world. The agendas listed above seek to express a holistic and synthetic outcome in which the equal educational treatment and opportunity of minority students is assured in science classrooms through culturally relevant pedagogy. Pomeroy's view of multicultural science also invokes a postmodern notion of curriculum and teaching that challenges the foundational claims of Western science and its hegemonic system of rules and regulations. A new postmodern politics in science education is valorizing diversity, difference, and heterogeneity so that there is no longer a binary opposition between good science versus bad science. In turn, multicultural science is developing from new epistemologies, new identities, and new political struggles while deconstructing modernist theories, concepts, modes of thought, and analysis so that progressive postmodern strategies, discourses, and practices emerge in the science classroom. With this definition in mind, let us examine promising programs that are implementing multicultural science curricula.

In the Navajo Nation, there is a current trend toward implementing multicultural practices in the science curriculum by creating a balanced approach toward learning that is harmonious with nature. In the Navajo language, this harmony with nature is called *hozho* (Keating, 1996). The indigenous science epistemology of the Navajo Nation has been rooted in the native knowledge of astronomy, agriculture, medicine, ecology, botany, and architecture that correlates with tribal perspectives but can also be linked to concepts in Western science. In his ethnobotany unit, Keating (1996) taught preservice student teachers to make connections between Navajo and Western science concepts by comparing the effectiveness of Navajo herbal medicine to penicillin using agar plate culturing. However, the emphasis was not on measuring and assessing quantitative effectiveness; rather, it was on how the processes involved in the experimentation can be related to their cultural contexts. In terms of teaching methods, an emphasis on observing nature in depth and a de-emphasis on qualifying nature with scientific explanations is a strong component of the Navajo science curriculum. The act of observing natural phenomenon also allows students to comprehend the natural world in diverse ways. After observations, a subsequent discussion on what students observed follows, but this discussion is not necessarily teacher-directed; instead, the students work together in cooperative groups and problem solve to demonstrate their solutions. Oral history also has a strong place in the Navajo culture, and assessing students through oral presentations in the science classroom is a culturally congruent practice.

Furthermore, by allowing minority students the freedom to voice their multiple solutions and interpretations, the science teacher encourages positive multicultural change by bringing diverse opinions into the discussion, allowing students to work collectively, and in turn building community in the classroom. Here the teacher becomes what Giroux (1991) calls a "transformative intellectual," since s/he is no longer the manager of student learning and instead encourages student learning that is collaborative and negotiated. The role of the teacher is important in the multicultural classroom because s/he can make curricular changes that allow minority students to be academically successful while still allowing them to build on and maintain their own indigenous identity. In *Finding Freedom in the Classroom*, Patricia Hinchey (1998) writes about how teachers can implement critical theory such as multicultural science directly into their classroom practices in order to build new classroom communities that empower students and teachers.

For example, in the Hawaiian school system, multicultural education is used to empower and educate children in several content areas. In "Native Hawaiian Epistemology," Meyer (1998) focuses on a Hawaiian epistemology that is largely shaped by sensory knowledge as opposed to "a universal set of empirical judgments" (p. 39). In the science curriculum, the natural environment plays a significant role and is largely defined by Hawaiian cultural practices, beliefs, and values. For example, Meyer interviews a Hawaiian school teacher who elaborates on how the Hawaiian epistemology shapes their sense of experience in the physical sciences:

> The notion that a rock exists as an inanimate object, especially in its creative stages, is totally foreign to the Hawaiian. Rock, especially fresh lava flow, has a spirit, and with the assumption of a spirit, pro-creation is possible. Thus, this belief that Pele (the volcano deity) is magma, Pele is lava, and that she is the one who controls the outpour-ing of this energy is within this dualistic concept. Pele is the creative force whose name signifies the physical and the spiritual essence of newly formed land. (p. 40)

The spiritual and phenomenological Hawaiian interpretation of rock and lava clearly shows insights gained from sensory knowledge that is essential to Hawaiian life but is also contradictory to Western science. By integrating the Hawaiian epistemology into the science classroom, diversity and differences are reinstated to create a web of signification that extends beyond Western science.

Another dimension to diversity in the science classroom is linguistic pluralism. In multilingual classrooms, the language of science can be-come a barrier to limited-English-proficient (LEP) students, who do not have a deep understanding of the scientific vocabulary in English. Even when scientific concepts are translated into the second language, they lose their intended meaning (Vira, 1997). Thus, if there is a large LEP student population, it is imperative to develop curriculum in the students' first language so that science learning is contextualized. Another reason for using the students' first language as a resource is to break down the silences of language minority students' voices in the science classroom and allow them to seek equity and access to the dominant curriculum through their native language. In order to empower student voices, the classroom must sustain a comfortable environment that is committed to supporting linguistic and cultural diversity.

In one particular multicultural science program, a colleague and I de-cided to use a two-way immersion bilingual method to create an inclusive language learning environment by preserving and enriching the LEP students' first language. Two-way immersion or dual language edu-cation occurs when students who speak a majority language such as English are taught in the same classroom as students who speak a minority language such as Spanish (Christian, 1994). The two-way immersion model develops language proficiency as well as academic proficiency in the two languages by presenting the same subject matter in both languages for both student groups. Therefore, a key aspect of our science class was the conjunction between the language of our students and the language of science, thus enacting a pluralistic perspective toward scientific literacy. We also used a two-way immersion bilingual framework for our class, so that students were "doing science" in both English and Spanish. In our two-way immersion solar energy science class, there were a total of 25 eighth grade students: 48% were limited-English-proficient immigrant students of Mexican, Central, and South American origins; the remaining, 52% were English-speaking students who were one-third Caucasian, one-third African American, and one-third Chicana/o. Even though the student composition was diverse in terms of racial and ethnic backgrounds, all the students in the class were considered academically at-risk by the school district because of low standardized test scores, English proficiency, socioeconomic status, and parents' education levels.

The syllabus for the two-way immersion science course was originally designed for a grant proposal that allotted monetary funds for secondary teachers to develop a special curriculum that integrates math, science, and technology. The theme of our science course was solar energy: a topic that addressed both the motivational and developmental needs of the adolescent students in the two-way immersion class. By creating a curriculum that engaged students in understanding and processing the complex relationships in solar energy through hands-on experiments and group problem solving, we were able to produce a motivational climate in the science classroom in which the students were intrinsically invested in their learning due to the higher levels of cognitive processing involved in the rigorous understanding of solar energy. Furthermore, instead of creating a classroom environment based on tracked ability, competitive grades, and rote memorization, as team teachers we established a student-centered environment based on "task-focused goals" that organized individual student learning in terms of constructivist knowledge and comprehensive individual growth throughout the school year (Anderman & Maehr, 1994). In other words, the diverse student groups worked together productively on 27 tasks total throughout the year, which required them to make connections across experiments, see patterns across language and content, and develop metacognitive, problem-solving processes that fostered their understanding of the solar energy curriculum.

The course curriculum started with the most basic concepts of solar energy, transitioned to the study of electronics, and finally spiraled to solar-powered transportation. Some of the activities in the preliminary module included (a) reading mythologies and folk tales about the sun from Aztec, Maya, and Egyptian cultures; (b) examining the role of the sun in the solar system; (c) studying the effects of solar light and heat; (d) building a solar collector to study the water cycle; and (e) using the Internet to research the role of the sun in the greenhouse effect. The second module of the course curriculum transitioned to electronics and solar-generated electricity, in which students first explored electricity and its properties, then built a variety of simple circuits, and ultimately used solar cells to power student-designed circuits. In the last module, solar energy came alive when heterogeneous student groups designed, developed, and demonstrated their solar-powered model cars at a Texas state competition in San Antonio sponsored by the National Renewable Energy Laboratory.

The instructional teaching in the solar energy science class focused on four essential methods: two-way immersion, cooperative grouping, team-teaching, and portfolio assessment. Two-way immersion methodology drew attention to the role of language in the science classroom by integrating limited-English-proficient students with their English-speaking peers in an academic context that promoted cognitive, linguistic, and social/affective development for both groups of students. Within this multicultural and multilingual environment, cooperative grouping provided the ideal classroom structure for two-way immersion instruction. Since the students had different levels of literacy, education, and language proficiency, they were constantly negotiating the meaning of words and ideas during their group activities (see Holt, Chips, & Wallace, 1991). In each heterogeneous cooperative group, there were two limited-English-proficient students and two English-speaking students working together on collective and collaborative experiments. Most often, there was at least one Chicana/o student in each group who acted as a bridge between the two groups of students because s/he was fluent in both English and Spanish. The Chicana/o students in our class were U.S.-born Mexican Americans (see also Morales & Bonilla, 1993). In the cooperative group setting, codeswitching between the two languages was evident among the students as they interacted with each other during group projects: "The sun has energia solar." The vicissitudes of language in the science classroom seemed almost natural because much of the English and Spanish vocabulary on solar energy is rooted in the Latin language. By the end of the year, both the English-speaking and Spanish-speaking students knew the solar energy vocabulary in both Spanish and English. However, many of the English-speaking students were hesitant at first to use the Spanish vocabulary. In fact, a few of the English-speaking students dropped out of the class because of this requirement. But once the class became comfortable with the second language, science content, and each other, the social dynamics changed in a positive direction, and the students worked well with each other across racial, ethnic, and linguistic lines. Their ability to transgress these borders was evident during the solar energy car race, when camaraderie was at its strongest as students cheered each other. Thus, there was a crosspollination of languages, knowledge, and experiences within our multicultural science classroom.

Team teaching was another essential method of instruction in the two-way immersion science class. It allowed each teacher to distinguish and demarcate the curriculum into symmetrical halves: instruction in the English language and instruction in the target Spanish language. One teacher assumed the responsibilities of preparing the lessons in English while the other teacher focused on the same lessons in the target Spanish language. Thus, for limited-English-proficient students, there was a positive transfer of solar energy concepts and schema from the target Spanish language to the English language and vice versa. During class discussions and cooperative group interactions, the LEP students were able to respond to whole-group questions in English because they had grounded their knowledge of solar energy in both languages (see Saville-Troike, 1984). In addition to meeting the linguistic needs of the students, team teaching also allowed the instructors to meet the students' academic objectives. Team teaching seemed to improve the academic content of the class curriculum, because two teachers were dually involved in brainstorming lessons in both languages; sharing expert knowledge in math, science, and technology; structuring and facilitating cooperative group experiments and lessons; diagnosing the needs of both the limited-English--proficient and English-speaking students; and exploring new methods in a multicultural and multilingual science class.

Since the two-way immersion science class integrated both academic content and language learning, the assessment methods also encompassed both the contextual knowledge of solar energy and the conceptual knowledge of vocabulary, writing, and grammar. Thus, the use of portfolios was an ideal method to assess students' progress in both science and language development. For each of the three curriculum modules, students completed two entries to include in their portfolios. Each portfolio entry had three key components: a photo montage of a pictured science activity along with a written description of the activity; a procedural analysis on how to conduct the specific experiment; and a journal log with the student's metacognitive reflection and self-assessment of the cumulative learning process detailed in the particular science activity. By using photographs, the student was provided with visual cues that prompted and elicited a written description of the experiment utilizing specific science vocabulary. In addition, students took the portfolios home for their parents to read and add comments so that parents were aware of their child's learning on an ongoing basis (see O'Malley & Pierce, 1992).

In conclusion, when envisioning a multicultural science classroom, educators must imagine interactive, collaborative activities such as cooperative and project-centered learning; cultural connections to science; differentiated, individualized instruction; and authentic and performance-based assessment. All of the multicultural science programs highlighted in this chapter integrate many of Pomeroy's (1994) nine agendas by adhering to a postmodern theory of science that celebrates difference and diversity and no longer conforms to the structural strains of Western epistemology.

REFERENCES

Anderman, E. M., & Maehr, M. L. (1994). Motivation and schooling in middle grades. *Review of Educational Research, 64*(2), 287–309.

Burbules, N. C., & Rice, S. (1991). Dialogue across differences: Constituting the conversation. *Harvard Educational Review, 61*(4), 393–416.

Christian, D. (1994). *Two-way bilingual education: Students learning through two languages.* Washington, DC: National Center for Research on Cultural Diversity and Second Language Learning.

Cobern, W. & Loving, C. (1998, April). *Defining "science" in a multicultural world: Implications for science education.* Paper presented at the annual meeting of the National Association for Research in Science Teaching., San Diego, CA.

Dreyfus, H. & Rabinow, P. (1986). What is maturity? Habermas and Foucault on "What Is enlightenment?" In D. C. Hoy (Ed.), *Foucault: A critical reader*. Oxford: Blackwell.

Foucault, M. (1977). *Discipline and punish: The birth of a prison*. New York: Vintage.

Foucault, M. (1970). *The order of things*. New York: Random House.

Gane, M. (1986). *Towards a critique of Foucault*. New York: Routledge and Kegan Paul.

Giroux, H. A. (1991). *Postmodernism, feminism, and cultural politics: Redrawing educational boundaries*. Albany: State University of New York Press.

Hinchey, P. (1998). *Finding freedom in the classroom*. New York: Peter Lang.

Holt, D., Chips, B., & Wallace, D. (1991, Summer). *Cooperative learning in the secondary school: Maximizing language acquisition, academic achievement, and social development*. Washington, DC: National Council of Bilingual Education Program Information Guide Series, Number 12.

hooks, b. (1994). *Teaching to transgress*. New York: Routledge.

Johannesson, I. (1998). Geneology and progressive politics. In T. S. Popekewitz & M. Brennan (Eds.) *Foucault's Challenge: Discourse, knowledge, and power*. New York: Teachers College Press.

Keating, J. (1996). Designing multicultural science curricula for American Indian High School Students. *Multicultural Education, 4*(1), 24–27.

Kliebard, J. (1995). *The struggle for the American curriculum*. New York: Random House.

Meyer, M. A. (1998). Native Hawaiian epistemology. *Cultural Survival Quarterly, 22*(1), 38–41.

Morales, R., & Bonilla, F. (1993). *Latinos in a changing U.S. economy*. Newbury Park, CA: Sage.

O'Malley, J. M., & Pierce, L. V. (1992, March). *Portfolio assessment: Experiments from the field*. Paper presented at the annual meeting of the Teachers of English to Speakers of Other Languages, Vancouver, British Columbia.

Pomeroy, D. (1994). Science education and cultural diversity: Mapping the field. *Studies in Science Education, 24*, 49–73.

Raizen, S. (1998). Standards for science education. *Teachers College Record, 100*(1), 122–144.

Rhoads, R., & Valadez, J. R. (1996). *Democracy, multiculturalism, and the community college.* New York: Garland.

Saville-Troike, M. (1984). What really matters in second language learning for academic achievement? *TESOL Quarterly, 17,* 199–219.

Sheridan, A. (1980). *Michel Foucault: The will to truth.* London: Tavistock.

Sleeter, C. (1996). *Multicultural education as social activism.* Albany: State University of New York Press.

Snively, G. & Corsiglia, J. (April, 1998). *Discovering indigenous science: Implications for science education.* Paper presented at the annual meeting of the National Association for Research in Science Teaching, San Diego, CA.

Sutman, F. X. & Guzman, A. C. (1993, March). *Teaching science effectively to limited English proficient students.* (Digest No. 87). New York: ERIC Clearinghouse on Urban Education.

Vira, S. (1997). The nature of science in a multicultural context. *Multicultural Teaching, 15*(3), 28–32.

CONTRIBUTORS

Carol R. Adkins, Ed.D. is an assistant professor of outdoor and environmental education at Northern Illinois University, DeKalb, Illinois. Her research interests include informal environmental education and Native American education.

Roberta Ahlquist, Ph.D. is a professor in the Division of Teacher Education at San Jose State University, San Jose, California. Her research interests include race relation/antiracist education and critical multicultural curriculum development.

Mary M. Atwater, Ph.D. is a professor in the Department of Science Education at the University of Georgia, Athens, Georgia. Her research interests include the study of sociocultural influences on science learning and teaching (multicultural science education) and the investigation of students' understanding of chemical concepts.

Norvella P. Carter, Ph.D. is an associate professor in the Department of Curriculum and Instruction and endowed chair in urban education at Texas A&M University, College Station, Texas. Her research interests are multicultural education, urban education, and education of teachers for diverse classrooms.

Denise Crockett, Ph.D. is an assistant professor in the Department of Education at Furman University, Greenville, South Carolina. Her research interests include the study of microcultures in science and technology fields and the investigation of culture, ethnicity, and gender in science and engineering classrooms.

Shirley Gholston Key, Ed.D. is an associate professor of Science Education, the assistant chairperson, and director of graduate programs in the Department of Urban Education at the University of Houston Downtown, Houston, Texas. Her research interests include cultural inclusion, preservice science teacher education, elementary science education, multicultural education, urban education, science education of diverse learners, and education of teachers of diverse learners.

Samina Hadi-Tabassum is a doctoral candidate in the Department of Curriculum and Teaching at Teachers College, Columbia University, New York, New York. She is also an adjunct instructor in the Department of Teaching and Learning at New York University. Her research interests include multicultural theory, science education, critical theory, and linguistic anthropology.

S. Maxwell Hines, Ph.D. is an associate professor and graduate coordinator of secondary science education in the Department of Curriculum and Teaching at Hofstra University, Hempstead, New York. Her research interests include science teacher education, the sociology of science, and ethnicity, class, gender and exceptionality in science teaching and learning.

Julie Kailin, Ph.D. is an assistant professor in the Department of Educational Policy and Community Studies at the University of Wisconsin – Milwaukee. Her research interests include the theory and practice of antiracist and multicultural education, the history of American education, and race relations education for teachers.

Patricia J. Larke, Ed.D. is a professor in the Department of Curriculum and Instruction at Texas A&M University, College Station, Texas. Her research interests are multicultural education, issues affecting teachers of color, and educating teachers for diverse classrooms.

Cathleen Loving, Ph.D. is an associate professor in the Department of Teaching, Learning and Culture at Texas A&M University, College Station, Texas. Her research interest is the relationship between perceptions of the nature of science and science teaching.

Peter Ninnes, Ph.D. is a senior lecturer in sociology of education at the University of New England, Armidale, Australia. His research interests include poststructural and postcolonial studies of science curriculum, critical discourse analysis, and theoretical trends in international comparative education.

Bernard R. Ortiz de Montellano, Ph.D. is a professor emeritus of anthropology at Wayne State University, Detroit, Michigan. His research interests include Mesoamerican archeology and myth, Aztec medicine, health and nutrition, and Hispanic culturally relevant science.

Alberto J. Rodriguez, Ph.D. is an associate professor of science education in the Department of Curriculum and Instruction at New Mexico State University, Las Cruces, New Mexico. His research interests include sociotransformative constructivism (i.e., the intersection of multiculturalism and social constructivism to improve science teaching and learning), the use of video as a tool for research and teacher professional development, and the study of voice and representation in qualitative research.

Paul McD. Rowland, Ph.D. is a professor of curriculum and instruction and environmental sciences and director of the Center for Environmental Sciences and Education at Northern Arizona University, Flagstaff, Arizona. His research interests include Native American education, science and environmental education, and the assessment of the effectiveness of educational practices.

Erich Santos, M.S. majored in chemistry with an emphasis in chemical education in the Department of Chemistry at Texas A&M University, College Station, Texas. His research interests include chemical education and multicultural education.

Charles E. Simmons, J.D. is an education writer in Detroit and associate professor of English at Eastern Michigan University, Ypsilanti, Michigan. His research interests include media studies, multicultural education, environmental justice, and human rights.

Gail Singleton-Taylor, Ph.D. is an associate professor in the Department of Curriculum and Instruction at Old Dominion University, Norfolk, Virginia. Her research interests are multicultural education, reading education, and educating teachers for diverse classrooms.

INDEX

Studies in the Postmodern Theory of Education

General Editors
Joe L. Kincheloe & Shirley R. Steinberg

Counterpoints publishes the most compelling and imaginative books being written in education today. Grounded on the theoretical advances in criticalism, feminism, and postmodernism in the last two decades of the twentieth century, Counterpoints engages the meaning of these innovations in various forms of educational expression. Committed to the proposition that theoretical literature should be accessible to a variety of audiences, the series insists that its authors avoid esoteric and jargonistic languages that transform educational scholarship into an elite discourse for the initiated. Scholarly work matters only to the degree it affects consciousness and practice at multiple sites. Counterpoints' editorial policy is based on these principles and the ability of scholars to break new ground, to open new conversations, to go where educators have never gone before.

For additional information about this series or for the submission of manuscripts, please contact:

> Joe L. Kincheloe & Shirley R. Steinberg
> c/o Peter Lang Publishing, Inc.
> 275 Seventh Avenue, 28th floor
> New York, New York 10001

To order other books in this series, please contact our Customer Service Department:

> (800) 770-LANG (within the U.S.)
> (212) 647-7706 (outside the U.S.)
> (212) 647-7707 FAX

Or browse online by series:

> www.peterlangusa.com